THE
PUBLIC
DIMENSION
OF
FOREIGN
POLICY

THE
PUBLIC
DIMENSION
OF
FOREIGN
POLICY

David D. Newsom

Indiana
University
Press

BLOOMINGTON AND INDIANAPOLIS

The paper used in this publication meets the minimum requirements of
American National Standard for Information Sciences—Permanence of
Paper for Printed Library Materials, ANSI Z39.48-1984.

MANUFACTURED IN THE UNITED STATES OF AMERICA

Library of Congress Cataloging-in-Publication Data

Newsom, David D.
    The public dimension of foreign policy / David D. Newsom.
        p.   cm.
    Includes bibliographical references and index.
    ISBN 0–253–32960–4 (cl : alk. paper). — ISBN 0–253–21024–0 (pa : alk. paper)
    1. United States—Foreign relations—Decision making.   2. Freedom of the
press—United States.   3. Constituent power—United States.   4. United States—
Foreign public opinion.   I. Title.
JX1417.N49   1996
327.73—dc20   95-20450

1 2 3 4 5 / 01 00 99 98 97 96

Dedicated to my wife, Jean,
without whose support, suggestions,
and cogent advice
this book would not have been possible.

CONTENTS

PREFACE

This book is about the public dimension of United States foreign policy. One part of that dimension involves *expression* by officials, filtered and amplified by the print media, radio, and television. The other part lies in the marketplace of ideas with its developed *pressures* on policy. Both parts meet in the Congress, the ultimate venue of the public dimension.

Foreign policy is made within government in a process that is at the same time confidential and public. Although some of the proceedings of government are closed, the success of policy making in the American democracy ultimately depends on public acceptance and support. That is why an understanding of the public dimension is important.

In Washington, the White House, numerous agencies, and nearly every cabinet department are involved, challenging the legislative branch in the constitutional "invitation to struggle." Beyond official agencies are circles that include the information media, the academic world, think tanks, advocacy organizations, and lobbies. Each in its particular way seeks the attention of the U.S. public and its representatives in Congress.

Few issues of foreign policy escape entanglement in this institutional web. Some have been perpetual concerns, fed by the emotions and interests of significant parts of the U.S. population. These have included the security of Israel, the existence of apartheid in South Africa, the future of Cuba, and the conflict in Northern Ireland.

During the Cold War, the agendas related not only to policies toward the Soviet Union, but also to actions and personalities in Vietnam, Afghanistan, Angola, and Nicaragua. Those who saw problems in these areas as part of a global confrontation with communism were pitted against those who insisted these were regional problems to be treated, not through sponsoring conflict, but through economic and social development. The ideological debate preoccupied Washington's organizational arena for three decades.

As the century ended, new subjects emerged and old issues received new attention: the environment, population, the impact of technology, and trade. Organizations previously immersed in Cold War political issues adjusted their priorities to meet these new interests.

Throughout thirty-five years of government service, I have been an observer of this process. As a public affairs officer and ambassador overseas and as a policy official in Washington, I have been fascinated by the intricate interplay of official and public forces involved. At Georgetown University and, more recently, at the University of Virginia, I have distilled this interest into courses on public information and foreign policy. This book is an effort to capture the essence of this interest for the student of international affairs and the interested citizen both in the United States and abroad. The ways of Washington can be mysterious to the American at home as well as the foreigner.

The comments and conclusions are personal observations growing out of my involvement. This work undoubtedly would have benefited from more scientific and statistically supported surveys of each of the elements described in the text. Neither time nor resources permitted such an approach. My own impressions have been supplemented by the work and observations of others. Although scholars may find much to question, I hope this book may encourage deeper probes into the interplay of forces that make policy.

A full picture of the public dimension requires a discussion of organizations and activities, especially the press and television, with which I have had only peripheral experience. I approached these areas with some trepidation, only to find in participants' statements and writings observations that confirmed my own impressions. I have drawn on these observations at some length; they tell the stories of strengths and weaknesses better than I can.

Although this book focuses on Washington, the nation's capital is only the hub of a nationwide process. Initiatives and concerns flow to the capital from every corner of the United States. The perceptions of events and policies that emerge from the intricate interaction in the branches of government flow back to the country through the press and organizational networks.

This work is also the story of my personal voyage through the intricacies of official and public pressures. I have, in some places, inserted my own recollections growing out of experience that spans service in seven administrations—from Truman to Carter—and observations as an informed observer of three more—Reagan, Bush, and Clinton. Each president and each secretary of state has had his own style of handling the public aspects of policy and dealing with the information media. This is, moreover, being written in early 1995, a period of upheaval and change in the U.S. political process. Individuals and organizations that are prominent and influential as this book goes to press may be in changed circumstances on the date of publication. Nevertheless, I believe the conclusions of this work will apply to most administrations; the variations in the personal styles of officials do not eliminate basic elements present in the communications of every administration with the public.

Many good books have been written covering aspects of the subjects of this volume. Books on government-press relations have been written either as memoirs, scholarly studies, or from the point of view of journalists. Two recent books deal comprehensively with think tanks. Several are devoted to lobbies. International relations texts touch on the process. In seeking a text for my courses, however, I could find none that presented a comprehensive view of the interplay of forces in Washington or that struck an adequate balance between the problems of the policymaker and the understandable desire of the press and the public for information and influence.

I am writing, of course, primarily from the perspective of a former official. That perspective, however, is tempered by early training and experience as a journalist, by friendships and conversations with those from newspapers and television who cover international affairs, and by a strong belief in the importance of the First Amendment in our democracy.

Books evolve in the process of writing, and this one is no exception. It began as an exposition of the government-media relationship. My original intention was to emphasize how this relationship creates perceptions that influence how people react to policies and events. I soon came to realize that although perceptions are a significant part of the picture they are but the outward manifestation of the deeper contest of responsibilities, ideas, and pressures involving many players in policy formulation. The result, therefore, is a story not only of the perceptions created of international events and policies but also of the debate over what to do about these events and policies.

The process takes place in circumstances of unparalleled freedom. The book begins, therefore, with a look at the constitutional bases of freedom and the right to petition. Chapter 2 then describes how government speaks—and why its statements are not always clear and candid. The next three chapters look at the images produced by the information media and the inescapable conflicts between the demands for information and the need for concealment in a democratic society. Subsequent chapters treat the various elements in the marketplace of ideas, beginning with the need for and sources of money. Then observations follow on academia, think tanks, advocacy organizations, and lobbies. Chapter 11 deals with the Congress—where the pressures converge—and includes four case histories of issues before Congress: SALT II, Nicaragua, South Africa, and Angola. A final essay projects the public dimension into the twenty-first century.

ACKNOWLEDGMENTS

Many friends and colleagues have helped make this book possible.

I am indebted first to those at the University of Virginia who have made time and facilities available and have introduced me further to the mysteries and opportunities of academic life. I owe thanks to many colleagues of the faculty, but, in particular, to Prof. R. K. Ramazani, of the Department of Government and Foreign Affairs, who encouraged me in these pursuits. Nor could this have been accomplished without the diligent and capable assistance of graduate students who, often with difficulty, interpreted my requests for research help: Kevin Markland, Eric Thompson, and Yves Taylor. Christina Smith not only assisted with early research but authored the case studies on Nicaragua, South Africa, and Angola, and saw me through the final stages of the manuscript.

The list would be long indeed if I were to mention all of those who, during my Washington years, helped me understand the networks that are the subject of this book. In the preparation of this volume, I have turned to friends in the world of journalism: John Finney, Murray Gart, Irv Chapman, Bill German, and Hodding Carter. David Pearce, a former journalist, now a foreign service officer, contributed valuable observations. Dorothy Thomas of America Watch gave me a sense of the work of the advocates. Alice Neff Lucan, attorney at law specializing in First Amendment cases, provided valuable help on chapter 1. Rosemary Neaher Niehuss of the office of Henry Kissinger helped confirm my recollection of a meeting in Morocco. Pat Holt shared his expertise on the U.S. Congress. Nancy Eddy and Judy Harbaugh checked facts relating to think tanks. To all of them I am most grateful.

I have listened and taken from all, but the responsibility for the thoughts, as well as any errors, is mine.

THE
PUBLIC
DIMENSION
OF
FOREIGN
POLICY

1

The Legal Basis

In November of 1973, I accompanied Henry Kissinger on his first official travel as secretary of state, a trip to North Africa. At a lunch on the first stop, Rabat, the Watergate scandal was very much on the mind of King Hassan of Morocco. President Richard Nixon had been a special friend of his country. The king pressed the secretary of state to explain why a ruler as powerful as the president of the United States could not simply have silenced the voices that plagued him during the crisis. Kissinger could only explain that, under U.S. law, even the president could not suppress open criticism, a concept difficult for an absolute monarch—and many others—to understand.

This book begins with an examination of that legal basis for freedom; a recognition of that basis is essential to comprehending the multitude of influences that bear on the making of United States foreign policy and the limitations of official responses.

Although the concept has at times been challenged and limited, the right to criticize, express views, and even publicly disclose secrets without fear of subsequent penalty is deeply embedded in American society. Nothing sets democratic systems more clearly apart from others than freedom of speech and of the press. Authoritarian societies insist that all forms of public expression should be used to enhance support for a ruling regime and its policies. Even in the democratic societies of

Europe, the comment is heard—at times with envy and at times criti-
cally—that the U.S. press has too much power and reveals too many
secrets.

In many countries—perhaps most—foreign policy is "an affair of
state," a prerogative of the ruler, and the rules and practices governing
public expression are different from those applied to the discussion of
domestic issues. The British constitution has no bill of rights; revelations
and criticism of official actions are limited by the Official Secrets Act
(OSA), the Law of Confidence, Privacy Laws, and Contempt of Court
statutes. The OSA gives the government power to prohibit in advance
publication of national security information; the Law of Confidence
makes information the property of the government. Government information is made available to reporters through a lobby system of selective
briefings that establishes a cozy relationship between officials and British
reporters.

In France, press freedom came with the Revolution, yet current laws
place limitations on that freedom. Libel is more harshly defined and can,
in some cases, include facts ascertained to be true. Specific laws ban
discussion of certain subjects without government authorization: parliamentary investigations, and items affecting the credit of the nation,
public morals, and the military. Criminal as well as civil sanctions are
possible in the case of some offenses. The Foreign Office is understood to
be the primary source of foreign policy news. Journalists are required to
carry identity cards. In addition, until recently all television was govern-
ment-owned. Newspapers tend to be identified with political parties, and
close, informal understandings often exist between publishers and politicians.

Ironically, the information environments closest to that of the United
States exist in Germany and Japan, where constitutions crafted on the
U.S. model after World War II are still in force, with similar safeguards for
speech and the press. In Japan, however, custom and political tradition
place some limits on attacks on policies and officials. Control is exercised
through powerful links between media organs and politicians and
through press clubs closely associated with individual ministries.[1]

In less democratic societies, the means by which information is
controlled are legion. If publications are not owned either by the government or the single party of the state, they are subject to direct censorship
or to licensing and other forms of intimidation that lead to self-censor-
ship. Distribution may be in the hands of a monopoly friendly to the

leadership. Laws of sedition and libel protect officials from criticism. Import controls are used to divert newsprint and machinery to friendly organs. Favors in the form of advertising, subsidies, preferential access to officials, and tax breaks are granted to political supporters.

The Constitutional Basis

The free environment in the U.S. has been created primarily by two clauses in the First Amendment of the U.S. Constitution: "Congress shall make no law abridging the freedom of speech, or of the press . . . or the right of the people peaceably to assemble and to petition the government for a redress of grievances." This chapter looks at the development of the first clause as it has applied, through history, to foreign policy. The second clause and its application to the growth of foreign policy lobbies is examined in chapter 9.

Throughout two centuries of the nation's history, the courts have interpreted the "freedom of speech and of the press" clause to permit free criticism of officials and official actions, including those relating to foreign policy. In so doing, the courts created the environment for the interplay of diverse and partial images that so often marks the national debate on foreign policy.

Not everyone in the early days of the nation agreed that foreign policy should be thrown into the cauldron of free expression. Alexander Hamilton in the Federalist Papers doubted whether an adequate definition of freedom of the press relating to any subject could be established:

What signifies a declaration that "the Liberty of the Press shall be inviolably preserved"? What is the Liberty of the Press? Who can give it any definition which does not leave the utmost latitude for evasion? I hold it to be impracticable; and from this I infer, that its security, whatever fine declarations may be inserted in any Constitution respecting it, must altogether depend on public opinion, and on the general spirit of the people and of the Government.[2]

Even Thomas Jefferson, in a letter to James Madison from Paris on August 28, 1789, suggested a draft of an amendment on press freedom that would have provided an exemption for foreign affairs:

The people shall not be deprived of their right to speak, to write, or *otherwise* to publish anything but false facts affecting injuriously the life, liberty, or reputation of others, or affecting the peace of the confederacy with other nations.[3]

Madison rejected this limiting suggestion, however, and drafted the First Amendment as it was subsequently adopted.

The Sedition Act

The type of interplay of partisan action that marks the Washington scene today was foreshadowed early in the nation's history. In the last decade of the eighteenth century, the United States was caught between the French and British, at war in Europe. Each belligerent sought to use and intimidate the new country. The French, having been helpful during the Revolutionary War, urged the Americans to tilt toward Paris. A pro-French group included Thomas Jefferson, recently minister of the United States in Paris. Others, including George Washington, were not friendly to the British but wished to avoid European entanglements. At the same time that Americans were considering their new constitution, French partisans sought to carry the message of the recent French Revolution to the United States, creating what many in America saw as a threat to the fledgling institutions of their new country. At that moment, the political leak was born.

A journalist, Benjamin Franklin Bache, grandson of Benjamin Franklin and one of Jefferson's more ardent followers, obtained a copy of a letter from French Foreign Minister Charles Maurice de Talleyrand to President John Adams and published it before Adams had received it.[4] Adams was furious (as more recent presidents have been). Incidents such as this, and the intensity of the controversy, led to the passage in Congress of the Sedition Act of July 14, 1798, the first effort in the new nation's history to limit the freedom of the press. The act provided for fines and imprisonment for those found guilty of seditious libel: any attempt to weaken or defame the government or laws of the United States or to defame the president or other federal officials. In accordance with principles that had been introduced in earlier colonial cases,[5] the act required proof of malice and intent; truth could be given as justification and a jury would determine the law as well as the fact.

Jefferson and Madison led the fight against the act and, upon Jefferson's election as president in 1800, those who had been prosecuted under the act were pardoned. The act expired on March 3, 1801, the day of Jefferson's inauguration as president.

The fate of the Sedition Act firmly established that the government cannot determine what should be published and that no exception is provided, even for foreign affairs and national security issues. Nevertheless, public and congressional tolerance of dissent rose and fell with circumstances, including wars and the Cold War. The right to publish freely would be challenged several times during the two centuries of the nation's history. Even during the Civil War, the press remained largely free.

Limits of Freedom

Patterns of control of information still common in many countries never became part of the American system. With very few exceptions, such as the *Christian Science Monitor*, newspapers and publications were not owned by political parties, religious bodies, or labor unions as has been the case in much of Europe. In spite of wartime restrictions, the U.S. has steered clear of ministries of information and other official mechanisms found in most countries of the world for exercising government control over the press. Private ownership of the means of dissemination and opinion has prevailed.

The most untrammeled exercise of the right and power of the private media to influence international events occurred in the steps leading up to the Spanish-American War. In the last decade of the nineteenth century, the *New York Journal*, owned by William Randolph Hearst, a flamboyant journalist out of San Francisco, and Joseph Pulitzer's *New York World* were locked in a no-holds-barred battle for circulation. The two newspapers seized on the insurrection against Spanish rule in Cuba and competed in portraying the struggle in exaggerated and jingoistic terms. Frank L. Mott in his *American Journalism* describes the process: "Lurid pictures of mutilation of mothers and killing of babes, of the execution of suspects, of imprisonment in filthy and fever-charged stockades were drawn both in words and by the pencils of artists."[6] In one widely reported but never authenticated story, a photographer sent by Hearst to Cuba to document the trouble telegraphed to Hearst, "Everything is quiet. There is no trouble here. There will be no war. Wish to return." Hearst is said to have replied, "Please remain. You furnish the pictures and I'll furnish the war."[7] The campaign continued even after the Spanish government accepted U.S. conditions for reforms on the island. President William McKinley opposed going to war with Spain, but, when the battleship *Maine* was blown up in Havana Harbor on February 15, 1898, war was declared. McKinley could not resist the public pressures generated by the images of the situation created by Hearst and Pulitzer.

In the 1890s, the two publishers could prevail in their efforts to stir national emotions, despite the opposition of the president, because the nation was in a mood of "manifest destiny," of expansion. No serious threat or challenge existed to its sense of security or to its self-image as a dynamic, powerful young nation.

That sense of security was to change with World War I. That war brought a perception of serious threats reaching even into U.S. society, both from the Central Powers in Europe and from the emerging Bolshevik revolution in Russia. For the first time, in 1917, the U.S. government created its own information agency, the Office of War Information, with a mandate to disseminate the official version of events both at home and abroad. In June 1917, Congress passed a measure giving the government the power to impose criminal penalties against those providing false or damaging information. The Espionage Act (to be heard from again in 1990) provided punishment of up to twenty years in prison for (1) false statements that tended to interfere with military or naval operations or promote the success of enemies of the United States; (2) actions causing the disruption of loyalty or insubordination among soldiers and sailors; and (3) efforts to obstruct enlistments and recruiting. The act was followed in October 1917 by the Trading-with-the-Enemy Act, authorizing censorship of all messages sent abroad, and a new Sedition Act in May 1918. The latter imposed heavy fines and imprisonment for the writing or publication of "any disloyal, profane, scurrilous, or abusive language about the form of government of the United States or the Constitution, military or naval forces, flag or the uniform of the army or navy of the United States."[8] Under these acts, not only was the concept of "prior restraint"—prohibiting in advance the publication of an item—accepted but so also was the authority of the postmaster to block the dissemination of suspected publications.

The legal test of the Espionage Act came in the case of the *Masses*, a monthly journal that published four articles attacking the war and the military draft and was blocked from mailing by the postmaster. Learned Hand, then a federal trial judge, enjoined the postmaster from prohibiting the mailing, but the prohibition was upheld in March 1919 by the U.S. Supreme Court in the case of *Schenck* v. *United States.*[9] Each Supreme Court consideration of First Amendment law adds new language and new dimensions to the compounding case history; *Schenck* v. *United States* was no exception. Justice Oliver Wendell Holmes wrote a one-paragraph opinion for the majority:

> But the character of every act depends upon the circumstances in which it is done. The most stringent protection of free speech would not protect a man in falsely shouting fire in a theatre and causing a panic. It does not even protect a man from an injunction against uttering words that may have all the effect of force. The question in every case is whether the words are used in such circumstances and are of such a nature to create a clear and present danger that they will bring about the substantive evil that Congress has a right to prevent. It is a question of proximity and degree.[10]

Although Justice Holmes had been prepared to acknowledge the limits on freedom in war time, he used the concept of "clear and present danger" in a slightly different form in a dissent in 1920 in the case of *Abrams* v. *United States.*[11] The Abrams defendants were Russian refugees who threw pamphlets off the top of a building in New York City. The pamphlets urged a general strike to protest the decision of President Woodrow Wilson to send troops into Russia. The Court upheld their conviction on the grounds that their effort urged resistance to the war altogether. Holmes, however, dissented, referring again to the power of Congress to limit expression in cases of "the present danger of immediate evil or an intent to bring it about." He added, "Now nobody can suppose that the surreptitious publishing of a silly leaflet by an unknown man, without more, would present any immediate danger that its opinions would hinder the success of the government arms or have an appreciable tendency to do so."[12] Justice Holmes's term "clear and present danger" was to reappear frequently as a test for the justification of actions against publications, although not always accepted by the majority.[13]

Prior Restraint

Much of the action continued to be in the courts. Two other cases prior to 1970 were significant in expanding the limits of freedom. At the heart of the first case was the question of "prior restraint"; at the heart of the second, questions involving libel.

Court opinions that have implications for foreign policy often come about through decisions that bear no relationship to foreign affairs. This was the case both in the issue of "prior restraint" and that of the right of a public official to sue a newspaper for libel.

In 1927, Floyd B. Olson, the county attorney in Hennepin County, Minnesota, obtained a judge's order to close the *Saturday Press,* a muck-raking weekly newspaper in Minneapolis.[14] The offending articles charged that a Jewish gangster was in control of gambling, bootlegging, and racketeering in Minneapolis and that many officials, including the Chief of Police, were in cahoots with the gangsters. The closing was based on a 1925 Minnesota Public Nuisance Law that declared anyone operating "a malicious, scandalous and defamatory newspaper" was guilty of a "public nuisance" and the offending newspaper could be closed, unless the publisher could prove the story was truthful and published with good motive. The publisher, Jay M. Near, took the case to court, and, in 1931, the U.S. Supreme Court in the case of *Near* v. *Minnesota,* by a vote of five to four, struck down the law as unconstitutional, regardless of whether the article was true or false. The Court ruled that the plaintiff had recourse in suits after publication, but could not prevent publication. As Anthony Lewis has written in *Make No Law, Near* v. *Minnesota* "liberated American expression from a confining English practice, the ready use of prior restraints on publication."[15] Once more, in this case, the thread of tradition reaching back to the earliest days of the Republic appeared. Chief Justice Charles Evans Hughes, in the majority opinion, quoted from James Madison's attack on the Sedition Act of 1798 in the Virginia Resolutions:

> Some degree of abuse is inseparable from the proper use of everything and in no instance is this more true than in that of the press. It has accordingly been decided by the practice of the States, that it is better to leave a few of its noxious branches to their luxuriant growth, than, by pruning them away to injure the vigour of those yielding the proper fruits. And can the wisdom of this policy be doubted by any who reflect that to the press alone, chequered as it is with abuses, the world is indebted for all the triumphs which have been gained by reason of humanity over error and oppression?[16]

Near v. *Minnesota* established a strong tradition in the United States against actions to prevent publication. As an expert noted, "Although the first amendment is not an absolute bar to prior restraints, the Supreme Court has repeatedly said that 'any system of prior restraints comes to this Court bearing a heavy presumption against its constitutional validity.'"[17]

A related issue was the right of a public official to respond to criticism through libel suits against offending publications. Fear of such suits can be an inhibiting factor in the willingness of a publication openly to challenge the portrayal of policy or events by an official. Before World War I, libel was largely a matter for the states. Courts increasingly tolerated attacks on public officials, excusing falsehoods if the attacks were made in good faith and with a probable basis for believing them to be true. In 1964, however, in a landmark case, *New York Times v. Sullivan,* the issue was moved to the federal Supreme Court.

On March 29, 1960, the *New York Times* had published an advertisement by a civil rights group portraying the treatment of black protesters in Montgomery, Alabama, and implying brutality and harassment on the part of the police. L. B. Sullivan, a city commissioner in charge of the police, sued, insisting he and his officials had been defamed. The Alabama courts upheld the commissioner, but the U.S. Supreme Court overturned the decision and in its ruling extended to citizens throughout the country a constitutional privilege to criticize public officials. If the criticisms were false and defamatory, it became the burden of the plaintiff to show "actual malice," that is, in the language of the Court's decision, "with the knowledge that it was false or with reckless disregard of whether it was false or not . . ." defined as "a reckless regard for the truth." The Court made it clear that its purpose was to "unshackle free political debate." In his conclusion to the opinion, Justice William J. Brennan, Jr., wrote:

> Thus we consider this case against the background of a profound national commitment to the principle that debate on public issues should be uninhibited, robust, and wide-open, and that it may well include vehement, caustic, and sometimes unpleasantly sharp attacks on government and public officials. . . . The present advertisement, as an expression of grievance and protest is one of the major public issues of our time, would seem clearly to qualify for the constitutional protection.[18]

Criticism of foreign policies and of foreign affairs officials was not exempted from this decision.

Era of Disenchantment

Following World War I, when the United States assumed a greater international role, questions of how foreign policies and situations abroad were pictured became increasingly relevant.

The trend was substantially accelerated after World War II when the global position of the United States became dominant and the Cold War with the Soviet Union took center stage in foreign and strategic policy considerations. In the 1950s, the national consensus upheld the U.S. view of the worldwide struggle. Support was strong for participation in the North Atlantic Treaty and the Korean War. The mass media covered the war, as it had others before, in a patriotic spirit and without questioning official statements on the conflict and its progress.

Journalists in both the print media and radio, in the same period, led the way in challenging the substance of the exaggerated anti-communist charges and actions of Senator Joseph McCarthy. Among those in the print media were Murray Marder of the *Washington Post* and Phil Potter of the *Baltimore Sun*. In the emerging days of TV, Ed Murrow in what was then a courageous act denounced the senator on a CBS broadcast in March 1954, well before the opening of the congressional hearings that ultimately brought McCarthy down. Much of the press, however, reported his attacks on the State Department without challenge.

The almost automatic acceptance of the news as it was portrayed, whether by the executive or the Congress, came to an end in the next decade, the 1960s. It was spurred in part by television, which brought contradicting images directly into the nation's living rooms, in part by the rise of a new, more skeptical, less satisfied generation, and in part by a growing realization in the press that government versions of events could not be trusted. The 1960s and 1970s saw major assaults on the power of officials to portray events abroad in terms favorable to government policy.

James Reston, noted *New York Times* columnist, attributes the start of press disenchantment with government to actions of the Central Intelligence Agency (CIA), starting with the Bay of Pigs incident in 1961 when an attempt by anti-Castro rebels, with CIA help, to land in Cuba turned into a disaster.[19] The *Times,* however, remained sensitive to government secrecy. The newspaper learned of the training for the invasion and Tad Szulc, whom Reston describes as "one of the *Times'* designated scoop artists," filed a story from Miami saying that the attack on Cuba was "imminent." The managing editor overruled the makeup editors, reduced the item from a major front page story, and removed the word "imminent." Reston writes that the makeup editors were angry at the change and "were encouraged in their anger when Kennedy later remarked to Catledge [the managing editor] that if we had made more of the story maybe he would have avoided what he called a stupid mistake."[20] The *Times* was persuaded by the Kennedy administration to hold a story that the navy was planning to intercept Soviet ships during the Cuban missile crisis in 1963, but that was a rare occasion.[21]

Disenchantment with government became acute during the long war in Vietnam when correspondents on the ground began to suspect that official accounts of battles and of casualties were being altered to continue to project a positive picture of the war and its progress. Reporters contributed to a growing national skepticism and opposition to the war and were increasingly influenced by that mood in their own reporting. At the same time, questions were raised by those supporting the war regarding the patriotism, balance, and perspective of the mass media. In one event, the Tet offensive, even some members of the press believed that reporters and cameras presented a distorted picture.[22] The national consensus on foreign policy that had held for so long was collapsing, opening the way for a myriad of portrayals of situations abroad and intense debates at home.

James Boylan, in his article "Declarations of Independence,"[23] describes the attitudinal change among media professionals in the 1960s. He mentions the lessening of a blind acceptance that "Papa knows best," referring to government statements. "The press," he writes, "no longer saw itself as part of an American team." The tendency grew to look for lies, to challenge the official line, and for reporters and editors, not government officials, to determine what should remain secret.

The controversy over the coverage of the war in Vietnam ultimately reached the courts when the question of prior restraint recurred in the case of the Pentagon Papers. In 1969, Secretary of Defense Robert McNamara had commissioned a Pentagon researcher, Daniel Ellsberg, to prepare a "History of U.S. Decision Making Process in the Vietnam War." The result was a classified review of the debates within the government that surrounded the highly controversial U.S. involvement in Indochina. Ellsberg, an opponent of the war, made the documents available to the *New York Times*. The *Times,* preparing its editions in secret, began publishing the leaked report in June 1971. The government immediately sought an injunction to prohibit the *Times* from further publication of the documents. The *Times* stopped, but the *Washington Post* then began to print the forbidden papers. Another injunction stopped the *Post* and the effort was taken up by the *Los Angeles Times*. By this time, the *New York Times* had appealed to the U.S. Supreme Court. Taking up the matter on an urgent basis, the Court ruled in *New York Times* v. *United States* that the government failed to meet the heavy burden necessary to justify prior restraint. Hearkening back to the case of *Schenck* v. *United States,* the Court said that the government had not been able to show that the publication of these two-year old documents would constitute a "clear and present danger" to the security of the United States.

The Pentagon Papers case was also part of a larger challenge to the government's right to create and retain secrets. For the first time, major newspapers were prepared openly to publish an item stamped "secret." It opened the way to other major leaks of sensitive information, of which the most famous of the era disclosed the rifling of the files of the Democratic Party offices in the Watergate apartment complex. The "burglars" were later traced to the White House. The story emerged through revelations to two *Washington Post* reporters, Bob Woodward and Carl Bernstein, by an as yet unidentified source referred to as "Deep Throat," and was further elaborated on and followed by *Time,* the *Los Angeles Times,* and the *New York Times*. Although the Watergate affair was not directly related to the coverage of foreign policy issues, it did further stimulate the confrontation between government and the media on all issues. Investigative journalism became the popular road to media fame, and foreign affairs issues were fair game for such probing.

Contradictions between the truth and what government claimed to be the truth that arose from the Pentagon Papers and Watergate cases not only led to a further loss of confidence in government but also eroded the idea that government was the sole arbiter in determining what was in the national interest, and created pressures for still greater disclosure. Congress in 1966, responding to these pressures, passed legislation, unique in the world—the Freedom of Information Act. Under this act, private citizens could petition government agencies for the release of documents from official archives even if they were classified. Some exceptions were granted, including "items specifically authorized by executive order to be kept secret in the interest of national defense or foreign policy and determined to be properly classified." These exceptions, however, were limited by the requirement that, when challenged, agencies had to demonstrate in court that their refusal came clearly within the provisions of the act. Officials in foreign affairs agencies who wished to deny release would, for example, be required to demonstrate that a true national defense or foreign policy issue was involved and that the document had been properly classified. The CIA sought blanket release from the provisions of the act. As the result of this effort in 1986, operational files of the CIA are exempted from search, review, or disclosure.[24] Other intelligence material could be sought on the same basis as information in the foreign affairs and security archives.

Government agencies were accused of delaying release and, in 1986, Congress strengthened the act, requiring agencies to make a determination within ten days whether to comply with the request and to take action on appeals within twenty days.[25]

Libel

The 1960s and 1970s saw increasing challenges to the official portrayals of events, spurred in part by a more conservative mood in the country exemplified in the election of Ronald Reagan as president in 1980. Images that had been created in the media were challenged, primarily through two high-profile libel cases that also cast doubt on the methods employed by some news organizations in their presentation of events.

The first was a suit brought in 1984 by Ariel Sharon, a former minister of defense of Israel, against *Time* magazine. On September 16, 1982, Christian Phalangist militiamen invaded two Palestinian refugee camps in Lebanon—Sabra and Shatila—and massacred an estimated 700 inhabitants of the camps, reportedly in revenge for the assassination two days before of the Phalangist leader and president-elect of Lebanon, Bashir Gemayel. *Time,* in reporting on the event, stated that Sharon, then defense minister, had visited the Gemayal family after the assassination and had "reportedly discussed . . . the need for the Phalangists to take revenge."[26] *Time* also stated this information was contained in a secret "Appendix B" to a report of an Israeli commission investigating the Israeli role in the massacres. Sharon brought suit, arguing that *Time* had falsely and with malice accused him of directly inspiring the massacres.

The subsequent trial revealed questionable processes in *Time's* handling of the story. David Halevy, a native Israeli employed by *Time,* had reported that Sharon gave the Gemayel family "the feeling" that he understood their need to take revenge.[27] In the New York editorial offices of the magazine, the words "gave them the feeling" were changed to "discussed." The jury determined that *Time* was guilty of both defamation and falsehood, but, drawing on the case of *New York Times* v. *Sullivan,* also determined that *Time* had not acted with "actual malice." As one review of the case commented, "In the face of a trend in which news organizations rely on appellate courts to rescue them from hostile juries, this panel endorsed a concept of libel law designed to discourage litigation by public officials."[28]

In the second case, General William Westmoreland, who had been the commander of U.S. forces in Vietnam, brought suit against the Columbia Broadcasting System (CBS) for a program on January 23, 1982: "The Uncounted Enemy: A Vietnam Deception." The television film charged that there had been "a conspiracy at the highest levels of military intelligence" to "suppress and alter critical intelligence on the enemy."[29] The broadcast sought to show that Westmoreland had understated the number of North Vietnamese troops infiltrating into the South because the true figures were far higher than previous projections. According to the CBS program, intelligence officers had been ordered to make arbitrary cuts in the statistics to avoid an angry reaction from President Lyndon Johnson. The controversy over the broadcast was further fueled by the research of a *TV Guide* reporter claiming that CBS reporters had produced a biased story.[30] An internal CBS report, according to various news sources, found that the network had violated its own standards through interviewing mostly people who supported the program's thesis, coddling sympathetic witnesses, and coaching others. In one case, according to the CBS report, the network filmed one interview a second time because they were unhappy with the first interview.[31] The trial once again brought into question the procedures by which the mass media used information and framed issues. General Westmoreland, however, like Ariel Sharon, was unable to prove "actual malice" on the part of CBS and, on February 18, 1985, after five months of trial, costing roughly $2 million, he settled the case with a compromise settlement statement.[32]

Secrecy

In two cases reflecting events in the 1980s, the court did set limits in matters of the release of information relating to national security. The first was the case of *Snepp* v. *United States.* Frank Snepp, an ex-CIA official, in a book called *Decent Interval,* drew on his experiences as an intelligence officer in Vietnam and used material from intelligence files without clearance from the agency, although upon leaving the agency, he had agreed to seek such clearance. The agency sued, claiming that his failure to obtain clearance constituted a breach of contract. Anthony Lewis describes the Court's decision:

> The Supreme Court agreed that it was [a breach of contract] and granted the extraordinary relief sought by the government. First, it enjoined Snepp—for the rest of his life—from ever again writing or speaking without prior CIA approval about intelligence matters that he learned while an agency employee. Moreover, the CIA was to be the judge of whether he had learned something as an employee, so he had to submit for clearance anything that touched on subjects he had dealt with while there. . . . Second, the Court imposed what it called a "constructive trust" on Snepp's earnings from *Decent Interval*, meaning that he had to turn over to the Treasury his advance from the publisher and all royalties.[33]

The second case involved the release of three photographs obtained by a secret intelligence satellite of a Soviet aircraft carrier under construction. The photos were sent by a naval intelligence analyst, Samuel Loring Morison, to the British naval publication *Jane's Defense Weekly,* which in turn distributed them through the Associated Press to U.S. newspapers. The *New York Times* printed one of the photographs on August 8, 1984. Morison was indicted under the Espionage Act of 1917 not only for the distribution of the photos, but also for the theft and illegal possession of naval intelligence reports about an explosion at a Soviet naval base. Morison's defense lawyers argued that the Espionage Act was intended only to apply to the passage of information to an enemy, not to the press. Morison was nevertheless convicted, and the conviction was upheld on appeal in April 1986. In a concurring opinion on the case, Judge J. Harvey Wilkerson acknowledged the need for secrecy in the conduct of certain national business and listed the dangers if secrecy in some instances cannot be enforced:

> When the identities of our intelligence agents are known, they may be killed. When our electronic surveillance capabilities are revealed, countermeasures can be taken to circumvent them. When other nations fear that confidences exchanged at the bargaining table will only become embarrassments in the press, our diplomats are left

helpless. When terrorists are advised of our intelligence, they can avoid apprehension and escape retribution. The type of information leaked by Morison may cause widespread damage by hampering the effectiveness of expensive surveillance systems which would otherwise be expected to provide years of reliable information not obtainable by other means.[34]

Wilkerson went on to express a point of view that, perhaps, best balances the needs of government for secrecy and of the press for disclosure. He did so by quoting from a speech delivered by Justice Potter Stewart at Yale in 1975.

> But this autonomy [of the press] cuts both ways. The press is free to do battle against secrecy and deception in government. But the press cannot expect from the Constitution any guarantee that it will succeed. There is no constitutional right to have access to particular government information or to require openness from the bureaucracy. . . .
>
> The Constitution, in other words, establishes the contest, not its resolution. Congress may provide a resolution, in at least some instances, through carefully drawn legislation. For the rest, we must rely, as so often in our system we must, on the tug and pull of the political forces in American society.[35]

As the 1990s dawned, the limits of freedom of speech and the press in the United States had been defined and extended, although still with some limits. Greater skepticism placed constraints on the degree to which the government could credibly describe events in the face of an aggressive, often hostile, press. The actions of courts virtually eliminated the right of officials to respond to charges and criticisms. Newspapers, magazines, and television, although sensitive to possible libel actions, felt a strong degree of protection because of the demonstrated difficulty of proving "actual malice." But the courts still saw the need to support government in its efforts to preserve secrets—within the proper definitions of secrecy.

But the new decade also brought the end of the Cold War and, with it, demands for even greater limits on secrecy. Many also saw this as an opportunity for greater openness. In an article in the *Washington Post,* Congressman Lee Hamilton, a member (and later chairman) of the House Committee on Foreign Affairs, wrote: "The end of the Cold War provides an opportunity to promote greater openness in government. We should reform the entire system through which information is classified for national security."[36] As the government and the press grapple with the more complicated post–Cold War world and its conflicting and opposing images, this plea is likely to be heard more and more.

2 Government Speaks

The public dimension of foreign policy begins with the government. What the president or the secretary of state or any of the myriad of government spokespersons may say is the raw material for the challenges, the debates, and the pressures that ultimately determine support for policies.

The news organizations, print, television, and radio, are today a presence—whether seen or unseen—whenever Washington officials meet to consider action. News on the air may set the agenda. Awareness of deadlines can determine the timing of announcements. Concern over unauthorized leaks restricts attendance at official meetings. The question, "What shall we say to the press?" follows most decisions. The question is welcomed by those with the skill to manipulate, feared and avoided by others. In today's world, the link between foreign policy and what is said publicly is inseparable.

The drafting of public statements may represent the most important official decisions of the day in setting priorities and determining courses of action. The stakes are high; they may involve serious threats to the nation and to others: war, terrorism, famine, revolution. Silence or a statement of indifference toward an issue can lead others to challenge significant U.S. interests. Bold threats unsupported by action can weaken the nation's diplomatic credibility.

Public statements on foreign policy are the product of a complex process embracing politics, bureaucracy, diplomacy, and, often, personal ideologies and ambitions. In nearly every administration—certainly since World War II—a secretary of state's day begins with a review of the public aspects of foreign policy. Although the wider dimensions of issues may be discussed, the early morning meetings usually focus on questions raised by the morning headlines or news shows. Participation is limited to a few key staff members—determined often more by the secretary's personal relationship with the officials than by their precise duties. Secretary of State Cyrus Vance held such a meeting each day at 7:40 A.M. As undersecretary for political affairs, I was included, along with the deputy secretary, Warren Christopher, the head of the policy planning staff, Anthony Lake, the executive secretary of the department, Peter Tarnoff, and the assistant secretary for public affairs, Hodding Carter.

After such meetings, consultations take place with other executive departments. Whether the process involves the president, cabinet officers, subordinates, or advisers, the words, written or spoken are carefully drafted, reviewed, and coordinated. The results of these deliberations are revealed through daily briefings,[1] at the White House and the State and Defense Departments. Briefings are supplemented by periodic press conferences, interviews, statements at ceremonies, speeches, and appearances before congressional committees. Whatever the occasion, the words represent national policy.

The nature of the briefings was changed during the Carter administration when, for the first time, television cameras were introduced for live coverage. The free give and take between the press official and reporters that can later be modified in print is no longer possible before the camera. Caution on the part of the government became even more pronounced.

As chapter 1 demonstrated, U.S. government officials have few levers, under the law, with which to exert control over the flow of information. To gain public support and understanding they must create persuasive images of events and policies by other means. The results are not false, but neither do they always represent a complete picture.

Americans wish the pronouncements on foreign affairs that ultimately come from government were clearer, more informative, and more candid. The terms "fudge factory" and "foggy bottom," applied frequently to the Department of State, represent the measure of public frustration. Shortly after the Clinton administration came into office, the *Washington*

Post, under a headline, "At Briefing, No News Is Old News," commented on the new press team:

> Whether the subject is health care, or Haiti, or the economic address Clinton will deliver tonight, the daily briefings are an exercise in minimalism. Reporters repeatedly rephrase their questions in a dogged attempt to shake loose snippets of news. [George] Stephanopoulos and 31-year-old Dee Dee Myers, the press secretary, firmly hold their semantic ground.[2]

So why are official statements so often elliptical, equivocal, and obtuse?

Reasons for Caution

There are reasons for the caution and semantic evasion. Since the end of World War II, the United States has occupied a world position of unprecedented power. Nations abroad have listened for statements from Washington for clues to the direction of that power: adversaries have looked for weakness; allies have looked for support. In the Third World, where exaggerated suspicions of U.S. manipulation have existed, listeners have searched for conspiracies. Among friends in the Third World, what Washington says has created expectations—often unrealistic—of economic or military assistance.

In many situations, particularly in crises, fundamental differences exist between the objectives of government and the interests and needs of others. How public information is handled plays a role—not always successfully—in the government's ability to manage these differences. One example lies in the conflicting interests present for the U.S. government and U.S. citizens in the days preceding the revolution in Iran in 1978-79.

As the situation in Iran began to deteriorate, the United States had five principal objectives: (1) to evacuate approximately 45,000 U.S. citizens, military and civilian; (2) to maintain a friendly government in Iran for as long as possible; (3) to protect sensitive equipment and sites related to monitoring under the prospective Strategic Arms Limitation Treaty; (4) to dispose of approximately $12 billion in military sales agreements; and (5) to establish a relationship with a new regime should one take power.

Each of these objectives required different and at times conflicting information strategies. The evacuation required providing information and advice to the American citizen community without creating undue alarm or further undermining the shah's weak government. The maintenance of a friendly government required reassuring statements that were not totally divorced from the reality of a collapsing regime. The protection of sensitive equipment required making members of Congress and others in the government aware of the problem without attracting the political attention in Iran that might speed up demands for withdrawal of the installations. Efforts to renegotiate military equipment contracts required a minimum of publicity if the beleaguered military in Iran were to cooperate. Holding out a hand to a possible successor regime required avoiding negative statements that would make future cooperation difficult.

In each case, however, press interest was high and information was available to individuals and groups outside the influence and control of the authorities in Washington. Individual Americans as well as their Iranian partners were aware of U.S. government efforts to encourage their departure—and many did not like what they were being asked to do. Some, like Ross Perot, attempted to manage departures of employees on their own.[3] Efforts to bolster the shah's government through positive statements ran directly counter to the reports on television and in the print media of the deteriorating situation. Members of Congress opposed to the ratification of the SALT agreement went public with their knowledge of the vulnerability of the installations in Iran as further argumentation against the treaty. Military contractors were aware of the renegotiation of the military sales agreements. The question of U.S. efforts to establish a relationship with a successor regime became embroiled in an ideological debate within the government between those who thought the shah could survive and those who saw the handwriting on the wall. Inescapably, the debate became public knowledge.

In the end, only two of the objectives were achieved. The American community was withdrawn from Iran without casualties. The military sales agreements were renegotiated and much of the equipment destined for Iran shifted to other buyers. In a period dominated by dramatic television coverage of the revolution and media reports of dissension within the administration, however, these successful efforts received little public attention, either in the press or in official announcements.

Against this same background, the official public efforts to support the shah not only failed but may have further complicated what slim chance existed for good U.S. relations with the Khomeini regime. Throughout the final days of the revolution, U.S. official statements continued to express support for the shah, even when such a policy seemed more and more unrealistic. The State Department feared that any change in public support would accelerate the shah's downfall. Some in the National Security Council staff hoped that, by such reiterations, the shah might be encouraged to take forceful action on his own.

U.S. officials do not face dilemmas every day as difficult as those in Iran in 1979. Each day does, however, bring new problems and the need to digest information and create the images necessary to support policy. Such creation must be a constant and carefully managed activity, not totally divorced from the reality of what is happening on the ground.

The Check List

No formal checklist exists for those who speak or prepare drafts for those who do. Words flow out of experience, intuition, and awareness of the possible consequences of what is said. For those preparing public statements in response to a crisis or a problem, at least ten questions cross the mind, whether consciously or subconsciously.

1. How much do we know? Crises can happen without warning. The first knowledge for officials may come from a brief item on CNN. For government to react publicly on the basis of fragmentary information is unwise, however startling the news. Diplomatic communications lag behind news. Even when such communications are received, the information can be incomplete or contradictory. The intelligence community may be divided on its significance or reluctant to provide data that might reveal sources and methods.

The shooting down of Korean Airlines Flight 007 on September 1, 1983, illustrates the problem. The first news was that an airliner had "disappeared." An hour passed before the fact that the Soviets had shot down the plane was revealed by Japanese and U.S. intelligence sources. But many questions remained unanswered. Why was the Korean plane off course? Did the Soviets confuse it with a U.S. reconnaissance plane in the vicinity? Was the decision made at a high level in Moscow? Could the confirming information obtained by communications intercepts be used without compromising the method? Given the complexity and delicacy of relations with the USSR, the stakes were high. As Secretary of State George Shultz comments in his memoirs, "The debate now shifted, with even greater intensity, to what our public statement should be and who should make it. . . . A decision had to be made now about how the United States would treat this disaster. What was said in the next hour or so would shape our reaction in a fundamental way."[4]

2. *Do we need to say anything?* In the case of Korean Airlines flight 007, some statement was imperative. The news was out and much depended on the reaction. Shultz and President Reagan decided on a factual statement of what was known, adding only, "The United States reacts with revulsion to this attack. Loss of life appears to be heavy. We can see no excuse whatsoever for this appalling act."[5] Yet, in many cases, it is appropriate to ask whether any comment is necessary or wise. Events abroad, especially those involving crises or military risk, are news and gain wide public attention. Officials cannot ignore such news. Yet premature comment or comment on an issue in which the U.S. is not involved can create problems. Statements are rushed out before policies have gelled; decision makers are whipsawed by TV imagery and public opinion. When Secretary of Defense William Perry, during a critical period in the siege of the Bosnian Muslim city of Gorazde in April 1994, commented that the U.S. was not about to use military force to save the besieged town, his remarks had to be quickly toned down by the White House.[6] As in this case, statements from U.S. officials have impact far beyond Washington. The attacking Serbs could base their strategy on the assumption that the U.S. would not intervene; in contrast, the Bosnian Muslims resentment at the lack of outside support could only deepen. What Perry said may well have been true, but to the warring parties it represented an American intrusion into the action—favorable to one side, unfavorable to the other.

The impact on the public, especially of television pictures, means that responses to events cannot be indefinitely delayed without suggesting indecision or efforts to conceal. "No comment" will hold off unwarranted assumptions by the press for only so long. Hodding Carter, State Department spokesperson in the Carter administration, believes that officials too often panic and feel they must make statements when they may not be necessary—but for most, the pressure is too great.[7]

3. *If so, how much do we say?* Few issues in the relations between the press and the government awaken more criticism or create more serious concerns than the question of the right of government to dodge the truth. Numerous articles by journalists attack the government for lying.[8]

It is the policy of the government not to lie. A Department of State memorandum to "All Public Affairs Officers," dated February 16, 1982, states, "Apart from time, we need four things from officers in the Department." One of those listed is:

> We need *absolute honesty*. The Department's credibility is a matter of proud record over a long period of time, but it is tested anew every day of the year. As tempting as it may be in any given situation to shave the facts a bit, there is always another office which benefits on the same day in an equally tricky situation from the fact that the newsmen believe the Department's spokesman.[9]

But the matter is not that simple. Occasions frequently arise when presidents, secretaries of state, or other high officials believe it is not in the national interest for the press and public to be aware of diplomatic, intelligence, and military activities. Hard-pressed senior officials may have time only to say to their press officer, "Don't tell them a thing about that," making it clear that they do not wish to be disturbed again on that matter. The press officer is then left to interpret what the boss really wants. Such public relations disasters as the cover-up of the transfer of funds to the contras in the Iran-contra affair undoubtedly resulted in part from the combination of a hesitation to burden the president with details and a certainty on the part of lower officials that they knew the president's mind.

On the matter of telling untruths, the first question is, "What is a lie?" If the press spokesperson, aware that something has happened or is about to happen, when asked about it says, "I don't know," is that response a lie? Related is the question of how much the press official should know. Larry Speakes, White House spokesman in the Reagan administration, not only was not told about the forthcoming invasion of Grenada in 1983, but when he asked Admiral John Poindexter whether rumors about it were true, he was told, "Preposterous."[10]

In such cases, the next level of untruth is a direct denial that such an operation is going to take place. In the case of military and covert intelligence operations, alternatives exist. The general outline of policy can be laid out without being precise on actions. The press can be briefed on a background basis and trusted to hold the story until it is officially released. The lack of confidence in the media, with few exceptions, makes that option unrealistic.

Although the press and the public may have little sympathy with the concept, for foreign affairs officials secrecy is the normal mode—whether in planning or in the midst of a crisis. The fear of the consequences of disclosure may appear exaggerated to the reporter. The official, often working long hours and under great stress, has much at stake both personally and professionally, and an excess of caution appears justified. To the practitioner, the successful development of foreign policy requires an initial period in which all alternatives can be examined within the government away from the interventions of special interests and pressure groups, whether foreign or domestic. For the public to accept closed-door decisions, policymakers must demonstrate that they have the necessary political support, expertise, and judgment to make responsible decisions away from public glare.

Theoretically, an open debate on a policy in formation in a democracy is desirable. Unfortunately, in recent years, open debates on foreign policy are more often opportunities for the most determined, vocal, and best financed elements in a debate to have a disproportionate influence on the outcome.

In 1979, the Carter administration was attempting to create a centrist alternative to the Nicaraguan dictator Anastasio Somoza. Somoza was engaged in a civil war with leftist Sandinista elements and was given little chance of victory by most observers. He had, however, a small but powerful group in Washington defending his interests, including two members of Congress. A meeting on the morning of June 8, 1979, was held in the State Department with, as I recall, thirteen persons participating. By two o'clock in the afternoon, the late edition of the *Washington Star* appeared on the streets with a front-page story accurately recounting the options considered in the meeting. The story was repeated with greater detail in the Saturday edition.[11] This leak immediately stimulated a strong counter effort against any options that implied the departure of Somoza, seriously complicating the possibilities of a peaceful alternative.

In perhaps the most studied crisis of the post–World War II period, the Cuban missile crisis of 1962, most observers accept as essential to its resolution the secrecy within which decisions were made. For thirteen days in October, not only the world but most of those in government were unaware that President John F. Kennedy and his small group of senior advisers were debating options in response to the deployment of Soviet missiles in Cuba. During that period, I was responsible for two White House visitors, President Ahmed Ben Bella of Algeria and Hassan al-Ridha, the crown prince of Libya. I was at least twice in the White House and had not the slightest indication that serious matters were occupying the leadership. Clearly, the management of that crisis would have been far more difficult—if not impossible—if leaks had created a wider national debate on what should have been done.

Precisely to avoid outside pressures, both the Nixon and Carter administrations were able to keep secret their moves toward normalization with China until the initial steps had been taken. Henry Kissinger, then Nixon's national security adviser, feigned illness in Pakistan and was able to make a secret trip to Beijing in July 1971 to meet with Zhou Enlai. Carter limited knowledge of his China initiative to no more than a dozen officials, and completed the process begun by Nixon through secret negotiations in 1978. Premature disclosure of either step would have embarrassed the Chinese and led to strong efforts by congressional supporters of Taiwan to block the move.

The process of diplomacy requires confidentiality. Negotiations with others cannot be productively pursued if tactics and positions are revealed prematurely. Few believe it would have been possible for President Carter to have achieved the breakthrough in Middle East negotiations and the peace treaty between Egypt and Israel in 1979 if the press had had full access to the day-to-day deliberations at Camp David.

Diplomacy also requires effective consultation with other countries. Such consultation in turn creates the need to protect information received from other governments and the names and origins of sensitive sources. Other governments will be reluctant to share candid assessments of their own political problems or of the international scene if their comments are not safeguarded. Individual foreigners, whether dissidents or officials, will be afraid to share their private views without some assurances of confidentiality.

Reporters and academics frequently challenge government officials to demonstrate where genuine harm has resulted from premature disclosures of foreign affairs information. To the official who may be seeking carefully to manage a crisis or to prepare a significant initiative, many cases come to mind.

In February 1979, when the American Embassy was first seized in Tehran, the United States planned to move six helicopters and a contingent of Marines to eastern Turkey to prepare for the possible evacuation of U.S. citizens from Iran. The Turkish government, always sensitive to foreign—even NATO—forces in its country, consented on condition that the deployment not be publicized. The news of the deployment leaked out of the Marine base in Camp LeJeune, North Carolina, and, on

February 12, the *New York Times* carried a story revealing the planned destination. The next day, the Turkish foreign minister withdrew permission for the deployment.

After the embassy hostages were seized in Iran in November 1979, President Carter decided to send former attorney general Ramsey Clark and a Senate staff member, William Miller, on a secret mission with a presidential message to Ayatollah Ruhollah Khomeini. The Iranian officials agreed to the visit, but emphasized that it had to be kept secret. When Clark and Miller arrived at Andrews Air Force Base outside of Washington, however, they were confronted with a battery of reporters and TV cameras. The story, including pictures of the departing plane, broke on the NBC evening news on November 6, despite efforts by Jody Powell, the White House press secretary, to dissuade NBC from carrying the story. The publicity caused second thoughts in Iran, and Khomeini ordered that no one in Tehran should talk with them. Whatever possibility might have existed for an early dialogue with Khomeini was ended.[12]

4. *What about the politics?* In an ideal world, those preparing official statements and recommendations would do so based solely on their perception of the nation's interests and international consequences of an action. The State Department, in contrast to the White House, maintains, in theory at least, an approach above politics. Inescapably in a democracy, however, politics intervenes. Those in elected positions and their appointees have the ultimate responsibility. In the case of the United States, how will the president and his administration appear: strong, weak, uninformed, undecided, inconsistent? How does what is said position an administration for the next election?

Constituencies are also a factor. Will industry, agriculture, labor be affected? Each constituency is important politically and yet may have different interests and perspectives in a foreign policy matter.

An experienced State Department official will know that certain international issues are loaded with domestic political dynamite. If statements, in particular, that relate to issues of concern to potent ethnic lobbies are not checked by the White House, trouble can ensue. In at least two occasions in my career, once in the Johnson administration and once under Carter, the Department was forced to retract statements relating to the status of Jerusalem because of objections from the political operatives. Similar pitfalls exist on issues relating to Greece and to Ireland.

5. *How will what we say affect our bureaucratic and personal positions?* Battles within the bureaucracy are not only over policy. Senior officials in

executive departments will have in mind how media coverage of policies or events will affect the standing of their department in the executive branch as a whole. Standing means cabinet and legislative clout. Tugs of war have taken place between secretaries of state and defense over which department will release an important national security decision. The Department of State wishes to maintain control on foreign policy issues, but faces mandates presidents give to others, whether the Defense Department or the Central Intelligence Agency. In some administrations, the intense rivalry between the Defense Department, the National Security Council staff and the State Department has been marked by acrimonious debates over public statements. Former Secretary of State George Shultz, in his book, *Turmoil and Triumph,* reports how Secretary of Defense Caspar Weinberger sent an unclassified letter (almost certain to be leaked) to President Reagan before a summit meeting with Mikhail Gorbachev of the Soviet Union in November 1985. The letter urged the president not to give Gorbachev either a commitment that the United States would continue to abide by SALT II or to agree to any narrow interpretation of the Anti-Ballistic Missile (ABM) Treaty that might interfere with the development of the Strategic Defense Initiative. In Shultz's view, the letter was "written and leaked deliberately to hamstring the president and sabotage the summit."[13]

At lower levels of the bureaucracy, fear plays a role. Many a subordinate official in the United States government has felt some empathy for those in authoritarian societies where thought and speech are closely controlled. Especially in U.S. administrations in which sharp divisions exist or which feel beleaguered by public attacks, a pervasive sense exists throughout the government that unauthorized speech will reflect badly not only on the official involved but on the secretary of the department as well. In the administration of President Jimmy Carter, deeply divided between National Security Council staff and State Department positions on policy toward the Soviet Union, lower level officials in the State Department were circumspect lest their comments complicate the problems of the secretary of state in his contest over policy with the White House.

At the upper levels, ego comes into play. Washington is a city of ambitious people; a positive public image is essential to their survival. Competition for position leads inevitably to the use of the press and TV to advance personal agendas as much as to inform. Those with great egos will consider primarily how information can be released—or withheld—

to enhance their individual prestige and position. When preparing a statement, officials ask themselves, "How will this statement affect me?" President Lyndon Johnson wanted the option of making important announcements himself; if decisions of his administration leaked before he could do so, he would often cancel the decision. Personal and official motives meld together and are often indistinguishable.

6. *Will we offend any audiences?* Public statements on foreign policy reach a variety of audiences. No one who prepares or issues a statement can be under the illusion that only the immediate audience is hearing. Electronic communications and print can carry statements before small and obscure audiences to affected corners of the world. In some cases, statements unnoticed in the United States but published in foreign media come to the attention of U.S. correspondents abroad and are then sent back to America. The re-transmission may not be immediate, but delays do not diminish the impact.

The diverse audiences include, among others, the Congress, special interest groups, allies, adversaries, and international organizations. An official statement that confirms corruption or weakness in a country receiving aid can be immediately seized on by a committee of the Congress as a reason for cutting assistance to that country—even when other policy reasons would support its being continued. The lack of admission that such conditions exist can be criticized in the Congress as evidence either of ignorance or inattention to corruption or human rights on the part of the administration. During the Cold War years, administrations struggled with statements related to countries like the Philippines and Zaire where oppressive rulers were tolerated because of the security interests involved. Statements to Congress in regard to a country like Saudi Arabia had to avoid discussion of such issues as the position of women and the criminal code in order to minimize offense to a significant friend.

Because of the importance of the United States to the security of a host of nations around the world, allies pay close attention to U.S. official pronouncements. Consideration of allied sensitivities is important but is at times overshadowed by domestic requirements. In recent years, ideology has affected U.S. official statements. President Ronald Reagan's statement in 1981 that an exchange of tactical nuclear weapons might be possible without escalation into a wider nuclear war may have pleased his domestic followers, but it caused serious consternation among the friends of the United States in Europe.[14] Reagan's application of the term "evil empire" to the Soviet Union was intended primarily for the audience of evangelical Christians he was addressing on that day, yet it was read throughout the world as an indication of a confrontational official attitude.[15] Adversaries take seriously what the United States is saying. Some, such as the former Soviet Union and Iran, saw such statements against the backdrop of their own perceptions of the United States as a threat.

Those who prepare and make statements on behalf of the United States must remain conscious of the threat that can be posed to American citizens abroad in times of crisis. Overly belligerent statements can, in such circumstances, trigger reactions ranging from an increase in military activity to threats against individuals. Although it was never proved, many involved in efforts to rescue Ambassador Cleo Noel and his deputy, Curt Moore, from terrorists in Sudan in 1974 believe that President Richard Nixon's statement during the crisis that "the United States would not submit to blackmail" led the terrorists to conclude that negotiations were not possible and, subsequently, to kill both Noel and Moore.[16]

7. *Is our statement sufficiently positive?* Admissions of failure or inability to resolve a problem are not welcome. Even though in retrospect many a public official would have been better off to have acknowledged problems and failures at the time they happened, the political culture is generally afraid of candor.

One issue that especially bedeviled the Clinton administration was that of Bosnia. Hemmed in by campaign rhetoric that spoke of rolling back the Serbs and of war crimes trials for their leaders, they gave uncertain signals on policy.

On March 24, 1993, the situation in Bosnia was becoming increasingly bleak. Neither the European nations nor the United States were prepared to take forceful action against Serbian attacks on Muslim civilians. The peace plan negotiated by Lord Owen of Britain and former secretary of state Cyrus Vance was gaining little support. The only action taken by the United States in direct support of humanitarian aid was the decision to airdrop supplies to beleaguered Muslims. On that evening, Reginald Bartholomew, who had been appointed a Special U.S. envoy to work on the problem of the conflict in the former Yugoslavia, appeared on the MacNeil-Lehrer News Hour. In it, he turned a discussion of the negative to the positive—a clear example of this second principle:

MacNeil: The United Nations authority is being flouted daily by the Serbs in all kinds of examples we have seen. What practical steps does the United States think or advocate to strengthen the United Nations' hand there?

Bartholomew: Well, I think what we're doing in the sense of the kinds of support that we've been giving to the, giving to the humanitarian effort, and here may I say I, I would just simply like to note that when the President took the decision on the airdrops at the time you might recall that there was some questioning as to how effective they would be or whether they were more than a gesture.

MacNeil: I questioned you about it.

Bartholomew: You did, indeed, question me about it. I just note Larry Hollingsworth [representative of U.N. High Commissioner for Refugees] speaking of their absolutely critical role in the case of, in the case of Srebrenica.[17]

Closely associated with the positive statement is the claim of success. "Take credit for achievements; leave disasters to others" remains a political axiom. It applies both to individuals and to countries. Europeans have blamed the Americans for their foreign policy problems and vice versa. Americans have done it to each other. Following the Gulf War in 1990–91, controversy raged in Washington over what the United States had said to Saddam Hussein before the war that might have encouraged him to believe that it would not respond to aggression against Kuwait. Much of the blame was permitted by Secretary of State James Baker to fall on April Glaspie, then U.S. ambassador to Iraq, although copies of her instructions subsequently released made it clear she was following dictates from the secretary of state. Secretary Baker was asked about his responsibility by R. W. Apple of the *New York Times* in a *Meet the Press* program on September 23, 1990:

Apple: April Glaspie . . . made it quite clear in quite explicit language—as I said, authorized by you—that the United States took no position as between Kuwait and Iraq in this border dispute. Why was she told to say that?

Baker: Johnny, I think what you see here has best been characterized, if I might say so, by a very good article that Ed Yoder wrote yesterday in the *Washington Post,* and what he called all of this as "retrospective scapegoating," and he characterized it as shameful. . . .

Let me tell you what the signals were that were sent to Saddam Hussein before this happened.

Signal No. 1 was to slap foreign policy export controls on exports to Iraq. Signal No. 2 was to cancel or suspend the Commodity Credit Corporation program with Iraq. Signal No. 3 was to prohibit the export of a number of items that we and some of our allies thought might be useful in terms of missile or nuclear proliferation. So now we've got some 20/20 hindsighting going on that's been highly critical, frankly, of some very fine career public servants of the United States.

Apple: Nobody's trying to criticize April Glaspie. They're trying to criticize you.

Baker: What you want me to do is say that those instructions were sent specifically by me on my specific orders. I'm not going to deny, Johnny, what the policy was, but I'm going to say to you that there are probably 312,000 or so cables that go out under my name as Secretary of State.[18]

8. Is our statement consistent? When preparing a public statement, it is a virtual axiom in the State Department always to look at what was said on the issue in the last previous statement. Members of the White House and State Department press corps, long-time residents of Washington, and observers of the bureaucracy also have long memories. They are quick to look for inconsistencies, especially on critical issues. Statements, for example, on the U.S. view of the status of Jerusalem always get special scrutiny. President Reagan was tripped up in the Iran-contra affair in large part because his actions in providing arms to Iran were in sharp contrast to his previous statements about that country. When inconsistencies are noted, the usual response is to say that the U.S. position has not changed; circumstances have.

Consistency is especially necessary during times of crisis when the slightest change in wording may be interpreted as a change in policy. In 1979, when the shah of Iran was under increasing pressure to leave his country, Hodding Carter, the State Department spokesperson, was asked each day if the United States supported the shah. Despite indications of the weakening of the shah's position, Carter repeated the same phrase, "Yes, we support the shah." To have done otherwise would have sent a signal of a weakening U.S. position with consequences for the effort to make a smooth transition in Tehran.

For many nations abroad, consistency means doing for them what the United States has done for others. During the Gulf War, official spokespersons frequently mentioned that the United States did not condone the acquisition of territory by force. Such phrases immediately raised questions among Arab states about why this did not also apply to the U.S. attitude toward the Israeli occupation of Arab lands. Others seek to demand comparable attention on the basis of U.S. statements on human rights. When the U.S. criticizes the oppression and lack of democracy in Haiti, for example, why does it not make similar statements about China or Zaire? Each statement on an internal condition in a country, whatever the circumstances and however unique the particular situation may be, creates a precedent that will be applied by advocates for other areas.

The problem of maintaining consistency in official statements has constantly plagued the U.S. government. Presidents and their staffs, however, have traditionally been reluctant—except in circumstances in which their own prestige was at stake—to exert discipline within the bureaucracy. Presidents have obligations to each of those whom they have appointed to lead executive departments; they would prefer to avoid being caught between them. Constant monitoring by presidential staffs to ensure conformity and cooperation among the bureaucratic elements is beyond the capacity of a busy White House.

Often the effect of public statements is blunted when actions read as "signals" are inconsistent with official statements. From the recent post-mortems on the Cuban missile crisis of 1962, it seems clear that Nikita Khrushchev, before deploying nuclear missiles to the island, genuinely believed—as did Fidel Castro—that the United States was planning to invade Cuba. He had as background the failed Bay of Pigs invasion in April 1961, plus a number of other signals and statements. A strong economic embargo had been imposed against Cuba. According to Raymond Garthoff in his *Reflections on the Cuban Missile Crisis,* the Soviets were aware of an October 1961 directive from President Kennedy to the Joint Chiefs of Staff to draw up contingency plans for an invasion of Cuba. The Kennedy administration, Garthoff noted, "was also responsible after November 30, 1961, for sending sabotage and diversionary units of Cuban emigres on raids into Cuba under an action plan called "Operation Mongoose."[19] The Soviets and Cubans were undoubtedly aware of these efforts. In the spring, summer, and fall of 1962, a series of large-scale U.S. military exercises were conducted in the Caribbean. On

September 20, 1962, a Senate resolution, passed by a vote of 86 to 1, stated that the United States was determined "to prevent by whatever means necessary, including the use of arms, the Marxist-Leninist regime in Cuba from extending, by force or the threat of force, its aggressive or subversive activities to any part of the hemisphere."[20] To a suspicious Soviet Union, such a statement would appear to provide a pretext for military action if the United States decided to take it. As Garthoff comments, "It was thus not unreasonable for Cuban and Soviet leaders to be concerned in 1962 over intensified U.S. hostile action against Cuba, including the possibility of an invasion."[21]

Against this background, the Kennedy administration sought in public statements to deny any intention to invade. But the statements were always a balance between denial and an expressed determination to use force against Cuba if U.S. interests were threatened. President Kennedy spoke to the American Society of Newspaper Editors on April 20, 1961, just after the Bay of Pigs disaster. He said, "Any unilateral American intervention, in the absence of an external attack upon ourselves or an ally, would have been contrary to our traditions and to our international obligations." Yet his speech was full of other phrases indicating that "if the nations of this hemisphere should fail to meet their commitments against outside Communist penetration—then I want it clearly understood that this Government will not hesitate to meet its primary obligations, which are to the security of our Nation!"[22] In the same vein was this statement by Ambassador Adlai Stevenson to the United Nations General Assembly on September 21, 1962:

> Now, in direct answer, let me say to the representatives of the Soviet Union and of Cuba that we are not taking and will not take offensive action in this hemisphere. For, as the President of the United States made clear last week, we and other countries of the Americas will not be deterred from taking whatever action is needed by threat from any quarter. While we will not commit aggression, we will take whatever steps are necessary to prevent the government of Cuba from seeking to subvert any part of this hemisphere. We shall work closely with our inter-American partners, and this intention does not, of course, derogate from our right, a right anchored in the United Nations Charter, to protect our vital national security.[23]

The most skillfully drawn public statements, seeking to balance a determination to isolate Cuba with a note of restraint could not dispel the impression given by other actions that led to one of the most serious crises of the post–World War II period.

9. *Have we chosen the right words?* Words are the life blood of diplomacy and politics. Presidents are invariably tempted to use them in expansive rhetoric that may imply or promise more than is intended. Presidential rhetoric is a form of diplomatic currency that requires careful hoarding. When presidents speak too often and without careful preparation, not only does the rhetoric lose its power and prestige, but the risks are high of errors and misunderstandings.

In every country, whether democratic or authoritarian, political leaders take a special interest in foreign policy. Not only are the issues exciting; they are also crucial to the security of the nation and, often, to the future of the individual leader. Kings, prime ministers, and presidents enjoy the drama and the exposure of summits, visits, conferences, and speeches that put them at center stage. Domestic issues may be more important, but they do not usually command the same audience.

The power of the United States, especially in the post–World War II years, has created a worldwide impression that, whatever Washington wants to do, it can do. Public expressions by U.S. officials, therefore, are seen against the background of the nation's assumed capacity to act. When American officials speak of their strong belief in freedom and democracy, the statements create expectations that the U.S., if it really believes what it says, will work to establish such freedom and democracy. An announcement that the United States "supports the independence of Country X" may immediately create hopes of a U.S. military intervention. An observation that the United States "is greatly interested in the economic development of Country Y" can lead to unrealistic expectations of economic aid. Washington has often in the past been pressed to make such statements either in lieu of more forceful action or on the occasion of the visit of a foreign dignitary. Administration officials had to face the problem of explaining lowered realizations later on. Rhetoric, whatever its intended purpose, can have a cost in the anger of the disappointed.

Although officials of the Bush administration insist that statements during the Gulf War calling for the Iraqis to overthrow Saddam Hussein did not give encouragement to resistance forces in that country, it is hard to disassociate the tragic expectations of the Kurds and the Shiites from hopes raised by presidential rhetoric. An example is Bush's comments in remarks to the American Association for the Advancement of Science on February 15, 1991:

But there's another way for the bloodshed to stop. And that is for the Iraqi military and the Iraqi people to take matters into their own hands—to force Saddam Hussein, the dictator, to step aside, and to comply with the United Nations resolutions and then rejoin the family of nations.[24]

When a militarily powerful nation publicly calls on others to rise against their government, it is naive to think that those affected will not assume that this means a willingness of the powerful nation to come to their aid.

Leaders often speak on their own. President Carter's statement after the invasion of Afghanistan that he had not previously understood the Russians did not come out of a staff conference. The same could be said of Secretary of State James Baker III's statement that the U.S. response to the Gulf War in 1991 was based on "jobs." Leaders can—as they often do—set aside the recommendations of staffs. When President Carter visited the shah of Iran in December 1977, he was advised that conditions in Iran were becoming uncertain and that any public statement should avoid too close an identity with the shah. Carter ignored the advice, believing, as many of his predecessors had believed, that it was important not only to be polite on such occasions, but also to give the shah strong support. The consequence was his embarrassing and well-reported statement—thirteen months before the shah was overthrown—that the Iranian monarch "represented an island of stability" in the region.

The drafting of official statements involves a carefully considered use of words. This advice may seem obvious, yet it is meant to convey more than a truism; it is meant to refer, also, to the time often spent in deliberation over one or two words in an official release. Words are at the heart of public expressions and carry perils of their own.

Some words when associated with certain issues imply positions of the parties. Ronald Reagan's use of "freedom fighters" to describe the contras in Nicaragua or the resistance in Afghanistan clearly implied sympathy. "Terrorists" or even the more neutral "guerrillas" suggests a less favorable stance. Middle East policy issues are minefields in which words become identified with the position of one side or the other on the nature of a final peace. "Self-determination" to both Palestinians and Israelis means ultimately a Palestinian state; for that reason Israelis have consistently protested its use by the United States.[25]

10. And finally, do we have a persuasive rationale for our action? The preparation of an official statement often begins with a search for a rationale that will be persuasive both at home and abroad. The problem is not great if the reasons for action are clear and can be explained without adverse diplomatic or political reaction. This is not always the case; what is an acceptable rationale in one country may not be in another. An administration must then determine how it can sell what it is about to do to a variety of audiences. Questions must be answered: What national interest is involved? Will the explanation bring us the authority and resources required from the Congress? Will the public support whatever risks or sacrifices may be necessary? Will allies and adversaries accept the rationale as a convincing basis for cooperation? In legally minded Washington, can we provide a basis in law—whether national or international?

Finding a proper rationale for action was seldom a problem in the Cold War; officials needed only to cite the Soviet threat. Few in the United States or the non-communist world quarreled with the rationale for U.S. sanctions applied against the Soviet Union following the Soviet invasion of Afghanistan in December 1979. But by the 1980s, the power of the Soviet rationale began to fade. Ronald Reagan, with all his persuasive powers, could not convince the American public that the contras in Nicaragua were "freedom fighters," holding up the interests of the West against the Cuban/Soviet threat.

By contrast, the search for a persuasive rationale was even more pronounced in the several justifications presented for major U.S. deployments to the Gulf after the Iraqi invasion of Kuwait in 1990, a time when a collapsing Soviet Union no longer presented a basis for U.S. actions. When President George Bush decided to send troops to Saudi Arabia, he faced not only a variety of possibly inhibiting public attitudes, but also the national sensitivities involved in putting together a coalition of Arab and European states. The primary U.S. interest was clear to knowledgeable observers of American policies in the region: the preservation of access on reasonable terms to the oil supplies of the Gulf. Beyond that, many were concerned by the implied threat to the security of Israel of Saddam Hussein's declarations and acquisition of weapons of mass destruction. Ironically, as is occasionally the case, the specific concerns could not be strongly emphasized in public statements; other rationales needed to be found. Despite the heavy dependence of Americans on fossil fuels, the concept of sending armed forces to "protect the oil companies" or the "oil rich sheikhs" was unpopular politically. Similarly, any stress on the security of Israel would risk diminishing support among Arab states for Washington's policies in the Gulf.

In official statements in support of the Gulf War, words and concepts were needed that would avoid these pitfalls and, at the same time, build support for military action in a deeply divided Congress and from a public skeptical about executive motives. What followed was a series of statements by different speakers, with emphases tailored to audiences of varying political tendencies. Although a thread of consistency existed, the result of the strategy was a public impression of an uncoordinated search for a rationale for the deployment and of a none-too-successful effort to disguise the real reasons.

David Hoffman of the *Washington Post* described the administration's dilemma:

> Bush devoted the autumn months to midterm congressional campaigns and his remarks on the stump often underscored the difficulty that he had in offering the country a compelling rationale for the Gulf deployments. He tried saying, delicately, that it was about oil, but polls showed that the American people did not support military action over oil supplies. He several times compared Saddam to Adolph Hitler, but this also seemed hyperbolic. . . . At yet another point, Bush emphasized Saddam's nuclear potential, but experts said it was not clear that Iraq was on the verge of obtaining nuclear weapons. [Secretary of State] Baker, too, stumbled in trying to articulate the stakes, saying at one point [November 13, 1990] that Saddam threatened the world's economic lifeline "and to bring it down to the average American citizen, let me say that means jobs. If you want to sum it up in one word, it's jobs." Baker was widely criticized for the condescending tone of his remark.[26]

A more detailed examination of the administration's statements will illustrate the dilemma Hoffman outlined. In his first address to the nation on the deployment, President Bush, on August 8, 1990, said: "I took this action to assist the Saudi Arabian government in the defense of its homeland."[27] He added reference to "four simple principles" that were repeated, with some variations, in most statements on the crisis: the withdrawal of Iraqi forces from Kuwait; the restoration of Kuwait's legitimate government; the security and stability of the Persian Gulf; and the protection of American lives abroad. Oil was mentioned as part of the "high stakes" in the region; Israel was not.

The president stated the goals in somewhat different terms in his address to employees at the Pentagon on August 15:

> Our action in the gulf is about fighting aggression and preserving
> the sovereignty of nations. It is about keeping our word and standing
> by old friends. It is about our own national security interests and
> ensuring the peace and stability of the world.
>
> We are also talking about maintaining access to energy resources
> that are key—not just to the functioning of this country but to the
> entire world. Our jobs, our way of life, our own freedom, and the
> freedom of friendly countries around the world would suffer if control
> of the world's great oil reserves fell into the hands of Saddam Hussein.[28]

In a statement at a news conference on August 30, the president
added "the shape of the post-postwar world" to the stakes.[29] Secretary
Baker, in an appearance before the House Foreign Affairs Committee on
September 4, reworded the stakes, placing emphasis on the invasion as "a
political test of how the post–Cold War world will work," and on the need
to "show that intimidation and force are not successful ways of doing
business in the volatile Middle East—or anywhere else."[30] Dependence
on access to the energy resources of the Persian Gulf was given as a third
stake. The objectives previously enunciated by the president were repeated with a revision to take into account the need to release Americans
then held hostage in Iraq. Finally, the secretary outlined the broad
international support being given to U.S. efforts.

In less formal statements, however, the president went beyond the
prepared rationales to speak of Saddam Hussein as "another Hitler" and
to draw frequent analogies to the appeasement in Europe in 1939.[31] Vice
President Dan Quayle, in a speech at Seton Hall University on November
29, referred to America's victory over the Soviet Union in the Cold War
and the need to continue two other strategic objectives in the Middle
East: "the prevention of any local Middle East power from achieving
hegemony over its neighbors," and securing "the uninterrupted supply of
oil at a reasonable price."[32] He also, for the first time in an official
statement on the issue, mentioned "We do not think Israel's existence . . .
should be threatened," and introduced the issue of "weapons of mass
destruction."[33] President Bush picked up the latter theme in a statement
at a news conference on November 30:

> We're in the gulf because the world must not and cannot reward
> aggression; we're there because our vital interests are at stake; and

we're in the gulf because of the brutality of Saddam Hussein. We are dealing with a dangerous dictator all too willing to use force, who has weapons of mass destruction and is seeking new ones and who desires to control one of the world's key resources—all at a time in history when the rules of the post–Cold War world are being written.[34]

In this statement, the president also introduced the themes of the "immorality" of the invasion and the "precedents" such actions might create for others. Vice President Quayle further stressed the morality issue in remarks to a conference of the Foreign Policy Research Institute in Washington on December 18:

Some critics of the Administration have questioned these [the stated goals] of the administration. In particular, they have questioned the morality of coming to the defense of what they call a "feudal," "reactionary," and "repressive" regime . . . .

This is precisely the warped and evil morality used by Stalin and his henchmen to justify their infamous campaign of terror during the 1930s. The people of the Soviet Union have turned their backs on the morally demented legacy of Stalinism. And so shall we.[35]

The various statements paved the way for a narrow vote in Congress in support of military action against Iraq. But the legacy of skepticism over the hyperbole of some of the statements remained.

3 The Reporting Dimension

I f officials close meetings with a query about how to deal with the press, public discussions on foreign policy almost as frequently lead to complaints about "the media": It's the media's fault we don't understand issues. The media is unfair or inaccurate. The media exaggerates, sensationalizes. You can't believe what you read or hear.

The free and active information services in the United States through their reporting and circulation of opinion play a key role in shaping perceptions of events and of government responses. The images they convey press government and people to action. Their screens and pages filter and challenge what officials say. Inevitably, the news organizations share with officialdom the burden of being a target for public frustration in a complex world.

As an official for many years with access to both government messages and the daily newspapers and newscasts, I have concluded that there is little of international significance that is not covered by the news organizations. In Washington, at least, the government has few secrets. Certainly there have been items I found inaccurate or incomplete. Inevitably time lagged between decisions and their disclosures. Those reporting and selecting the news are inescapably limited by the economics of the business, the boundaries of time and space, and access. In what they present they cannot wander too far from the interests and conventional wisdom of their readers and listeners. But these do not add up to the ideological bias which many, unhappy with the message, charge the messenger.

With the rise of a new breed of talk show hosts, primarily conservative in outlook, and utilizing new cable channels, TV networks, radio, and book publishing, the relationship of opinion to information has become an issue. A comment in the *Los Angeles Times* illustrates this:

> There are now more than 20 public affairs talk and interview shows on television, and their proliferation, combined with the decline of the Washington columnist, "can't help . . . diminish the quality of conventional wisdom" and the public discourse that ensues, says Robert Merry, managing editor of Congressional Quarterly.
>
> "There's a show biz imperative to spout off," Merry says. "You don't survive on these shows if your aim is to . . . dig deep into the complexities of Washington happenings and emerge with wisdom.... You survive on these shows by being quick—provocative."[1]

Hodding Carter, State Department spokesman in the Carter administration, calls the Washington-based TV talk shows "the most insidious, the most destructive [force] to independent thinking. The best of the shows put a premium on essentially superficial reactions. Insight and any depth of analysis, any nuance, is completely gone."[2]

This chapter is intended to deal with news organizations — those which see their mission as the objective transmittal of the events of the day, supplemented by editorials, columnists, and analyses with the intent of providing a broad range of opinion. Nevertheless, the existence of the new talk show phenomenon of highly ideological, often vitriolic commentary, exemplified by such voices as Rush Limbaugh, cannot be ignored in any discussion of the influences that shape perceptions and attitudes toward foreign policy. Such voices, given access to the public through new cable channels, book publishing, and the effective use of radio and television, make no pretense of objectivity. Their influence is reflected in think tanks and in Congress. Limbaugh was given credit by many observers for the mobilization of Republican sentiment in the 1994 congressional elections. He was a speaker at the Heritage Foundation conference for new members of Congress.

Although the insistence by such conservative voices on the bias of the "liberal media" can be challenged, a full examination of the influence of the newspapers, radio, and television on public perceptions of international events requires an examination of common criticisms of the news business—many of which come from those directly involved in it.

Although usually referred to as "the media," as if it were one national institution, the organs of public expression that carry international news in the United States are far from monolithic. They vary in ownership, in style, in politics. They include (as of 1993) 1,735 daily newspapers and more than a dozen weekly magazines of news and opinion.[3] Broadcast organizations include three major television networks plus Cable News Network (CNN), Public Broadcasting System (PBS), National Public Radio (NPR), and numerous local TV and radio stations. Except for PBS and NPR, which receive partial government subsidies, all organizations are private, for-profit, commercial ventures. Although the electronic networks require government licensing to ensure fair frequency allocation, in none is the content subject to government control.

The television networks, CNN, PBS, and NPR are national in coverage. Major newspaper chains, such as Knight-Ridder and Gannett, also have national scope, and at least three newspapers, *New York Times, Wall Street Journal,* and *USA Today,* through multiple publishing, circulate on a national level.

The major news organizations gather information through their own reporters and correspondents, but they and all others depend also on wire services, principally the Associated Press and Reuters. Major newspapers, *New York Times, Washington Post,* and *Los Angeles Times,* also sell their news to other publications. Electronic news services feed programs such as MacNeil-Lehrer.

Any description of information sources in 1995 must be qualified; technical advances lead to predictions of electronic newspapers, 500-channel television, and instantaneous computer communication that may make today's media dramatically outmoded. Yet such predictions are qualified by estimates of cost and questions concerning public acceptance. For some years to come, the public is still likely to receive its news and images of events abroad through the techniques that currently exist.

Even current techniques represent a radical change in the way international news is gathered and presented. Thomas Rosenstiel of the *Los Angeles Times* describes the change:

> Where once Walter Cronkite and Howard K. Smith described events and showed film footage that might be several days old, today

CNN regularly airs videotape as soon as it comes in—pictures that are unedited, that even the CNN journalists have not seen, pictures without narration.

The change has been driven by technology with an almost Darwinian inevitability, as videotape replaced film, satellites replaced wires and satellite dishes became so portable they could be carried in suitcases. In a few years, video signals will probably be sent over phone lines, meaning that TV can be transmitted from anywhere.[4]

The Primary Media

The medium with the greatest impact on both public perceptions and policies today is television. It is also the medium with the greatest limitations in terms of broad, in-depth coverage of events.

Visual images have always had the greatest effect on public emotions. Matthew Brady's photographs and the sketches in *Harper's Weekly* did it in the nineteenth century. *Life* magazine aroused the nation over Japanese atrocities in China in the pre-television 1930s. Today television, with its capacity for dramatic visual projection, follows that tradition. And it is to television that most people turn for their news. A News Interest Index issued by the Times Mirror Center for the People and the Press on January 10, 1991, during the Gulf crisis, reported that 82 percent of persons surveyed said they had been getting most of their Gulf news from television. A National Opinion Ballot Report of the Foreign Policy Association reported on a survey of participants in the organization's Great Decisions Program.[5] Of those who said they paid "a great deal" of attention to the coverage of international affairs, CNN, network news, and the MacNeil-Lehrer News Hour ranked high as sources of information. In a 1984 *Newsweek* poll in response to the question, "Where do you get most of your news about current events?" the responses were: television, 62 percent; newspapers, 56 percent; radio, 13 percent; and magazines, 9 percent.[6] In 1990, the *New York Times* estimated that 40 million Americans still tuned in to the nightly news.[7]

Quite apart from the absorbing impact of pictures, television stimulates causes, encourages interest in disasters, conflict, and repression, and affects political attitudes. Television does this both by providing the technology that permits politicians to speak directly to audiences, and by transmitting news and programs. The *New York Times* on December 14, 1994, reported how Newt Gingrich, new speaker of the House of

Representatives, skillfully used C-Span in his rise to the political top. Said the *Times:*

> It really was just coincidence, but Newt Gingrich and C-Span arrived at the House of Representatives at the same time. Since then, 1979, they have come of political age together, with the media-savvy Republican Representative from Georgia, set to become Speaker in January, knowing instinctively how to exploit the unblinking television eye in the House and revealing himself to be one of the smartest chiefs in the global village.[8]

Michael Mosettig, a producer for the MacNeil-Lehrer News Hour, describes TV's power on the international scene:

> What is important about what we do, in this age of television and imagery, is which slice of life gets conveyed. From nearly every major event or crisis, there comes a certain shot, a certain sequence, that seems to capsulize the event. Sometimes that picture is as important or more important than the totality of the coverage. China is again an example. The picture, of course, is of the young man against the tank, rather like a bullfighter staring down the bull purely by the power of his presence and courage. Go back nearly 22 years ago to another example. The picture of the Viet Cong on the grounds of the U.S. Embassy in Saigon that had such a powerful effect on American public opinion. That had a more powerful effect than the cold reality that the Tet offensive was a costly and militarily unsuccessful roll of the dice by the communists. The power of the picture is why so many people try, and sometimes succeed in, manipulating us. Whether it's Mike Deaver at the White House, Anwar Sadat flying into Israel, the men around the Ayatollah Khomeini who thought they could stage-manage American public opinion during the hostage crisis or the people who hijacked TWA 840 in Beirut four years ago—all knew the reach and power, not just of our medium, but of particular pictures and images and the connotations a picture could carry.[9]

The events in China and Vietnam mentioned by Mosettig were only two in recent years that demonstrated this power. On October 23, 1984, the last item on NBC's Nightly News was a three-and-a half-minute report on a famine in Ethiopia filmed by the British Broadcasting Corporation. As reported by Peter J. Boyer, then chief of the Atlanta bureau of the *Los Angeles Times,*

It was a jarring piece, movingly narrated by BBC correspondent Michael Buerk. "The faces of death in Africa," [Anchor Tom] Brokaw called it.

The impact was immediate and overwhelming. The phones started ringing at NBC and at the Connecticut headquarters of Save the Children. . . . The next night, NBC aired another BBC report and, again, the response was staggering. CBS and ABC a week later aired more reports on the famine—with even more response, more reports. The story had exploded.[10]

The explosion continued into further coverage by all media and into massive international relief efforts. In 1991, similar coverage of war and famine in neighboring Somalia led not only to a global relief effort but to international military intervention.

But TV's concentration has not only been on immediate disasters. Without doubt, the electronic medium has been a potent force in bringing extended conflict to public attention and, through the technology of the tube, bringing warring parties to talk. As will be discussed in the next chapter, this was dramatically illustrated by Ted Koppel's Town Meeting programs that brought antagonists together in both the Middle East and South Africa.

Television is given substantial credit for spreading the word and the stimulus of the revolution of 1989 in Eastern Europe. In a paper published by the Atlantic Council, "The Media: Partners in the Revolution of 1989," Johanna Neuman, senior diplomatic correspondent for *USA Today,* writes:

> The truth is that the news media, no more than the Kremlin, cannot make a revolution. People, and passion, make revolutions. But a Soviet leader deciding not to send in the tanks—contrast Budapest 1956 and Prague 1968—can clear the stage for a revolution without bloodshed. A media spreading the news so quickly it defies the ability of censors to use their blue pencils can speed the players to the stage. And one thing more: a media that for forty years brought news of a different way of life—a message confirmed by travelers and culture, underscored by social memory and oral history—can keep alive hope, deepening an audience's resolve to take action into their own hands.[11]

With all the conspicuous power of television, however, questions remain regarding both the completeness and accuracy of its pictures of events and its ultimate impact on policies and actions. The scene taken by the camera and chosen by the news director may be only a vignette, omitting elements of a larger picture, and may, on occasions, be staged. Nevertheless, by the rapid transmission of news and images, television does, to a considerable extent, "set the agenda." It brings issues to the fore and creates pressures for official statements and policy responses. In *News That Matters: Television and American Opinion,* by Shanto Iyengar and Donald R. Kinder, the survey conducted by the authors concluded that if, over a period of time, television dedicates most of its news coverage to a particular subject, then, when the public is asked—days later and outside the context of television viewing—what is the major problem facing the country, they will be likely to mention that subject. At the same time, the authors conclude, "We do not mean to suggest that television's power to set the agenda and to prime citizens' political choices is unlimited. In fact, our studies suggest clear limits to television's power."[12]

Marvin Kalb, former television reporter and now director of Harvard's Shorenstein Barone Center, commented in a *New York Times* op-ed piece on the shortcomings in TV's coverage of the Gulf crisis of 1990-91:

> The crisis is clearly a big story, but it has yet to invade prime time. With few exceptions, there has been little serious reporting or analysis between 8 p.m. and 11 p.m.—the most precious terrain for any commercial network. But it's hard to crack through the corporate fix on ratings and profits. Worse, many producers and correspondents, bruised from earlier battles, seem resigned to accommodating this corporate mentality.[13]

In the panoply of information organizations, major newspapers continue to occupy a significant place. Their influence, however, is less with a mass audience than with opinion setters and, to some extent, policymakers. In the Great Decisions survey, also noted above, 36 percent of those who paid "a great deal" of attention to international affairs listed newspapers as a primary source and 21 percent, news magazines.

In any consideration of news sources, the newspapers of the medium-sized cities should not be forgotten. William German, editor of the *San Francisco Chronicle,* contributed this:

> Some of the newspapers below the very top level are covering the world with their own correspondents or are using one of the army of

free-lancers available all over. We have had our own people in Far East, Middle East, Central America, Western Europe, Balkans, etc. Gives readers a new perspective. Has inherent dangers (we have to be wary of journalists we don't know that well). In many cases these journalists are more independent of government pressure because they don't attract immediate attention (especially in Washington) . . . new communication technology . . . makes all this possible without a world-class budget commitment.[14]

The wide audience for both television and print does not necessarily suggest equally wide public confidence in the media. A *Newsweek* poll taken in 1984 showed a declining public confidence in newspapers. Thirty-four percent of the respondents in the poll said they had confidence in newspapers, compared with 51 percent in 1979. Confidence expressed in television news also declined—but from a lower base. Thirty-eight percent of respondents said they had confidence in television in 1979 and only 26 percent said so in 1984.[15]

What are the limitations faced by the news media in their quest for a full presentation of a day's events? First, news organizations are private commercial enterprises. They are at the mercy of economics.

Economics

The resources available to bring the external world into American households are finite. The news received, therefore, represents a choice in expenditures; much of the total world picture does not reach viewers, listeners, and readers in the United States. The cost to a television network to send producers, reporters, and cameramen to a foreign story is, at a minimum, $100,000 per day. With the takeover of all three networks by holding companies more concerned with profit than coverage, news programs are seen more than ever in terms of the "bottom line." This has meant both a greater emphasis on the entertainment value of news programs and less costly and adventurous news coverage.

The print media are also facing new economic constraints. The advent of television has meant a decline in newspaper and news magazine readership. The number of daily newspapers has declined; most cities are now one-newspaper towns. National chains own a greater proportion of newspapers. That decline and the development of new interactive shopping channels on television have resulted in serious competition for the advertising dollar, with long-range prospects for newspapers in their current form in question. Such uncertainty naturally breeds restraint in the stationing of correspondents overseas and in extraordinary coverage of events. Particularly in television, economic factors have led to a reduction in the permanent assignment overseas of full-time correspondents. This means more dependence on "parachute journalism" with the correspondent and camera crew moving from place to place as events dictate. The major newspapers, however, despite economics, have maintained their major bureaus in world capitals. In 1994, the *Washington Post* operated 22 overseas bureaus while the *New York Times* had 24.

The general reduction in the number of American news organizations with full time representatives overseas has meant a greater dependence on nationals of other countries, either as full-time correspondents or "stringers." As William German noted above, however, this has perils. TV film from unfamiliar sources can hide biases of the cameraman. This has been especially true in Bosnia where, in dangerous areas, outside networks have been forced to rely on Serb or Muslim "stringers." Reporters with different backgrounds may not understand the interests of American listeners and readers. At the same time, U.S. audiences have benefited from many non-American journalists who have been willing to cover stories in areas where Americans either cannot or may be unwilling to go.

Competition

The news that reaches the United States from abroad is the result not only of economic choices, but also of fierce competition. As newspapers and television networks face increasing economic problems, competition for audiences and readership becomes more and more intense. Compete or die is not just an aphorism. That competition leads in some instances to imaginative and innovative coverage such as ABC's Nightline. But it also leads to the tendency for all organizations to concentrate on the same stories and the same areas; they do not want to be caught short.

News is where the cameras and reporters happen to be. One result of this competitive instinct is that once one organization reports a development, the tendency is then for every other competing organization to follow. A natural outcome of a journalistic "sheep" instinct is that those events that gain the most public attention are those that take place where

TV and press representatives happen to be. This concentration of media organizations in one area covering one event may well distort both the importance and the nature of the event and lead to the neglect of other significant happenings. The seizure of the hostages in the American embassy in Tehran in 1979 received far more attention in the United States than the seizure of the U.S. ambassador in Bogota, Colombia, at the same time; the cameras were in Iran.

Not only does the concentration in one region distort, but so does the presence of cameras on a single street. Many are the reports of demonstrations that form as soon as TV cameras appear, whether in Iran, China, or Somalia. Little doubt is left about the real audience of the demonstrators when, in a land where English is little spoken, signs in various forms of English are thrust before the cameras. The cameras represent a way of reaching a Western audience.

When major events do occur, television organizations, in particular, make major efforts to "get on the scene." The Iraqi invasion of Kuwait caught the networks by surprise and none had crews or correspondents in Kuwait. The only eyewitness reporter was Caryle Murphy of the *Washington Post*. Radio and print media representatives are better positioned to get quickly to regions of unexpected crises because they have less equipment to carry. In a *Washington Post* story at the time, Ed Turner, top news executive of CNN, was quoted: "This story's a bitch. In a wired universe, where up-links and transponders are so common, here you've got a whole area of the world that's off-limits to us. We could get in the bowels of the Soviet Union for the Armenian earthquake and we could stay in [Tiananmen] square in Beijing, but we can't get a frame out of there."[16]

Access and Sources

The question of gaining access in times of crisis raises difficult issues. If access is only at the mercy of a government, should the media representatives accept limitations on their movements and censorship of their copy as the price of entry? Numerous reporters did ultimately get to Baghdad during the Gulf War and interviewed Saddam Hussein, presumably on his terms, giving the Iraqi dictator a major world forum. The question became even more acute after the air war started in January 1991 and Peter Arnett of CNN reported from Baghdad. The press argument that what Saddam Hussein says and what happens in Baghdad during a war constitute news is compelling. It would be impossible for the press to enter under such conditions without accepting controls. News organizations do attempt to indicate where censorship and conditions are being opposed and trust that the public will understand the conditions under which their reports are being sent.

Nevertheless, Saddam Hussein took full advantage of Western media interest. Cameras require scenes, and when such scenes cannot be found by producers, they fall prey to scenes provided by others. Walter Goodman, television critic of the *New York Times,* pointed out after the Iraqi invasion of Kuwait how Saddam Hussein, after forbidding cameras to show scenes of occupied Kuwait, was making use of Western television crews in Baghdad:

> President Saddam Hussein, at whose pleasure Western correspondents are in Baghdad, permitted them and their cameras into a hospital room for newborn babies. These are the targets of the embargo on trade, say the Iraqis; their milk and medicines are at risk. Is there in fact a shortage of milk or medicine? The question seems trivial beside the pictures, with their message that any threat to those sickly infants from any side and for any reason is unconscionable. Will many Americans be untouched by that principle?[17]

Somalia further demonstrated the vulnerability of TV cameras to a clever demagogue. Although the United Nations command concluded very early in the 1992 intervention in that country that Mohammad Farah Aideed, a warlord who controlled southern Mogadishu, was a major part of the problem, he made himself readily available to TV reporters. He clearly saw access to cameras as part of his strategy for gaining power. His ability to speak English helped. As a result, pictures of Aideed drawing large crowds in the Somali city dominated much of the coverage, giving viewers a misleading impression of his national power.

As Iraq and Somalia and numerous other international crises have shown, news reporting, whether by TV or the print media, is limited by the access granted to reporters and cameras and by the sources available. In authoritarian countries, American news organizations (not unlike diplomats) are often restricted to government officials; efforts to broaden coverage by speaking to dissident or opposition groups can bring expulsion. In such an environment, the ordinary citizen is afraid to be seen speaking with foreign reporters—and even more afraid to be quoted by one. Even in countries where access is freer, U.S. news representatives tend to seek out the English-speaking sources willing to meet with the foreign press. One result is a sameness of information and analysis that comes from correspondents tapping the same sources. The U.S. media thus often paint a picture of conditions and events representing the views of one segment of a society and miss the significance of other less accessible segments. One striking example was the coverage of Iran before the revolution when many of the indications of the serious threat to the shah's regime came in sermons in Shia mosques closed to foreigners. The concentration on official sources means, also, that the media is used—if not exploited—by regimes in power as well as opposition groups eager to get their point of view before Western publics.

Reporters who remain a long time in a country—or local correspondents for U.S. media—are likely to build friendships with significant local political figures. Such symbiotic relationships can affect the objectivity of someone reporting on local events. In the case of Ariel Sharon against *Time* magazine, discussed in chapter 1, David Halevy, the *Time* stringer in Israel, was accused of distorting his coverage of events because of his closeness to political enemies of Sharon.

American correspondents overseas also find sources in U.S. embassies, including the ambassador and other senior officers. Depending on the attitude and personality of the ambassador, the embassy can be a significant well of information and background assessments. Llewellyn Thompson, U.S. ambassador to the Soviet Union from 1957 to 1962, held regular meetings with American reporters and was a valuable source at a time when the USSR was closed generally to foreign journalists. In circumstances where deep policy differences exist at home, however, journalists are more suspicious of information coming from embassies.

Frank Smyth, a freelance journalist, raised questions about the reliability of the U.S. embassy in El Salvador during the civil war in that country:

> In the post–cold war era, ethnic rivalry may have replaced ideology as the most likely cause of conflict, but while all else changes one journalistic habit picked up during the past four decades will, in all likelihood, persist—the habit of relying heavily on the mission, as the U.S. embassy is known, for assessments and information. In an increasingly unfamiliar world, in fact, the temptation to do so will be even stronger.

What's wrong with this? A close look at coverage of the last of the cold war conflicts—the civil war in El Salvador—shows that all too often such reliance results in distorted news.[18]

Smyth then cites information that came from the embassy, later revealed to be either without foundation or incorrect, that included details about who was responsible for the murder of six Jesuit intellectuals in 1989 and assessments of the military success of the guerrillas.[19] Questions of access and sources exist in Washington as well. As the previous chapter has indicated, information is more freely available there, and sources are plentiful and often eager to talk to the press. Symbiotic relationships develop in the nation's capital as they do overseas, especially among top government officials and well-known columnists. Questions were raised, for example, during the Reagan administration about the objectivity of the conservative columnist George Will because of frequent meetings he was reported to have had with First Lady Nancy Reagan.

A veteran Washington journalist, Murray Gart, former *Time* correspondent and editor of the *Washington Star,* takes a different view:

> My experience suggests that so-called inside sources—sources that a reporter, like Will, get[s] to know well—are often much more reliable, better informed and far more useful than any of the alternatives official or otherwise. As long as the reporter takes care to check with others what he learns from the insider before rushing into print with a "scoop" what's wrong with inside information?[20]

Both the print media and television seek out as sources not only government officials but experts—or proclaimed experts—as well. Herein lie possibilities for distortion. Most information organizations genuinely seek a representative cross section of opinion in order to be as objective as possible. In an ordinary day, one can find opposing points of view presented on the op-ed pages of the major dailies and in the political talk shows on television and radio. Two difficulties arise: the question of who is an expert and, in television, the time allotted and the directions given.

Washington is full of proclaimed experts—academics, consultants, current and former diplomats both American and foreign, think tank members, and lobbyists. Many are eager to be seen and heard, although the quality of their knowledge, relevance, and delivery varies. Whenever a new crisis develops, newspapers, magazines, radio stations, and TV channels seek out people with some experience in the troubled region. The expert's knowledge may be recent or years old; it may be of the region or somewhere near by. Print media usually have the space for fairly full accounts. Except on a program like MacNeil-Lehrer, TV has little time, and looks for the person who can present an encapsulated statement of a complex issue in three minutes or less. Anyone who has appeared on a network show in such circumstances knows the experience: a quick thrust into the makeup room; a wait for the producer, usually running late; a brief greeting; a superficial question about one's background; and an admonition to keep comments brief.

Marvin Kalb, in the piece quoted earlier, commented on the experts used by television during the Gulf War:

> Networks seemed excessively dependent on retired admirals, generals, and former Secretaries of State and Defense. Expertise is one thing, cheerleading is another. On ABC, Adm. William Crowe "analyzes" U.S. military capability: "We'll clean their clocks." This kind of optimism, unchecked and unquestioned, resonates through the echo chamber that is the modern network. Superficial historical analogies, such as Saddam Hussein as Hitler, go unchallenged.[21]

Stephen Hess, a Brookings Institution scholar who has studied the media, insists that with the increased pressures of time television networks have their own agenda in seeking experts. Hess writes, "My hypothesis is [after appearing on numerous TV news shows] that TV news is increasingly dishonest in that increasingly its stories are gatherings of quotes or other material to fit a hypothesis."[22] After referring to the smaller operations occasioned by increased financial pressure on the networks, he points out that TV, unlike the print media, no longer can afford the luxury of collecting more information than it can use on a given day:

> In the TV news business, unfortunately, redundancy is now viewed as a problem to be solved; the goal, apparently, is to gather no more than can be used. As TV news increasingly has no use for information that is not scheduled to fit into a package, it loses interest in anyone who it has determined in advance will not be a sound bite. In other words, reporters tend to interview only those who fit into a

preconceived notion of what the story will be and a story's hypothesis becomes self-fulfilling.[23]

Time and Space

Not only are resources finite, but so are the windows through which news is presented. The evening network news must confine the news of the world of the day to 22 minutes. CNN has 24-hour coverage, but even its capacity for lengthy, in-depth analyses is limited. A full column story—600-700 words—in a newspaper is too long for most readers. Av Westin, a television news producer, describes the problem in *New York* magazine:

> Television news is obsessed with time. It deals in seconds within a broadcast and in getting on the air. When the big red sweep-second hand hits the twelve on the studio clock, the news goes on the air—not a second before, not a second after. When the red hand hits 28 minutes and 29 seconds, it goes off.[24]

The limits of time and space require editorial judgments both as to how much of a story is told and which stories are told. That judgment, whether made by the news director of a network or the editorial conference of a daily newspaper, is based on what the judges consider important in the context of the listenership and readership of the medium. In both mediums, the judgment is subject to the shifting currents of events. On one occasion, NBC sent a crew for three weeks to Germany for a planned ten-minute segment in advance of a German election. Because of the pressure of events, when the segment was finally aired it was cut to a minute and a half. In the United States time constraints favor domestic news and lead to frequent expressions of disappointment from foreigners who find little about their problems either on U.S. television or in most newspapers. One of the most striking—and embarrassing—evidences of this concentration comes in the frequent TV pictures of the president or secretary of state standing beside an important visiting dignitary, answering questions from the press that are totally unrelated to the visitor's country. Furthermore, the visitor is seldom identified by the commentator.

The practical limits of television time mean that only a few items can be covered by network news in comparison with items in newspapers. In a survey I made of international coverage in three newspapers, *New York Times, Washington Post,* and *Los Angeles Times,* in comparison with network news during the week of July 1-7, 1992, five items of foreign news was the maximum for television while the three newspapers averaged better than ten items a day.

The limits of time and space mean that the emphasis is always on the immediate; attention shifts from one crisis to another even though basic problems remain. Richard Harwood, ombudsman for the *Washington Post,* in a May 1993 column asked: "Where are the wars of yesteryear?" and listed the crises that preoccupied journalists for brief periods which, once the journalists had left, were virtually forgotten: Nicaragua, Lebanon, Grenada, Panama, and even the Persian Gulf War.[25]

The Human Factor

News and pictures of foreign events come to the United States through human effort—reporters, correspondents, cameramen, producers. Each media representative faces a series of considerations: competition (Can I get it there first?); credibility of sources (Are they telling me what I want to hear?); news management (Am I being used?); relations with officials (How will what I write affect my access to sources?); complexity (How can I make this understandable to the viewers and readers?); deadlines (How many minutes [hours] do I have?).

The human factor in what they present, and how, cannot be excluded. A strong political bias or negative attitude based on disagreeable experiences can obviously affect the images sent back by reporters and the scenes chosen by cameramen. Edward Jay Epstein describes the significant role of the journalist in the intermediary stage of the news process:

> Surrounding almost any happening is a confusing, confounding blur of information. The journalist—who seldom, if ever, witnesses the entire event—must reconstruct it from a welter of conflicting assertions, fragments of evidence and possibly some eye witness accounts. (The only events that journalists can count on witnessing in their entirety are those staged especially for the media, such as press conferences and interviews.) In sifting through the data surrounding an event, the journalist must have some overall view of reality to help him put together a coherent picture. Some statements might be

emphasized and highlighted; others, played down or omitted entirely. Indeed, the journalist often organizes the material to coincide with what he believes is the true meaning of the happening. For instance, television reporters covering a political rally commonly find that from the same audience they can choose a picture either of a participant cheering with enthusiasm or of one yawning with boredom. If they select the former, they provide a visual cue indicating approval; if they select the latter, they signal disapproval.[26]

The leading news organizations and especially the newspapers have made efforts in the last few decades to recruit journalists with knowledge of areas and language. David Remnick of the *Washington Post* in Russia, Robin Wright of the *Los Angeles Times* in the Middle East, and Henry Kamm of the *New York Times* in Asia are examples. But many of those who are assigned overseas must cover wide areas, working, for example, on African issues out of Johannesburg or on Asian issues out of Hong Kong. The policy means constant travel, little knowledge in depth of the regions where significant news is taking place, and frustrations and hardships that must, inevitably, affect the attitude of the correspondent toward the subjects about which he or she is writing. Wherever they are, they tend to remain in capitals and large cities near communications and support. Journalists are not welcome in many countries where they are traditionally seen as gossips or are paid either to print or not to print. Appointments are hard to make, telephones do not work and, if they do, people will not use them, and many in other lands are averse to answering questions. Transportation is uncertain and power sources unreliable. The U.S. media representative faces bureaucratic delays and suspicion, if not outright hostility. Jack Smith, an ABC news correspondent, described the life thus:

> The fact is, you have to be slightly mad to become a foreign correspondent. At least, it helps.
> The work is hard, and sometimes un-rewarding. The constant travel takes a terrible toll on your personal life. And the living is unhealthy, if not dangerous.
> Washington, by contrast, is an easy place for a reporter to work out of. To enlighten one of my benighted colleagues recently—a man who wants to work overseas—I told him to imagine that no one at the White House spoke English; that Larry Speakes, President Reagan's press secretary, wore a pistol which he regularly pointed at you; that

your TV equipment always broke down; and that you had diarrhea most of the time. That, I said, is what being a foreign correspondent is all about.[27]

Distortions and Stereotypes

Despite a generally conscientious approach to the coverage of international events, the nature and limitations of the American media inescapably create biases that result in partial and, at times, distorted pictures of events and policies in the United States and beyond.

The approach is basically U.S. and Western centered, both in the choice of news and in the cultural context within which it is presented. This orientation is inevitable, not only because journalism is dominated—although less and less so—by white males, but also because of the need to appeal to American readers and listeners. Disasters get attention primarily if American citizens are casualties. The internal problems of Lebanon in the 1980s were overshadowed by the focus on the U.S. Marine presence.

Further, reporters from the Western media are catering to editors and listeners and readers at home who look for the unusual and the dramatic. The positive development rarely makes news. Even as dramatic an event as the fall of the Berlin Wall in November 1989, to the surprise of media observers, attracted less than expected interest. The size of audiences for the three network news broadcasts was less than the year before; special reports that aired on ABC, CBS, and NBC scored ratings that were mediocre or meager or worse. Even CNN viewing declined.[28]

The concentration on problem areas outside of Europe and America gives the impression that a whole region, such as Africa, is troubled. That disasters and scenes of extreme poverty or famine are news in America is constantly seen and resented by peoples in the Third World as media bias. Concentration on the disasters in Somalia and Liberia during the early 1990s meant little attention to more positive developments that were taking place elsewhere in Africa—in Mali, Niger, Tanzania, and Zambia.

In response to space and time limitations and in efforts to explain complex problems, coverage becomes oversimplified; no place exists for lengthy explanations or nuances. Perhaps in recognition of the American love of sports, foreign events are seen as sports contests—zero-sum games: who wins, who loses.

Much of the responsibility for the superficiality of current coverage is laid at the door of television. Richard W. Jencks, a former CBS executive, was critical of the medium with which he was long associated:

> According to one poll, the major source of news for Americans is television, so quality news-gathering by experienced journalists in the field—those with investigative skills and intimate knowledge of their beats—is truly important. But unfortunately, these are not always the chief qualities that keep correspondents in the field and on the payroll. As beneficial is a winning on-air appearance and personality.[29]

Jencks went on to note other weaknesses: correspondents are tempted to gain attention, to "adorn a tell story with daring and unsupported conjecture"; entire subjects of vital concern often "fall to journeymen correspondents without significant background in the field"; pictures of violent action, no matter how tactically insignificant, get precedence over "stories dealing with the broader matrix"; and television's insatiable demand for picture opportunities makes it possible "for government officials or other news makers to suppress or shape stories by denying or qualifying such opportunities or, on the other hand, staging spurious events in order to create them."[30]

Television inevitably leads to simplification which, in turn, risks stereotypes. The shorthand required to tell a story in a few minutes or a few inches results in generalized descriptions ("oil-rich sheikhs," "Islamic fundamentalists," "terrorists") that may be wrong or, at best, tell only part of the story. Edwin Diamond, media critic for *New York* magazine, criticized television's stereotypes of Japan: "These images are false and ultimately self-destructive. We could all profit by reevaluating old cultural notions. The inscrutable East belongs to the past. The Japanese are not ciphers; they can be understood by anyone who makes the effort."[31]

The simplified characterization of groups or events creates attitudes that may limit the official response. When a Soviet brigade, which had long been in the country, was "discovered" in Cuba in 1979, the intelligence note that was leaked referred erroneously to the unit as a "combat brigade."[32] The characterization heightened public and congressional interest, making it more difficult for the Carter administration to resolve the issue with the Russians. Similarly, when the *Washington Post* referred to the enhanced radiation weapon as a "killer warhead" or "capitalist bomb," those terms amplified the public concern over the weapon.[33]

Stereotypes are not only simplistic; they are judgmental. The "good guys" must be distinguished from the "bad guys." A *Los Angeles Times* article quotes Ben Bradlee, former executive editor of the *Washington Post:* "Television has created a compulsion to judgement. It takes too long to tell everybody what happened. . . . You've got to tell them 'This is good' or 'This is bad' and therefore you've got to be judgmental."[34]

Stereotypes of another form appear in efforts to find historical analogies to current events: "Does the current unrest in Egypt represent another Iran?" Journalists make extensive use of the rear view mirror;[35] what has happened in the past that is like what has happened today? Each revolution or setback of U.S. interests becomes a catchword to be applied to future developments—even though conditions may be very different.

Washington is both a source of news and a filter of information that flows in from around the world. Both functions are affected by the prevalence of conventional wisdom that can—and has—shut out indications of events and disasters to come.

> Unlike Paris or London, which are not just governmental capitals but financial, cultural, and communications capitals, Washington is purely a government capital; news coverage and commentary there generally move within a narrower range than in the other, more cosmopolitan capitals. When you have journalists with a great deal in common covering news within relatively narrow parameters, the likelihood of conformity—the pressure to conform—can be great.[36]

The press and the government are often criticized for failing to fore-shadow major developments—whether a revolution in Iran or the fall of the Berlin Wall. Yet, in the years before these events, their possibility seemed so remote that few editors would have regarded seriously, and published, predictions that they would happen. One of the most dramatic failures in recent years occurred when the Washington press totally missed indications of the Iran-contra scandal in 1986-87, although Hearst Newspapers outside of Washington first reported U.S.-Iran contacts as far back as July 1985. The secret U.S. overtures to Iran and the diversion of funds to the contras in Nicaragua attracted attention in Washington only on November 3, 1986, when East Coast newspapers reported an item from a relatively obscure Beirut newspaper, *Al Shirah*.[37] Speculation on why the press paid so little attention to rumors of the deal that were current in the capital focused on several reasons:

- •an elaborate effort to keep the operation secret;

•a coziness with sources, particularly Colonel Oliver North, who provided misleading information and insisted on anonymity;
•normal sources did not have the story;
•the story seemed too complicated;
•confidence in Ronald Reagan;
•concern over the national security and the safety of the American hostages in Lebanon.[38]

But, in addition, the story did not fit the conventional wisdom; it seemed too farfetched that a popular conservative president, Ronald Reagan, would be involved in such a scheme. Scott Armstrong, writing in the *Columbia Journalism Review,* noted also the lack of institutional memory in connection with this story. He commented:

> The sad lesson implicit in those five years of sporadically spectacular reporting is that the press corps does not read itself. There was no institutional memory. Breakthroughs by star reporters passed largely unnoticed by peers until months or years after they were first published or aired.[39]

Another failure of much of the mainline press occurred in the case of the U.S. role in the supply of weapons technology and finance to Iraq before the Gulf War. Despite extensive coverage in the London *Financial Times,* the *Los Angeles Times,* and ABC's Nightline, and a revealing story in the *Intelligencer Journal,* a 45,000-circulation paper in Lancaster, Pennsylvania, the major network news shows and other major newspapers paid little attention. Part of the reason given was the failure of major newspapers to take seriously Representative Henry Gonzalez, chairman of the House Banking Committee, who, by early 1990, was making charges of U.S. complicity in the arming of Iraq. Journalists were also discouraged by the attorney general, William Barr, from probing into the story on "national security" grounds. Ted Koppel of Nightline explained a further reason in the opening of one of his programs on "Iraqgate" in July 1992:

> There's a good reason why we in the media are so partial to a nice, torrid sex scandal. It is, among other things, so easy to explain and so easy to understand. Nothing at all, in other words, like allegations of a government coverup, which tend to be not at all easy to explain, and even more difficult to understand.[40]

The *Los Angeles Times* in 1989 conducted a survey seeking the answer to why the press seemed so bound by "conventional wisdom."

Why? Why do the media sometimes arrive at instantaneous consensus on issues, events, and individuals that would seem open to widely varying, even conflicting interpretations? How does this "conventional wisdom" develop?

Many of the more than 60 journalists and public opinion specialists The Times interviewed recently about the phenomenon attributed its growth to the tendency of reporters to talk to the same sources all the time. Others pointed to a "herd mentality" in the media—"the nation's herd of independent minds," in [Charles] Krauthammer's phrase. Still others cited conditions ranging from geographic myopia and ideological bias to manipulation by government officials, laziness, homogeneity, timidity and insecurity in the press corps and the absence of such volatile, fundamentally divisive issues as Vietnam, Watergate, or the civil rights movement.

But most of those interviewed said the growing trend toward consensus journalism derived largely from the pervasiveness and impact of television, with its demands for speed, brevity, and conformity.

These demands affect print reporters as well as television reporters; knowing that television will almost inevitably be first, newspaper and magazine journalists often try to provide the analysis that television may lack the air time to do. But in trying to rush this analysis into print to compete with the ever-increasing speed of television, many reporters and columnists reflexively reach for the simplest, safest, most obvious explanations.[41]

The *Times* article also points out that technology permits reporters to check quickly on the competition:

Technology has also made it possible for reporters to check their work against the competition in a way never before possible. A reporter sitting in his office or in a hotel room can watch Cable News Network and, simultaneously, call up on his computer screen several wire service reports of an event, even as he sits writing his own version. The tendency to conformity can be all but irresistible.[42]

Tom Wicker, veteran reporter for the *New York Times*, points out that the press rarely bucks the official consensus because, in what he calls

"The First Law of Journalism," "the American press is neither heroic nor villainous, but . . . mirrors rather well the character of the American community."[43] Conformity comes not only from the actions of reporters but from those of editors as well. David Shaw in the *Times* article points this out in the context of trips in which reporters accompany high officials overseas and have only themselves as sources, but the practice can apply in other cases as well:

> Not surprisingly, reporters who talk almost exclusively to each other often produce similar stories. And if one is tempted to offer a different view?
>
> "Suppose I wrote that the Bush NATO summit trip was a failure," says Jack Nelson, Washington bureau chief for the Los Angeles Times. "The editor would say, 'hey, wait just a minute . . . AP says it's boffo. UPI says the same thing. The network anchors seem to all agree that it was a success.' Suppose I wanted to go against the grain. . . . I didn't happen to go against the grain on that, but I would imagine that I would meet with some resistance."[44]

Henry Muller of *Time* is quoted in the same article:

> Any reporter who is reporting a story substantially differently from his colleagues is sure to get a lot of calls from home office asking why. . . . He's sure likely to get a lot of skepticism from his home office and maybe even some guidance to file stories that come closer to the mainstream view.[45]

Finally, there is the question of exaggeration. The accusation is common that "the media" have blown a personality or an event out of proportion. As this is being written, the press and television are full of the story of Sheikh Omar Abdul Rahman, the blind Islamic leader accused of being at the center of an extremist group that includes individuals suspected of being responsible for bombings and bombing threats in New York City. Egyptian officials accuse the U.S. press of building up the prominence of the sheikh. In a press free of government control, however, heavy attention to a figure strange to most Americans linked, however tangentially, to bombings and threats of bombings in the nation's largest city is inevitable. At the same time other newspapers, especially the *Los Angeles Times* and the *Christian Science Monitor,* made efforts through numerous articles on Islam to put the sheikh, his ideas, and his followers into some perspective.[46] Nevertheless, given the factors in the case, some distortion in the relative importance of the subject was inescapable.

American journalism, for all its limitations and faults, brings to the American public and the world the principal events of the day. If those events seem dramatic or out of proportion, such as the possible involvement of a Muslim sheikh in the bombing of the New York World Trade Center, it is the nature of the event. The press as the messenger cannot be blamed for giving attention to such items. Media "hype" exists, but is driven by the nature of the subjects, not, in most instances, by any desire to give undue prominence to matters that contain their own exaggerations.

4   Conflicting Objectives

Officials and journalists have conflicting objectives: the former wants to control information; the latter, to find it and release it. The public receives its perspectives on foreign events and policies largely through the interaction and frequent confrontation of these two views.

Except where people have direct access to government statements through the full broadcast or printing of complete texts of speeches, the news organizations become filters through which information and opinion reaches the public. That process of reporting, editing, and opining raises a series of issues that lie at the heart of the continuing differences of approach between officials and journalists in a democratic society. These include rights and responsibilities, information versus the sound bite, process versus politics, negative versus positive approaches, and the identification of sources. The most basic question relates to rights and responsibility.

Rights and Responsibility

Former Secretary of State Dean Rusk, in a letter to his predecessor, John Foster Dulles, expressed the view that journalists lack a sense of responsibility toward the country:

The press is another matter. There often appear to be deep divergences of interest between the Secretary of State and the reporters of a highly competitive press. Unless your press advisers fully understand this clash of interest and are constantly alert to it, their advice may not always be helpful. The competitive press finds it almost impossible to exercise discretion and a sense of public responsibility, with rare exceptions. If a man digs a secret out of an official or a department and takes it around to the Soviet Embassy, he is a spy; if he digs out the same secret and gives it to the Soviet Union and the rest of the world at the same time, he is a smart newspaperman. . . . Each [reporter] insists upon sitting in the chair of judgement to decide what should and what should not be made public. The private citizen, therefore, finds that he cannot have his representatives (the President—not the press) decide what, in the citizen's own interest, ought to be withheld temporarily from public knowledge.[1]

At least one veteran reporter takes issue with the suggestion that the press sits in judgment. In his view, the press has been too subservient to official views:

When it comes to the press challenging policy as it is being formed, I think the press is pretty toothless without the help of other watchdogs. It needs outside critics to begin raising questions. That was true in Vietnam. The press was very supportive, patriotic until people like [Senator William] Fulbright began raising questions; then it had the peg to begin belaboring the government.[2]

Most journalists will respond that, except in situations where lives or the safety of the nation are clearly in danger, they have no responsibility to the government. Some claim that their only responsibility is to their employers. In a television symposium on "National Security and the Press," Lyle Denniston, Supreme Court correspondent for the *Baltimore Sun,* startled the participants. If he were left to himself in the office of a high official, he said, he would have no compunction against looking at the papers, including confidential documents, on the official's desk and taking information from them. He works for an institution that gains its profit by selling news; his job as a reporter is to get the news wherever he can.[3]

Denniston's comments, considered extreme even by many journalists, sparked a discussion on the rights and responsibilities of the press.

Some of the journalists on the program insisted that, although they might not go as far as Denniston, the public had a "right to know." Retired Supreme Court Justice William J. Brennan insisted that the First Amendment created only the right to publish, not any right "to know." Retired officials on the program asserted that journalists had a responsibility to protect sensitive information.

Journalists, in response, insist that it is the government's responsibility to protect information. Further, they seriously question the rationale for much official secrecy. Not only do they believe too much is kept secret, but they are suspicious that government efforts to maintain secrets flow too often from the desire to avoid acknowledging personal and official errors.

Howard Simons, late managing editor of the *Washington Post* and curator of the Nieman Foundation, protested the degree of secrecy:

> If you live and work as a journalist in Washington long enough, several things about national security and the press become self-evident—and they are not always life, liberty, and the pursuit of happiness.
>
> The first thing that you learn is that it is impossible, not just improbable, but impossible to do your daily job without running into a secret.
>
> By one estimate, 20 million federal documents are classified each year—20 million. Of these, 350,000 are stamped top secret, a designation that means if the information in the document were disclosed, it would cause quote exceptionally grave damage unquote to the security of the nation. . . . It is a constant wonder how any of the four million Americans who have access to classified information can remember what is secret and what is not secret.[4]

Another charge leveled at the press and television is that, while officials are accountable for their actions, journalists are not. In an article in the Army War College magazine, *Parameters,* Richard Halloran asserts a common journalistic defense that the media are accountable "through a network of public opinion, constitutional and legal constraints, competitive pressures, and company policy":

> In many ways, the press is held as accountable as any institution in America, and, perhaps more so, given its visibility. The people to whom a newspaper is most accountable are its readers. If they don't

like what the paper reports, they stop reading it. If they don't like a TV news anchor, they switch him off. . . . But the press is voted on more than any other institution in America, and journalists more than any elected official. A daily newspaper or television network faces the voters every day, and is given a thumbs up or thumbs down. If the thumbs continue to turn down, the journalist can be out of a job or the newspaper out of existence.[5]

Leaks

The unauthorized disclosure of sensitive information—the leak— remains still the most challenging obstacle to the maintenance of government secrets. Every administration has faced the problem, yet, except for the Morison case (see chapter 1), no official has yet paid a penalty for leaking. The Reagan administration and especially Secretary of State Alexander Haig railed at leakers. In *Caveat,* Haig writes:

> Even at this very early stage, it was clear that the press had exceptional sources in the new Administration. Line-by-line quotations from my report to the President on a conversation with the Soviet ambassador were put into the hands of a television commentator in time for the evening news on the very day they were delivered to the White House. A story in *Newsweek* contained direct quotes from deliberations in the National Security Council. An NSC decision on Libya appeared in the papers on the day it was made. Plans for covert action in Central America were leaked to the *Washington Post,* then backgrounded to the major media. A secret submission to the NSC by James L. Buckley, the under secretary of state for security assistance, was leaked. I learned that my memoranda to the President were being made available to reporters in a method of leaking-by-proxy that suggests the Byzantine complexity of the methods involved in the craft of leaking.[6]

Why do leaks occur? Stephen Hess, in his book *The Government-Press Connection,* gives a typology of leaks, including the ego leak (to satisfy a sense of self-importance); the goodwill leak (a play for future favor); the policy leak (a straightforward pitch for or against a proposal); the animus leak (used to settle grudges); the trial-balloon leak; and the whistle-blower leak.[7] Other categories could be added:
   •the advance-spin leak. By releasing the substance of an important

document before the official date with favorable comment on the conclusions, the way is paved—it is hoped—for a favorable public reaction when it is released. Parts of a report on a Reagan administration commission on Central America, chaired by Henry Kissinger, were extensively leaked in both the *New York Times* and the *Washington Post* well before the official release. The leaks represented efforts by members of the commission with opposing views on the conclusions to get their points of view before the public.[8]

•the demonstration leak. Administrations at times believe not enough is known of significant secret efforts in support of policies. An official disclosure of such efforts might require an official response from an adversary. Leaks can always be denied. For many years during the Soviet presence in Afghanistan, U.S. help to the resistance was well known, leaked openly by officials but never formally acknowledged. The Soviets were well aware of the help but, in the absence of an official acknowledgement by Washington, could choose not to respond.

•the signal leak. Information is sometimes given out unofficially in order to warn another country of a possible reaction to policies or deployments. Secretary of State Kissinger, according to several sources, anonymously briefed reporters on reports that Cuba was building a base for Russian submarines at Cienfuegos and subsequently blamed the Pentagon for the leak. His purpose, according to Seymour Hersh in *The Price of Power*, was to send signals to both the Cubans and the Russians that the United States would not tolerate this intrusion of Soviet military power in the Caribbean.[9]

•the foreign leak. Not all embarrassing leaks come from U.S. sources. The most famous in recent years was the leak in the Lebanese newspaper *Al Shirah* that led to the revelations of the Iran-contra scandal in the Reagan administration. On some occasions, the foreign leak can be no more than the playing back to the United States of news from a foreign correspondent in Washington that no one noticed at the time.

•the professional leak. Many of the reporters who cover the White House and State Department have been in Washington much longer than most officials. They know how the government works and can detect the signals of major events. When, for example, black limousines carry recognized officials dealing with Latin America to an unannounced meeting at the White House on a Sunday afternoon when an issue such as Nicaragua is critical, the reporter knows what to do. He or she begins calling around to various officials. From the tone of voice or the hesitation of an unsuspecting bureaucrat the reporter can confirm that something is taking place. The diligent journalist—especially one who has worked in government—can also find significant unannounced information hidden in documents. Walter Pincus of the *Washington Post* broke the story of the decision to manufacture the neutron bomb after finding a reference to the Enhanced Radiation Weapon in transcripts of unclassified congressional budget hearings.[10]

Certain conditions lend themselves to leaks. The ideological divisions within and surrounding the Reagan administration undoubtedly led to leaks in support of or against policies. Dramatic words or phrases in documents make a tempting target for the leaker. In the case of the Soviet brigade in Cuba in 1979, the writer of the intelligence brief used the word "*combat* brigade," and the addition of the adjective may well have led to the ultimate leak of the brief.[11]

Advance planning on sensitive and controversial policy issues is especially vulnerable to leaks. When the U.S. is surprised by a foreign development, the demand arises for better contingency planning. Yet officials shy away from such planning, in large measure for fear of disclosures that would create problems with both domestic constituencies and foreign governments. Officials feel they have enough to deal with with current issues; they do not need the kind of manufactured crises created by hypothetical contingencies. During most of the 1970s and 1980s, for example, public knowledge of State Department planning that might have included either a rapprochement with Fidel Castro in Cuba or talks with the Palestine Liberation Organization in the Middle East would have set off a firestorm of counter pressures. Whether word of such planning on major, sensitive foreign policy issues is announced or leaks, the result is to alert all sides in a controversy to weigh in with both the executive and legislative branches of government. The public defense of such pressures may require a premature commitment not to consider some options or an agreement to call off the planning. An article in the *New York Times* on March 24, 1975 disclosed that the Ford administration was considering a "reassessment" of policy in the Middle East predicated on improving relations with the Arabs.[12] The information immediately generated counter pressures, including a letter signed by seventy-six senators, that ultimately required canceling the policy review.[13]

Leaks contain other perils for the policymaker apart from the possible damage to particular policies or initiatives. Leaks can have unintended consequences. In 1983, an official discussed with John Wallach of Hearst Newspapers the Reagan administration's problems in preventing the spread of communism in El Salvador and Nicaragua, pointing in particular to threats by Congressman Clarence Long, Democrat of Louisiana and chairman of the House subcommittee on operations, to reveal a secret CIA plan to mine the harbors of Nicaragua. The official clearly hoped the unpatriotic obstruction of the member of Congress would be the focus of the reporter's story; to Wallach, however, the plan to mine the harbors was the news. After checking an additional source, he ran the item in the *San Francisco Examiner* on July 17, 1983.[14] The result was not a public outcry against the congressional obstruction, as the official had hoped, but a denunciation of the United States in the International Court of Justice and a cancellation of the project.

Leaks become instruments by which officials seek either to promote or discredit policies; it is sometimes difficult to judge which objective is involved. An article in the *Columbia Journalism Review* of July–August 1988 reported the following regarding an Iran-contra leak:

> During the Iran-contra hearings, [Col. Oliver] North testified that "leaks" had led to the publication of information about the interception of an Egyptian plane carrying the suspected hijackers of the *Achille Lauro*. Indeed, North testified that he believed the leaks "very seriously compromised our intelligence activities." Shortly after, however, *Newsweek* revealed that "the Colonel did not mention that details of the interception, first published in a *Newsweek* cover story, were leaked by none other than North himself."[15]

The fear of leaks has also led to the making of policy in smaller and smaller circles. When any sensitive issue is to be discussed, the president and the secretary make certain that the smallest number of people possible are involved.

David Gergen, a White House counselor in both the Reagan and Clinton administrations, in the Frank E. Gannett lecture of November 25, 1986, said:

> For our part, our part in the press, we should at least acknowledge that sometimes the government is right to be concerned about its leaks. Something distinctly unhealthy has taken place in our public policy making of late. Fifteen years ago, I can well remember, aides to a President felt free to write candid memos and have serious, far-

reaching disagreements with each other—and the President—on paper. Watergate put the first stop to that: One quickly learned never to *write* anything on paper that you would be unhappy to see on the front page of the *Washington Post*. Now, that did make for a more efficient government—memos grew considerably shorter—but it also meant for less dissent and less open dialogue. By the time of the Reagan administration, leaks had become so bad that one learned not only not to write things down on paper but never to say anything controversial in a meeting with more than one person.[16]

Leaks immediately raise the question of responsibility. Reporters claim—and most of them correctly—that leaked documents come to them; they do not seek them out. The responsibility then rests with the official who takes the initiative in distributing a classified document and talking about sensitive matters. It remains true, also, that the top levels of government do not object to leaks as long as they control them. In the last analysis, as journalists insist, it remains the government's task to keep secrets.

Information versus the Sound Bite

Although the objective of most reporters is clearly to get as much of a story as they can, leaving the headline to the editor, to the public official the objective of the press seems too often to be an eye-catching opening lead or sound bite. The official or diplomat is trained to obtain as many details and as much understanding of an event or issue as possible. Observing a TV interview or being interviewed, they are struck often by the questions not asked by journalists. The media interviewer appears primarily concerned with highlighting failures, second-guessing officials, or extracting sensational comments. It is the phrase that will make the evening news or the front page, not the story, that becomes important. On May 20, 1993, Robert MacNeil, one of the most effective interviewers on television, discussed Somalia with Henry Kissinger, former secretary of state. At a critical time in that crisis, even MacNeil placed less emphasis on the details of the issue. His questions included, "What should President Clinton do now?" and "Let's talk basic things about how the American people feel about this at the moment and not geopolitics for just a moment." The final question was "Would you say right now that Americans could go to sleep tonight with a good conscience about their role in Bosnia, saying to themselves, well, we've done everything we should, we've done everything we could?"[17]

Charlayne Hunter-Gault, also of the MacNeil-Lehrer News Hour, on December 4, 1992, interviewed a group of senators who had just visited Somalia. Although gains were being made in the feeding of Somalis, her questions dealt not with positive aspects of the situation but with the possibility of a "quagmire."

> **Ms. Hunter-Gault**: All right. All three of you heard what Secretary Cheney just said about this end point, January 20th, being not necessarily in the real world, but that was the number, the date that Fitzwater, I think, threw out. And we have been hearing the word "quagmire." Are you worried about that?
>
> **Sen. Leahy**: Well, there's a big difference between not stopping exactly on January 20th and a quagmire. I think it would be a mistake to look at a calendar and say, if at such and such a time, the time of the inaugural or something like that we're not out of there, we're in a quagmire. I don't perceive that at all.
>
> **Ms. Hunter-Gault**: But what's your sense about how long it will take and how you can avoid the quagmire, based on what you've heard today?[18]

Tom Brokaw of NBC, in another program on Somalia the next night, interviewed Mohammad Farah Aideed, one of the most troublesome of the warlords. Not a single question dealt with Aideed's attitude toward his own people—a significant element in the puzzle. Instead, Brokaw asked Aideed how long he felt the U.S. troops should remain in Somalia—as if that were a matter for Aideed's decision.[19]

Process versus Politics

The official lives in a world of process, politics, and personalities. The journalist concentrates on personalities and politics: Who made the decision? Who was left out of the loop? Who was responsible for the failure? How will this affect the fortunes of the president?

Approaches are personalized—this is Reagan's war or Bush's policy; in only rare instances are decisions pictured as the result of a complex policy-making process. The participation of a large governmental machinery in the creation of policy is often ignored. Even veteran journalists do not seem to know the difference between an under secretary and an assistant secretary in government. For the official, the bureaucratic details and elements are important. A lack of understanding of process led journalists, for example, to erroneous conclusions regarding U.S. policy toward Iraq prior to the Gulf War. Kevin Juster, writing in *Foreign Policy* in the spring of 1994, points out that the press perpetuated the charge that Iraq purchased weapons with "loans" from the United States because of a misunderstanding of the nature of transactions under the Department of Agricultural Commodity Credit Corporation (CCC):

> The distinction between a "loan" and a "credit" is not simply a matter of semantics. The use of credit rather than a loan dictates both what is to be purchased as well as the direction of the cash flow. The foreign purchaser disburses money in exchange for agricultural commodities; it never receives any money. The only entities that receive money are the U.S. exporter (from the U.S. bank) and, on a deferred basis, the U.S. bank (from the foreign purchaser). Thus, assertions that Iraq received "loans" authorized by the CCC, that those "loans" were inflated, or that Iraq purchased weapons with such "loans" are incorrect; they are neither actually nor even theoretically possible given the manner in which the CCC program operates.[20]

The practitioner has other problems with much of the coverage of the foreign policy process. A policy is criticized without an examination of the alternatives; much of policy making is finding the least objectionable option among a list of undesirable choices. The role of Congress is usually neglected. The press attributes a degree of omnipotence to government, assuming officials had knowledge but did not act on it. Often the government knows less about an issue than the press believes.

Negative versus Positive

As was pointed out in chapter 2, officials seek the positive on any issue. Journalists naturally look with some skepticism on government claims of achievement. Too often, however, this skepticism seems to lead to an automatic perpetuation of the negative. Conventional wisdom in much of the media—albeit reflecting political judgments—has been that the Carter administration was a disaster in foreign policy, primarily because of the Iran hostage crisis. Little attention has been given in analyses of those years to achievements such as the Camp David Middle East peace accords, the Panama Canal treaties, and the opening to China.

Much of the coverage of the Clinton administration's foreign policy has focused on the disasters in Somalia, Bosnia, and Haiti. Less attention has been given to the relatively successful initial handling of relations with the former Soviet republics and the Middle East, two areas of even greater importance to the United States.

In 1992, William Branigan of the *Washington Post* did a lengthy series on the specialized agencies of the United Nations. Branigan emphasized the mismanagement and corruption in the international organization. Four accompanying articles gave profiles of four U.N. officials as examples of the weaknesses in the organization's structure; the fact that each had been dismissed or had resigned was barely mentioned; the impression was left that they were still working for the U.N.[21]

When President Bush gave his annual address to the U.N. General Assembly on September 21, 1992, the *New York Times* placed the emphasis on what he did not say; the headline read: "Bush, in Address to U.N., Urges More Vigor in Keeping the Peace: But He Does Not Offer Money or Staff, Nor to Pay U.S. Debts."[22]

Sources

Another bone of contention between officials and journalists relates to the identification of sources. Officials below the cabinet level prefer—and are encouraged to prefer—anonymity. Backgrounders are attributed to a "high-level State Department source" or a "senior administration official." At times, especially on overseas trips, cabinet level officials themselves will insist on such designations, considered to be both politically and diplomatically desirable. Because the statements are official policy, they avoid the identification of policy with any single individual and thus limit the personification of decision making. The practice also provides a greater opportunity to deny what was said.

Media organizations, especially the *Washington Post,* have long protested this practice. On one occasion, the *Post* ran a picture of Secretary of State Cyrus Vance with a caption, "high administration official," beside a story that attributed comments to such an official. On another occasion, when Secretary of State Kissinger was the backgrounder, the newspaper referred to a backgrounder by an official "with a German accent." John Wallach, writing in the *Washington Quarterly,* recounts another incident in which the *Post,* in its coverage of a backgrounder by Secretary of State Alexander Haig, to be attributed to a "senior official," ran a photograph of

Haig in a continuation of the story under a caption that read, "reasoning behind his views explained."[23]

On May 25, 1993, Peter Tarnoff, undersecretary for political affairs in the State Department, attended an "off the record" luncheon of the Overseas Press Club. His remarks suggested that the Clinton administration, as it focused on domestic economic troubles, expected to withdraw from many foreign policy leadership roles. He requested identification as "a senior State Department official." Reporters for the Washington Post immediately called the White House to determine whether this statement indeed represented U.S. policy and obtained contrary quotes both from the secretary of state and "a senior White House official." The next day, the Post, in its "Style" section, ran a long article, "Who Was That Masked Official? Media Chafe over Unnamed State Source." It seemed clear that the Post used the utterance of some possibly controversial remarks to emphasize again what they considered to be the absurdity of the practice of anonymous sources. The New York Times, which was not represented at the lunch, did not feel bound by the agreement and the next day published Tarnoff's name as the source.[24]

Officials become particularly vulnerable to such tricks on the part of the press in times when the media believes either that the government does not know what it is doing or that it is hiding something. I was similarly "mousetrapped" during the minor crisis on the Soviet brigade in Cuba in 1979. At a time when the secretary of state had laid down strict instructions that no public statements were to be made by officials on the subject, I, the under secretary for political affairs at the time, attended an "off the record" luncheon with reporters. I made the mistake of discussing several alternative explanations for the presence of the Soviet force without suggesting that the administration had accepted any one of them. Bernard Gwertzman of the New York Times noted reference to one that had not previously been mentioned by anyone; he assumed that this previously unmentioned explanation represented the department's thinking and ran with a story, quoting "a senior State Department official."[25]

A distinction is made in journalism between an anonymous source and a confidential source. A memorandum circulated to the Wall Street Journal staff described the distinction thus:

> An anonymous source is one whose name we've agreed to leave out of the paper but whose identity we may later need to disclose—in the event of a libel suit, for example—in order to show that we had good reason for using the information.

A confidential source . . . is one whose name isn't published and whose identity we are pledged to keep secret, even if that means losing a law suit or going to jail.[26]

An article in the *Columbia Journalism Review,* "Broken Promises," points out the growing pressure on reporters to disclose confidential sources. Unlike the Watergate case, in which *Washington Post* reporter Bob Woodward was able to keep secret the identity of his source, "Deep Throat," reporters must now disclose such sources to their editors who make the decisions regarding the maintenance of the confidentiality.[27]

The differences in attitudes and approaches recited in this chapter are inevitable in a circumstance marked by fundamentally different objectives. Despite this, close personal relationships exist between journalists and officials and often they change places. But, when they do, they exchange, also, the fundamental outlooks that go with their position. "Where you stand depends on where you sit," can be as well said of those who move from journalism to bureaucracy and back as of those who move within government. As this is being written, the deputy secretary of state, Strobe Talbott, the man who once wrote extensively for *Time* magazine of the discord within the Reagan administration, is heard denying reports of differences within the Clinton foreign policy team.

5 Key Issues

The differences between officials and reporters on disclosures rest fundamentally on varying perceptions of how the national interest will be affected. Reporters will accept that subjects and occasions exist in which public statements will be unwise, but they believe these to be few. They are largely skeptical about an official's justifications for withholding information. Officials follow the general rule that, if there is no demonstrable need for others to know the inner secrets of national security policies, no reason exists for releasing the information. Officials err on the side of caution in their control of information.

Media representatives insist in this debate that they represent the public and the public's right to know. Given the importance and, often, the drama of national security issues, this press argument is to some extent self-serving. Some evidence suggests that in national security issues the public believes the press is excessively intrusive and, although faith in government is far from deep, doubt also exists concerning the motives and patriotism of the press.

Confrontation between the government and the media is most severe in five closely related areas: national security, combat, terrorism, intelligence, and diplomacy.

National Security

For all forms of the mass media, national security items are significant news; they tap a broad interest among readers and listeners. Security issues, however, encounter deep sensitivities about disclosures. In peacetime, defense officials are especially apprehensive about the release of information on contingency planning, weapons development and deployment, budgets, and U.S. intelligence on potential adversaries.

The new global responsibilities of the United States that followed World War II created more complex and nuanced national security issues than ever before. The Vietnam War shattered a national consensus that had supported past wars—including the Korean War. Questions of war and peace in the U.S. domestic debate no longer revolved around supporting the nation in a conventional conflict with clearly marked adversary forces. They involved ideological disputes over the nature of the communist world and the degree to which foreign policy issues were related to the East-West struggle. Press-government clashes on national security issues were part of the debate and especially acute in the Reagan years when the administration pursued a more aggressive policy of military and covert intelligence activities.

The disputes extended to internal differences on policies toward non-communist countries, especially in the developing world. Indigenous African quarrels became arenas in the East-West conflict. Problems of Central America that had once been considered only in the context of the troubled Yankee-Latino relationship became, to many, part of the global confrontation.

The nuclear age brought new issues with significant moral and security implications and weapons systems of unprecedented complexity as well. Efforts to reduce the threat to human existence through arms control negotiations created new levels of highly technical diplomacy. Journalists faced the problem of reducing complex issues to understandable news.

A few journalists fully understood the concept of deterrence, including its various manifestations through mutually assured destruction and flexible response. Efforts to simplify for public consumption questions involving the MX missiles or the "two-track" intermediate nuclear force policy of NATO often involved writers and broadcasters in arguments with proponents or opponents who saw efforts to explain as volleys in the ideological debate. This became especially true when President Reagan launched his Strategic Defense Initiative plan on March 23, 1983.

Each of these issues brought new tensions between the press and the government in large measure because the press became the public arena in which many of the policy and ideological issues were fought. Interest groups, think tanks, and expanded congressional staffs on both sides fed the debate.

Differences were pictured as personal rivalries. Strobe Talbott's book, *Deadly Gambits,* portrayed the internal differences on policy toward the Strategic Arms Reduction Treaty as essentially a contest for power between Richard Burt, then in the State Department, and Richard Perle, assistant secretary of defense for policy.[1]

The substance of many of the arguments between officials and journalists over national security issues concerned the seriousness of the damage caused by press revelations. This damage assessment was further complicated because information considered classified by officials could often be put together by journalists through diligent research in open sources.

The *New York Times,* in an article on August 30, 1987, showed how Tom Clancy, author of *The Hunt for Red October,* was able to demonstrate to Navy officials who had accused him of using classified information in the book that all the information had come from open sources.[2]

Journalists point out that in many cases material is classified that must be known to the Russians. In 1986, a Navy Department employee, Ronald Pelton, was convicted of espionage. The *Washington Post* was severely criticized for reporting the details of information Pelton had sold to the Russians. In the *Post's* response, Benjamin Bradlee, then executive editor of the newspaper, compared this disclosure to information on the bombing of Cambodia:

> Trouble starts when people try to sweep a lot of garbage under the rug of national security. Even some very highly placed people.
>
> Like President Richard Nixon in 1969, when he described a *New York Times* exclusive report on the secret bombing of Cambodia as an egregious example of national security violation.
>
> That's right out of Kafka, when you think about it. The Cambodians certainly knew they were being bombed, and since only the United States was then flying bombing missions in Indochina, they certainly knew who was bombing them. If the Cambodians knew, the Vietcong knew. And if the Vietcong knew, certainly their Soviet allies knew immediately. So what was all *that* about?[3]

In an earlier case, in 1984, the *Post* was accused by Secretary of Defense Caspar Weinberger of an irresponsible security breach in publishing a story about the payload of a secret space shuttle mission. The *Post* replied in an editorial:

> The general outline of the story and many of its specifics had been floating around the governmental and journalistic worlds for months. They didn't get there from nowhere: They had been disclosed by military and civilian government sources. Readers of American publications—including this country's adversaries, of course—had long since been able to read virtually all of the material that was to appear in the Washington Post story. They had been able to read it elsewhere in the open—i.e. unclassified—literature. Some of this material had been printed in other publications, such as Aviation Week and Space Technology and broadcast on CBS. Some came from the Reagan administration's public testimony on Capitol Hill.[4]

The response from national security officials is that it is not only the knowledge that is important to an adversary, but also how the knowledge was acquired. The press may have the information, but they may not have an understanding of the implications of release.

Combat

Clashes between officials, both military and civilian, and the media are perhaps most acute under the pressure of actual military action. To the general concerns for secrecy in national security matters are added the operational worries about information on troop movements and operational plans. The press generally agrees on the need for confidentiality in such matters. Agreement dissipates, however, on questions of casualties, the course of the combat, and the coverage of actions and results in enemy territory. In such cases, what officials see as restrictions to avoid aiding the enemy, journalists may see as efforts to cover up disasters and errors.

Until the Vietnam War, U.S. journalists were given relatively free access to combat zones. Beginning with Vietnam, military commanders became more sensitive about the presence and activities of press representatives. Unlike the more or less conventional actions in previous wars, in Vietnam the United States fought a guerrilla enemy, difficult to locate and identify. A political controversy at home in the U.S. over the nature of the South Vietnamese regime—the American ally—added to the neuralgia of officials. As prospects for victory faded, press disclosures of failures and casualties became ever more resented, especially when they differed from the official version. With the debut of television came the negative impact on domestic support for the war caused by relatively instantaneous, dramatic, and bloody shots of combat.

Distortions of reality occurred on both sides of the debate. Officials did seek to play down or, on occasion, deny setbacks. By concentrating reporting and cameras on dramatic events, the press, however, may have missed positive aspects of the larger picture. This phenomenon was brought home most vividly in Peter Braestrup's account of the coverage of the Tet offensive in 1968.[5] Braestrup points out that the pictures of enemy invaders in the American Embassy in Saigon gave an impression of a disastrous U.S. defeat, whereas the military situation in the rest of the country was unfavorable to the North Vietnamese.

Media representatives in Vietnam protested military charges that their presence during military operations jeopardized security. Richard Halloran, writing in *Parameters,* took issue with this accusation:

> That is an allegation without basis in historical fact. An examination of the record in World Wars I and II, where there was censorship, and in Korea and Vietnam, where there were guidelines but no censorship, shows that rarely did the press endanger operational security. In Vietnam, Barry Zorthian, long the government's chief spokesman, has said he knows of only a half-dozen instances in which a correspondent broke the guidelines; three of those were inadvertent.[6]

Halloran's defense further highlights the differing objectives of journalists and officials, and not only in questions related to military combat. To the journalist, the reader's interest is paramount. To the official, items that are dramatic or sensational do not serve military or diplomatic objectives. The detailed complaints of a soldier about combat conditions will be avidly read at home; it could help to destroy morale in the field. Brent Scowcroft, President Bush's national security adviser, in a speech at Georgetown University on April 8, 1987, commented:

> What of the media? To whom are they accountable? Is it to the people, through the profits of the media enterprises which prosper? I think we all would recognize that a direct correlation between journal-

istic integrity and excellence and corporate profit is certainly open to question.[7]

A major confrontation occurred between government and the press at the time of the U.S. invasion of Grenada in 1983. With recollections of Vietnam in mind, military officials excluded the press from the invasion and sent back members of the press who had reached the island on their own. The resulting outcry brought about the appointment of a commission under Major General Winant Sidle to explore the relationship. The Sidle Commission report recommended the establishment of press pools to cover combat. The new arrangement was tried—without success, from the press standpoint—in the 1989 invasion of Panama. The controversy continued into the Gulf crisis of 1990-91. Again, defense officials and military personnel, still stung by the Vietnam experience, determined that they would manage the flow of information. Their decision extended not only to actual operations, but to contacts between individual reporters and military personnel. In the case of the Gulf War, the relationship was further complicated because much of the combat activity originated from Saudi Arabia, a country traditionally averse to journalists. In that conflict, journalists were angered by delays in the review of dispatches and by confusion between press policies in the field and in Washington, although many agreed to the pool arrangements. Instances were reported in which information was removed by censors in the field only to be revealed shortly thereafter by officials in Washington. Reporters also complained that changes were made for reasons of public relations rather than security; in one case, a reference to Air Force personnel as "giddy" was changed to "proud."[8]

Television coverage was criticized by some journalists as being too uncritical of the war. Marvin Kalb, director of Harvard's Shorenstein Barone Center on the Press, Politics, and Public Policy and a former NBC reporter, wrote in the *New York Times,* "Even a sympathetic look at television coverage suggests that there is a certain whiff of jingoism on the airwaves and in print, that there is not enough detached, critical skepticism. When the boys go off to war, the press goes with them."[9]

Liz Trotta, the first woman correspondent for an American television network in the Vietnam War, made similar comments in an interview with the *Christian Science Monitor:*

After working beside American troops in Vietnam, Trotta became an admirer. "I was gratified to see [in the Gulf War], albeit it was a short, shiny little war, that soldiers walked tall again," she said in a Monitor interview. . . . It was the newspapers and television networks, Trotta says, who failed in their Gulf War duty. They "rolled over" when they should have been fighting the "silly" pool-reporting idea designed to contain them, she says. Television settled for simply "a nice, Technicolor war. We had shifting sands on CNN; we had shiny jets. [The networks] had a very good time with the hardware."[10]

Much of the effort of the military was designed to present a sanitized picture of the war, one without blood and casualties. The fear was deep that images of actual combat and negative remarks by soldiers would weaken support for the war at home. As Walter Goodman of the *New York Times* commented, one result was that cameras focused on the potential victims of war, citizens in Baghdad, Westerners temporarily held hostage.

> For the television audience, the confrontation with Iraq has become a war of the innocents. The screen is dominated not by warriors but by wives, not men but boys, not armor but infants. . . . But given its inherent fascination with faces rather than causes, with personal loss rather than national gain, television is taking on the role of a deterrent to an expanded war.[11]

When the air war against Baghdad began in January 1991, Peter Arnett, a veteran war correspondent with CNN, was in the Iraqi capital. His presence raised another issue: Should journalists continue to broadcast clearly controlled and censored material from an adversary's capital? Those opposed to his staying feared that CNN would thus become a mouthpiece for Saddam Hussein's propaganda. Arnett stayed and, afterward, claimed that he was able to broadcast in such a way as to indicate Iraqi control but, nevertheless, to get out important news. The viewers seemed generally to agree.

Terrorism

The 1970s and 1980s saw a rash of acts of terrorism that presented special problems for both the news organizations and the government. Acts included hostage-taking, hijackings, ship-jackings, and bombings. The incidents raised questions of press access to terrorists, the broadcasting of messages from terrorists and hostages, media involvement in negotiations and approaches to families of victims.

The U.S. newspapers, magazines, and networks naturally gave greatest attention to those incidents in which Americans were involved, although statistically they represented a small proportion of the total victims; Britain, Germany, Italy, Turkey, and Spain suffered more. Many of the incidents in these countries were internal, and treated as police matters. The definition of terrorism depended in part on the perspective of the definer: in the case of Middle East terrorism, those sympathetic with the Palestinian cause tended to see acts even by extreme Palestinians as understandable. Nevertheless, as acts became more brutal and the origins and the purposes of the perpetrators became less clear, most countries—in the West, at least—tended to agree that acts involving innocent citizens constituted terrorism. Differences existed, however, in the European and American approach to terrorism, differences reflected in press policies. Stefano Silvestri, in "The Media and National Security," explains: "The Americans have approached terrorism as a sort of war to be fought with military means, while the Europeans have tended to see it as a political phenomenon requiring political response."[12]

The tensions that exist between journalists and officials in combat conditions are paralleled in terrorist incidents and especially in those involving hostages.

Acts of terrorism are filled with drama and tragedy, the stuff of news. In the opinion of those responsible for resolving or preventing such acts, the resolution of hostage seizures and the investigation of bombings and hijackings require secrecy. Officials resent public discussions of their efforts, particularly with those suspected of perpetrating the act. The reporter at times appears to be a self-appointed negotiator, provoking replies to questions from the suspected terrorist that can harden negotiating positions and complicate efforts at resolution. Reporters and camera crews are seen as falling too easily into the designs of the kidnappers or perpetrators, giving them forums that increase their stature and their bargaining power. Heart-rending transmissions of statements by captives and demands by captors create pressures on officials from families to relax policies against negotiating with terrorists.

Officials acknowledge that reporters often have access to individuals and sources of information not available to governments. Ideally, a basis should exist for an exchange between officials and journalists in crisis situations. The journalist, however, is reluctant to appear to be sharing information with authorities; the official is rarely confident that what is told to a journalist in confidence will not be disclosed.

In many terrorist situations, both governments and journalists are face to face with sophisticated uses of the media. In 1986 American, British, German, and French citizens were seized at random as hostages in Beirut. Captors delivered to television networks videos of the hostages, obviously made under pressure, in which the captives accused their governments of neglecting them or pled that they would be executed if governments did not act. The captors sought opportunities to tie such pleas into other events. When Nicholas Daniloff, the Moscow correspondent for *U.S. News and World Report,* was arrested in the Soviet Union, President Reagan made a personal plea to the Russians to release him. Within thirty-six hours, an Islamic Jihad announcement from Beirut echoed pleas from the Beirut hostage families that the president give the same amount of attention to their plight. Once Daniloff was released, the Beirut captors produced a tape in which two of the hostages, including a journalist, Terry Anderson, pleaded with Reagan, accusing him of neglect and urging him to make arrangements for their freedom as he had done in the Daniloff case.[13]

For terrorists, the television networks are the primary instruments through which they believe they can get their message to the public and negotiate over the heads of hesitant governments. The journalist believes that giving space and time to the demands of terrorists can facilitate a solution. Katharine Graham, chairman of the board of the Washington Post Company, has called news coverage "an insurance policy for hostages." In her 1985 Churchill lecture in London she stated, "As soon as hostages appear on television, they may be somewhat safer. By giving the terrorists an identity we make them assume more responsibility for their captives."[14] Publicity about hostages, in this view, makes it more difficult for terrorists to hide them or kill them. When government policy prohibits any official contact with terrorists, reporters, by their access, can probe the elements of possible solutions. At least some family members in recent incidents have welcomed this role by the media.

Not everyone agrees. Certainly some officials see the argument that publicity saves lives as a rationalization for media intrusions into sensitive political and personal events. Graham in her lecture quotes then–Prime Minister Margaret Thatcher, "We must try to find ways to starve the terrorist and the hijacker of the oxygen of publicity on which they depend." Graham, in responding to this, pointed out that terrorist acts are impossible to ignore, that specialists find no compelling evidence that a lack of coverage would stop terrorist acts, and that citizens have a right to know what the government is doing in such cases.

Perhaps the most dramatic confrontation between officials and reporters occurred in the hijacking of TWA Flight 847 in Athens in June 1985. At the first stop in Algiers, the Algerian government was prepared to attempt to release the hostages when news leaked that the United States was considering sending an anti-terrorism Delta Force team. The hijackers, in response to this news, forced the pilot to fly on to Beirut. At Beirut, an American sailor, Robert Dean Stethem, was killed and his body thrown on the tarmac.

During the crisis, reporters were in daily contact with Nabih Berri, representative of the Lebanese Shia, who was close to the kidnappers. One interviewer even volunteered to convey Berri's demands to President Reagan. The most controversial of the media actions, however, was a television interview of the hostages arranged with the captors and with the captors present. Alex Jones, in his *New York Times* analysis of the event, commented:

> In their role as a participant, the nation's networks broadcast statements and interviews with representatives of Amal, the Shiite Moslem militia that took responsibility for the hostages, and also transmitted interviews with the hostages that were carefully controlled by the captors.[15]

Jones also pointed out that journalists, fearful for their own safety, avoided asking questions that might offend the kidnappers, such as queries about Stethem's death.

Competition among the networks for access to hostages and captors was intense. Rumors circulated, denied by the networks, that some were paying for exclusive interviews. ABC gave a banquet for the hostages in Beirut and NBC flew hostage families to West Germany at the time of release in exchange for exclusive interviews.

Newspapers also followed the unfolding drama closely and published transcripts of TV interviews. It was the actions of the networks, however, that led to much soul-searching by media organizations. Some defended their actions, insisting that the publicity had helped resolve the issue and protect the hostages from harm. Morton Dean, for many years a correspondent for CBS News, commented in the *New York Times*:

> Now I hear that TV has become the terrorists' ultimate tool. This is a daffy and irresponsible charge. The competitive zeal with which

the networks chased after the story of the hostages should be celebrated as an example of what's right with the democratic system, not what's wrong with it.[16]

The journalists' actions in such cases also raise the question of whether the media have any responsibility to officials—either to share information or to ask difficult questions. In one extreme case, when authorities were seeking to track down Abdul Abbas, the terrorist responsible for the October 1985 seizure of the Italian ship *Achille Lauro* and the killing of an American passenger, Leon Klinghoffer, NBC located Abbas and had a telephone interview with him.[17] Does not the television network, in such a case, have a responsibility to the public to inform authorities of the suspect's whereabouts? Most media organizations would say "no." To appear to be assisting the authorities through sharing information would run grave risks for journalists, and make access to sources more difficult.

At the height of concern over the reporting of terrorist incidents and hostage situations, networks were urged to adopt guidelines for such crises. Some, such as Katharine Graham, believed guidelines were undesirable: "Even media-sponsored guidelines would be too broad to be useful or would be forgotten in the heat of a crisis." Networks, however, did try to respond. *Neiman Reports* published the broadcasting guidelines of the three TV networks relating to the coverage of civil disorders, acts of terrorism, and hostage-taking. The reports were uniform in their declarations that the news organizations must make the final determination of what shall be broadcast, and that they should not enter into any agreements to limit news coverage. Each of the three networks cautioned its personnel against using inflammatory catchwords or disobeying police commands. ABC and NBC admonished reporters to be unobtrusive (using unmarked cars, limiting lights, avoiding staging) and to take care not to become "participants." ABC and CBS urged caution in the use of the telephone in situations where such use might interfere with the efforts of authorities (CBS said "wherever feasible"). These two networks specifically approved the reporting of terrorists demands, but their guidelines urged that the networks not become "platforms" for the terrorists. The guidelines of both stressed that any suppression of news would adversely affect the network's credibility.[18]

Some points were unique. ABC was the only one specifically to state that nothing should be done "that could jeopardize the lives of hostages, or interfere with efforts by authorities to secure their safe release." ABC also recognized that "it is possible that even the most professionally detached team may by its very presence contribute to a disturbance by passively causing others to take action that they otherwise might not take." CBS encouraged its representatives to contact experts dealing with a hostage situation "to determine whether they have any guidance on such questions as phraseology to be avoided, what kinds of questions or reports might tend to exacerbate the situation, etc."

NBC emphasized "taste and judgement" as guidelines in hostage situations and mentioned that on three occasions the network had voluntarily withheld sensitive information from its news programs in hostage cases. The NBC guidelines urged that background and context be provided to coverage in order to remind audiences of "prevailing conditions." NBC was the only one to mention hostage families specifically: "We cannot subscribe to stipulations or recommendations that we ignore the hostages or their families—or even the hostage-takers—on the assumption that if we keep them off television the crisis situation will go away." NBC was also the only network to approve the payment of the travel of hostage families and purchase of "relevant diaries or photographic materials that fall within the category of memoirs." NBC's guidelines also had the most explicit statement of the role of television in such situations:

> There is no doubt that television has become a primary means of communications for terrorists, for hostages, and for the families of hostages. At times, television has also become one of the means by which the diplomatic parties involved exchange their positions and messages. One columnist has called television news "the international nervous system." We cannot ignore this modern communication function—even though we did not ask for it—and still operate as effective and honest broadcast journalists.[19]

Intelligence

In theory, the most objective official information on the nature of events should come from intelligence agencies. Relatively speaking, this may be true, but intelligence activities, too, are pulled into the political arena, and the press and television play a part in the pulling. This development has created perhaps the most contentious relationship of all between government officials and journalists. Officials of intelligence agencies believe near-total secrecy is essential in their work not only for operational reasons but for the personal safety of themselves and their co-workers as well. They fear that the release of even relatively innocuous information gained by clandestine methods can reveal how the information was obtained and jeopardize the lives of agents and informants. In some cases, revelations have dried up significant activities—at times with regrettable consequences.

Katharine Graham, in her Churchill lecture, acknowledged one:

> Tragically, however, we in the media have made mistakes. In April 1983 some 60 people were killed in a bomb attack on the U.S. Embassy in Beirut. At the time there was coded radio traffic between Syria, where the operation was being run, and Iran, which was supporting it. Alas, a television network and a newspaper columnist reported that the U.S. government had intercepted the traffic, and soon the traffic ceased. This undermined efforts to capture the terrorist leaders and eliminated a source of information about future attacks.[20]

Both newspapers and television have shown sensitivity to intelligence needs and have consulted with officials on information in media possession. As in every other issue, the media executives reserved to themselves the decision on whether or not to publish. As three of the most famous incidents involving the *Washington Post* suggest, it is difficult to assess the actual damage caused by the publication of sensitive materials.

In 1977, the *Post* learned that the CIA had been secretly funding King Hussein of Jordan. Although urged in consultations with officials not to publish the information, the newspaper did—on the eve of a visit by the king to Washington.[21] Since the king remained on his throne, the *Post* presumably felt no harm had been done.

In December 1984, the U.S. Air Force launched, for the first time, a space shuttle with a classified mission. All press was to be banned from the launch, and information on the time and nature of the mission was also banned. The *Post* challenged the necessity for this and, after talking with officials, concluded that publicity would not tell the Russians anything they did not already know.[22]

In the third incident, in 1986, a Navy intelligence officer, Robert Pelton, was charged with selling information on a secret sensing device to the Soviet Union. The CIA strongly resisted any revelation of the nature of the information sold to the Russians, in the courts as well as the press. Once more, the *Post* concluded that no serious harm would be done by describing what Pelton had disclosed.[23]

As those in the media like to point out, much of the damage comes because of leaks from within the intelligence community. In the last two decades such leaks have come about, in large part, because of the use of intelligence by opponents and proponents of disputed policies within the Agency. *The Soviet Brigade in Cuba* documents how Senator Richard Stone, desiring to gain favor with Cuban-American constituents in his district, obtained from intelligence sources classified satellite photos and information and created a crisis in U.S.-Soviet relations.[24]

Presidents have recognized that certain actions could only be justified by revealing classified intelligence information. To justify the U.S. raid on Libya in April 1986, Reagan revealed intercepted communications between the Libyan government and its Peoples Bureau in Berlin.

The open season on intelligence information began with the revelations of the hearings held under Senator Frank Church on U.S. covert activities in 1975. Another outgrowth of the Vietnam period and the controversies of the 1960s, the Church hearings lifted the veil on previously secret intelligence activities and created serious divisions within the government and the public over the appropriateness of such actions. On the fringe, counterculture publications such as *Counter Spy* challenged the clandestine service concept by revealing the names of CIA officers abroad. In the case of controversial intelligence actions, such as the assistance to the anti-Sandinista contras in Nicaragua, mainline publications were less inhibited in revealing secret operations. The debate over the release of classified intelligence information reached acute proportions in the Reagan administration with the appointment of William Casey as director of the CIA.

Casey, whose previous intelligence experience had been in wartime conditions, sought to stem the flow of classified information into the public arena. He required contractors and employees of the intelligence agencies to submit to polygraph tests, expanded the discretion of federal agencies to classify information for an indefinite period, required retiring officials to agree to submit all future writing for prepublication review, and sought to broaden the exemptions for the CIA under the Freedom of Information Act. In May 1986, Casey disclosed that he and other administration officials had discussed the possibility of prosecuting five news organizations (the *Washington Post,* the *New York Times,* the *Washington Times, Newsweek,* and *Time*) for publishing information about U.S. intelligence-gathering operations. Although the threat was never carried out, it led newspapers and TV organizations to examine more closely their policies on such information.[25]

Certainly no two elements of U.S. society have more contradictory obligations than the media and intelligence. In the debate over the respective roles, however, questionable rationalizations are created on both sides. The legitimacy of the demand for total secrecy by the intelligence agencies was undermined, especially in the Reagan administration, by attempts to hide actions that did not have congressional approval and were questionable under existing laws. The media, however, has put forward a "public right to know" as the basis for judgments on the publishing of secret data.[26] Many times in U.S. history some balance between these two views has been achieved. The fierce ideological differences that existed in the 1970s and 1980s, however, made any such balance difficult and precipitated the deep differences that existed during that period.

Diplomacy

In the world of intelligence, operatives assume that little is to be gained by public disclosure. The situation is different in diplomacy. A secretary of state may find it tactically useful to leak a possible negotiating ploy to put pressure on an opposing side. A national security adviser may tell a reporter about a policy option to test public reaction. A president may use a press conference to send a message to a country with which the United States has no diplomatic relations. Negotiators may publicly reject or reveal an adversary's position as a means of sabotaging or delaying an agreement. In the conduct of relations with other nations, the media can be a tool, especially in the United States.

The press and television—especially television—have become, inescapably, players on the U.S. diplomatic scene. Officials in crisis situations pay as much attention to CNN and the networks as to embassy dispatches. Television pictures of the Israeli bombing of Beirut in 1982 led President Reagan to telephone Israeli Prime Minister Menachem Begin to halt the bombing. The president sent the Marines back into Lebanon following television coverage of massacres in Palestinian refugee camps. In 1993, dramatic television pictures of a U.S. soldier's body being dragged through the streets of Mogadishu by a mob led to the expedited withdrawal of U.S. forces from Somalia.

Radio and television become channels for diplomatic messages when other relations are severed. Secretary of State Edmund Muskie purposely released a letter to the Iranian prime minister during the U.S. embassy hostage crisis of 1979.[27] Following the Iraqi invasion of Kuwait in 1990, when relations with Iraq were effectively severed, President George Bush and President Saddam Hussein hurled messages back and forth via television. Tom Shales, TV critic for the *Washington Post,* called the networks during the Gulf War a "de facto hotline" between Washington and Baghdad.[28]

Press and television are often ahead of governments when reporters seek interviews with emerging diplomatic personalities. When Mikhail Gorbachev emerged on the scene in the Soviet Union in 1985, there was tremendous curiosity in both official and public circles about this new Russian—his personality and his views. *Time* gained a diplomatic as well as journalistic coup when it arranged the first interview with him.[29] What a leader like Gorbachev says in such an appearance becomes part of his official commitment in relations with the United States. Officials in the Department of State had to take his comments into account as they crafted U.S. policy toward the Soviet Union.

The *Time* approach to Gorbachev was received more favorably than an approach made to the Russians by James Reston and Arthur Krock of the *New York Times* in 1952. In his book *Deadline,* Reston tells of the criticism he and Krock received in other publications and from the *Times's* own management when they sent a series of questions seeking to sound out Stalin's views on the election of Dwight Eisenhower as president.[30]

The central position of Washington in world affairs leads many nations to seek access to the American public—and through the public, it is hoped, to the Congress. The U.S. becomes an arena in which others present their causes and fight their battles. The aggressive and intrusive U.S. press and television become the channels for this access. No one has illustrated this more effectively than Ted Koppel of ABC's Nightline program.

Koppel has created a unique form of journalistic diplomacy in using modern communications technology to bring together political opponents—in some cases opponents who, for political reasons, cannot meet face to face.

In the light of dramatic breakthroughs in both South Africa and the Middle East it is fair to ask whether Koppel's pioneering efforts to use electronics to bring enemies together may not have played a part. In a broadcast from South Africa in 1985, he interviewed jointly (by split screen) the head of the African National Congress and the foreign minister of South Africa. On another occasion in Jerusalem on April 26, 1988 he brought together for the first time on worldwide television Palestinians and Israelis for an open discussion of their differences.

In a column in *Newsweek* magazine on April 8, 1985, Koppel addressed the question of why participants responded so well to the invitation to appear on his program:

> What was significant about "Nightline's" week in South Africa was not that blacks and whites of such diverse points of view agreed to appear together on TV, but their reasons for doing so. . . . Ask only why they bothered, and it becomes clear that once again we were engaged in that much misunderstood phenomenon known as "television diplomacy." . . .
>
> By participating in "Nightline's" week of broadcasts from Johannesburg, each of the factions with whom we spoke cast its vote, at the very least, for American participation in the process. . . . They were not substituting American TV for the diplomatic process; they were attempting to affect that process by addressing the curious amalgam which is the American political structure.[31]

One of Koppel's participants in the South African program was Oliver Tambo, then president of the African National Congress. The U.S. had virtually no official relations with the Congress or with Tambo. TV became a channel for communication with a significant South African political leader.

Until recently, the press and TV have been the principal channels through which leaders of the Palestine Liberation Organization have spoken to Washington. Secretary of State Henry Kissinger pledged that the United States would not recognize or negotiate with the PLO until the PLO met certain conditions. Although this was changed by the Israeli-PLO Accord in 1993, throughout the period when no official communication was possible the press was the PLO's link to the U.S. public—and government. Yasser Arafat, the leader of the organization, took every opportunity to communicate with the American public—and, presumably, listening officials—through newspapers and television.

Similarly, enterprising journalists such as Georgie Ann Geyer of the *Chicago Daily News* have sought out leaders of liberation movements in Africa and revolutionary movements in Latin America. In each case, to the journalist the interview is news, but, to some extent, the reporter is a diplomat, being used to send diplomatic messages to the American government. The day is past when such activities created serious political backlash in the United States as when Herbert Mathews of the *New York Times* went into the mountains of Cuba to interview Fidel Castro in 1957.

The efforts of foreign rulers to reach the American public through television can backfire. When Saddam Hussein held foreigners as "guests" in Iraq, presumably as shields against military action, he believed he could use TV to demonstrate compassion toward the guests. He invited TV crews to picture a session with the "guests" in which he was shown stroking the heads of children and chatting with their parents. As Walter Goodman, TV critic for the *New York Times* pointed out, Saddam badly misjudged the reaction:

> But having never performed for audiences further West [than the Arab world], he seems not to have understood that these pictures could only undermine the impresario. For what the camera brought most dramatically into America's homes were the captive children and their parents, along, possibly, with memories of other pictures of hostages.[32]

The most dramatic backfire came in 1986 in the case of President Ferdinand Marcos of the Philippines. Confident both of his personal appeal in the United States and his ability to predict the outcome of Philippine elections, he accepted a challenge to call a vote issued by George Will, Washington columnist, in a TV talk show. Once the election was scheduled, Marcos made himself continually available for TV interviews. He clearly hoped to convince the American public and, through them, the White House, that he was, for the United States, the indispensable man in the Philippines. He had seriously miscalculated the effect of his tactics. When he sought to claim an election victory that was not there, he was—before the very television cameras he had hoped to capture—forced to leave the country. Tom Shales of the *Washington Post* reported,

> Once the election wheels were set in motion, the campaign was played out on American TV as if Americans were going to be able to

vote. . . . Marcos and his opponent, Corazon Aquino, were roughly as available to the media as Democratic presidential hopefuls newly arrived in New Hampshire for a snowy primary.

Marcos looked bad, talked tough, conveyed corruption; Aquino maintained a relative dignity. U.S. policy began to turn. It didn't look good to be allied with this nasty little man on TV.[33]

Official Washington was swept up and, to some extent, swept along by TV initiatives in the cases cited. Government and the press found common cause in these diplomatic events.

In no way is the U.S. government likely to object to an opportunity like that provided by the *Time* interview with Gorbachev. That moment was a critical one in U.S.-Soviet relations and evaluating the personality and objectives of the new Soviet leader was vital. Neither does the government have any basis for objecting to press interviews with personalities with whom the U.S. has no official relations, although the risk is always present that such interviews may raise expectations of official support or undermine diplomatic efforts.

Nevertheless, officials have reservations about some journalistic actions, particularly when journalists in crisis situations pose questions directly relating to negotiating positions. In diplomacy, the timing and wording of questions are crucial. Periods occur in negotiations in which diplomats deliberately avoid asking questions of the other side for fear that the answers might establish a position from which it is difficult to retreat. Hypothetical questions are especially treacherous. Diplomats rarely ask them—or answer them. Such questions raise issues that might not otherwise be raised. The responses may represent the only answer the official believes he or she can give in public, yet may lock the official into a tough position from which it is difficult to retreat. An example:

Q: (to an Israeli prime minister) What if a peace proposal required that you withdraw totally from the Golan Heights?
A: That is impossible. We will never withdraw from the Golan Heights.

Journalists' questions may also provide opportunities to the foreigner unwelcome to U.S. officials. Foreign leaders, knowing that they are addressing the American public, may make demands for unrealistic amounts of aid or U.S. support for an extreme position in a conflict. In such cases, most leaders know exactly what they are doing; they are serving their own political purposes. What they are saying publicly may not represent what they believe or are prepared, in fact, to do. Reporters, however, appear to accept such statements at their face value.

Diplomatic differences can best be worked out in non-public conversations. An aggressive public challenge by a reporter may only bring about a reiteration of an extreme position that makes the retreat to a more realistic position more difficult. Journalists are not likely to respond to foreign officials with a realistic appraisal of what the United States can do; the public is left with an impression that the demands are serious, and the foreign official may believe the demands to be realistic. In some cases, the reporter in an article or commentary may put the foreigner's remarks in a realistic context but it is often left to the U.S. official to bring both public and foreign officials back to reality.

Shortly after the December 1979 invasion of Afghanistan by the Soviet Union, the United States began confidential internal discussions about resuming aid to Pakistan. Economic and military assistance had been suspended because of a suspected nuclear weapons program. In the internal deliberations, the figure of $400 million was proposed and informally discussed with congressional committees. The figure leaked, and a reporter asked President Zia al Huq of Pakistan what he would think of this amount. His answer was "peanuts."[34] Conceivably the final aid package could have been presented in diplomatic channels in a manner that President Zia would have accepted; his answer to the reporter made this impossible and created a temporary tension in U.S.-Pakistan relations at a critical time.

Diplomats cannot control the questions that journalists will ask. In a study of the public dimension of foreign policy, it is important to understand that a reporter's intervention at a critical moment in diplomatic negotiations can have consequences.

Radio and TV talk shows and the print equivalent, the op-ed page, have become significant transmission belts for the images and information that form the background of foreign policy decisions. The hosts and editors of such outlets are often influential personalities in their own right, but the ultimate influence of such programs comes from the individuals who appear as guests and writers. Who are these people? Where do they come from? How valid are their opinions and how disinterested? Subsequent chapters will address the several channels that play roles in forming the images and perceptions on which Americans, both official and private, base their world views.

6 Money

Beyond the realms of the government and the media lie the think tanks, academia, consulting services, public relations firms, and advocacy organizations. The nation is awash in institutes, centers, associations, and "watches," in addition to the departments of colleges and universities focused in whole or in part on international relations. Although the network is nationwide, Washington, in particular, is a veritable citywide university with continuing seminars, lectures, colloquia, and conferences for those who want to be educated or to educate others. Such organizations also have influence in shaping perceptions of international events and policies, although that influence is less clear and more subtle than that of officialdom and the press.

The key to the power and existence of these institutions, however, lies in the ability of those who lead them to find money. How they do it and where they find it is the subject of this chapter. No full understanding of the forces that govern this intricate institutional community is possible without a comprehension of the indispensability and influence of fund raising.

A few institutions are comfortably endowed, but most must compete in the world of donors for support. A prime qualification for leadership in nearly every think tank, advocacy organization, or university is the ability to bring in money; that is how executives spend most of their time.

Even membership groups like the Council on Foreign Relations have an annual fund drive.

If the First Amendment establishes the media's role in defining international events, the U.S. tax code nurtures the nonprofit sector that seeks to inform and influence the foreign policy process. Section 501 (C) (3) permits tax deductions for educational and charitable purposes. Other sections of the code authorize the establishment of charitable foundations and permit businesses to write off as expenses contributions to nonprofit organizations.

Fund Raising

When, after retirement, I was appointed director of the Institute for the Study of Diplomacy at Georgetown University, I realized that a part of my task would be to find approximately $250,000 per year to support the Institute, including my own salary. Father Timothy Healy, then president of Georgetown University, was once quoted as saying he would be prepared to hire anyone who could raise his own salary.

At the beginning, I was ignorant of this discipline. When I was introduced to the university's director of development, I became aware that "development" is the common euphemism for fund raising.

The person on whom the existence of an institution and, perhaps, personal livelihood may depend has the search for potential donors constantly in mind. The task can be discouraging. As one development officer told me when I began the process, "Take in your stride the first fifty rejections; you'll ultimately have a success." It was some time after I retired from the Institute at Georgetown before I approached a room full of people without wondering who among them might be interested in making a contribution to my organization.

During the ten years at the Institute, I learned much about fund raising from observing masters of the craft. Father Healy, by studied cultivation of alumni and friends of the university, increased the endowment several fold. Peter Krogh, dean of the School of Foreign Service at Georgetown, flattered, cajoled, and persuaded those with money to contribute approximately $2 million a year to the school. David Abshire, president of the Center for Strategic and International Studies, a think tank then associated with Georgetown University, built that organization primarily through a skillful tapping of sympathetic sources in Washington and beyond.

Fund raising is an art, but with a considerable amount of not-too-carefully concealed "scientific" research and calculation. The plans and purposes of an institution or individual must be aligned with the objectives and proclivities of prospective donors. Such donors must be found. In the cases of individuals, finding such persons and interesting them in a program or project may require the patient pursuit of a prospect through friendship and favors—sometimes over months and years.

Limitations abound. Donors, whether individuals, corporations, or foundations, want their money to go to projects resulting in tangible work: conferences, publications, studies—in other words, products. They want proposals that "break new ground," that are "timely," and, it is hoped, newsworthy. They want to please either themselves or their boards of directors. Administrative costs not attractive to donors must normally be siphoned off of project budgets. Very few corporate or foundation funders will provide money for buildings ("bricks and mortar"). Such large-scale capital outlays must normally come from individual major donors, often from persons not averse to having the family name on the cornerstone. Donors are rarely receptive to long-range, open-ended proposals; few, for example, will fund the establishment of new courses in a university, except in the case of chairs.

University administrations often cross swords with faculty and institute directors over how much of a project grant will go to the university for administrative overhead. The amount siphoned off can be as much as 50 percent.

Fund raising is not cheap. Landrum Bolling, former chairman of the Council on Foundations, estimates that, in one case, the costs of finding and soliciting donors amounted to 21 percent of the funds raised.[1] When institutions consider hiring a special fund raiser or inaugurating a major campaign, the prospect of returns must always be weighed against the expense of such activities.

Annual funding for all private sector organizations comes from sources both within the United States and abroad: individuals, direct mail and solicitation, corporations, foundations, governments, and revenue-generating activities such as conferences and publications. This applies not only to think tanks, special interest and advocacy organizations, and scholarly projects, but also to the vast array of charitable organizations dedicated to relief and development abroad.

The following chart illustrates by percentages (in 1993) the sources of revenue for six of the leading think tanks: Brookings Institution, Cato

Institute, Center for Strategic and International Studies (CSIS), Joint Center for Political and Economic Studies, American Enterprise Institute (AEI), and Heritage Foundation:[2]

TABLE 1: Think Tank Revenue Sources (%)

	Brookings	Cato	CSIS	Joint Center	AEI	Heritage
Foundations	38	89.8	84	53.2	37	25
Individuals	(1)	(1)	(1)	(2)	16	47
Corporations	(1)	(1)	(1)	28.8	38	7
Government	2	—	5	13	—	—
Generated Revenue (3)	35	10.2	11	5	9	21
Endowment (4)	25					

[Notes:
1. Contributions from foundations, individuals, and corporations are combined in institutions' reports.
2. Contributions from foundations and individuals are combined.
3. Includes conference fees, publications, computer network services, etc.
4. A breakdown of revenues for the liberal Institute for Policy Studies was not available.]

Although the institutions represent different points on the political spectrum, at least seventy-five corporate, foundation, and individual donors had contributed to more than one and, in some cases, to four. After the Republican sweep in the 1994 congressional election, the flow of money, primarily from corporations, shifted to conservative organizations, Republican members of Congress, and especially to the Progress and Freedom Foundation identified with House Speaker Newt Gingrich. Money clearly follows power.[3]

A similar chart for any series of special interest organizations such as those dealing with human rights, the environment, or population would probably show heavy dependence on major foundation grants and contributions gained through direct mail campaigns.

Anyone who receives mail in the United States is acutely aware of fund raising. Every post brings appeals from a host of privately funded organizations. Direct mail solicitation has developed as an important technique, especially for more conservative organizations. The best-known practitioner of this strategy is Richard Viguerie. David Ricci, in his book *The Transformation of American Politics,* describes how Viguerie built up a mailing list and enlisted it in support of New Right causes.[4] The conservative Heritage Foundation has also used this method effectively.[5]

Its appeals are straightforward and uncomplicated to those believers in sympathy with its neoconservative approach to both domestic and foreign issues. In some years, as much as 50 percent of the foundation's support came from small contributors ($50-$100), the result of postal appeals. Advocacy organizations, such as those working on human rights, population, emergency relief and Third World development, and the environment, also make extensive use of direct mail. Colleges and universities, too, solicit their alumni through the post.

Individual Giving

For think tanks and universities, the primary effort is directed at gaining large donations from individuals, corporations, and foundations. In the think tanks, money, access, and influence interact. Individuals give out of interest in a cause, issue, or ideology, but possibly the greatest lure is that of access to important personalities and specialized or restricted information. They may be corporate executives hoping to advance the interests of their company. They may be consultants seeking "inside dope," advice, or clients. In some cases, the donation is an ego trip—to have one's name associated with a book or project. Sometimes substantial fees are charged for the privilege of access. CSIS, for example, organizes business round tables in various cities for which business executives pay $5,000 to meet quarterly with high-level policymakers and CSIS scholars, including Henry Kissinger and Zbigniew Brzezinski. Undoubtedly, those who attend are interested in what the speaker will say, but the opportunity to rub shoulders with a famous personality is also a factor. Donor interest bears a direct relationship to the ability of an institution to attract senior policy officials, members of Congress, and international affairs "superstars" to committees and events. For many in the private sector world, formal appointments with policymakers are difficult. Institute events provide the chance to talk, to listen, and to plead a case. When this happens, their financial contribution pays off; they have purchased access.

Fund raising among the wealthy introduces an institute official to the world of the rich. It is a world of sensitivities, jealousies, and calculations. A common experience for fund raisers is an encounter with a wealthy individual who is unable to give, but who wants to "be helpful." Help consists of suggesting other wealthy friends who might be approached. At the same time, prospective donors do pay attention to what others may be giving. With this in mind, organizations list donors by categories. CSIS divides its donor list among those who contribute $250,000 or more; $100,000 to $249,999; $50,000 to $99,999; $25,000 to $49,999; $10,000 to $24,999; and under $9,999.[6] Brookings has organized the Brookings Council for individual contributions of $5,000 or more and corporate donations of more than $10,000.[7] The Heritage Foundation has the Windsor Society for those who have decided to provide future financial support "through their estates and other planned-giving programs"[8] on the theory that individual pride will lead them to opt for the higher gifts. Pressure is a factor. Some organizations will hold meetings of donors in which officers will designate an expected contribution on the basis of knowing an individual's income.

Tax considerations are important. A good development officer will know the tax code intimately and will helpfully suggest a way for both the individual and the institution to benefit. Especially for large gifts, a reduction in estate taxes may be a significant factor. Development officers spend considerable time discussing bequests with prospective donors. One of the largest donations to the Institute for the Study of Diplomacy during my tenure was from a retired Senate staff member who had made considerable money in the stock market. The man, a graduate of Georgetown, and his wife, then in their late seventies, had medical problems. The dean arranged for medical help and hospitalization; in the process he also found a lawyer to help them draft their wills. The result was a substantial bequest to the university for the Institute.

Although tax considerations may lead to a decision to give, where the gift may go is largely determined by either personal friendships, belief in an individual, interest in a field, or sympathy for a cause. Some donors build their gifts around individuals. In 1993, Edward Djerejian, former assistant secretary of state for Near East and South Asia, was appointed to head a new foreign policy institute at Rice University with funds raised and provided by former secretary of state James A. Baker III. Baker worked closely with Djerejian during the Bush administration and obviously had him in mind in the establishment of the institute. Similarly, Thomas Watson, former ambassador to the Soviet Union, provided funds for a new institute of Russian studies at Brown University and named Mark Garrison, who had been Watson's deputy in Moscow, as its head.

Understandably, confidence that the money will be used as the donor wishes weighs heavily in such decisions. One of the most substantial individual givers in recent times, Walter Annenberg, provides funds almost solely in the field of communications, an interest growing out of his long career in journalism.

Knowledge of a person's background and interest can backfire. One of the few genuinely wealthy men I came to know in my career was Dr. Armand Hammer, the president of Occidental Petroleum. I was ambassador to Libya when he made significant oil discoveries in that country. Dr. Hammer was also well known for his personal relations with key figures in the Soviet Union and had played a role in the ending of the war in Afghanistan. He had mentioned to me once that he had known Lenin and had an autographed photo of the Bolshevik leader. When I assumed responsibility for the Institute at Georgetown, I approached him for a contribution to the Institute on the basis of his role in diplomacy. Thinking it might be an inducement to a gift, I proposed that his mementos of the early days of the USSR be put on display. I never got a gift; I was told later by one of his associates that, for political reasons, he did not want public reminders of those early connections.

For the wealthy, financial considerations also become a factor, especially in matters of endowments. Most universities seek to protect endowment funds against changes in the economy by limiting the amount of interest income that can be used for the designated program. Usually this is 5 percent. Although this should be understandable to a potential donor, some are turned away by the prospect that their money will produce only a 5 percent return, especially during a period of high interest rates. Other devices are used, such as trusts that provide the full income to the project on condition that the fund will revert to the donor after a period of years, usually ten.

Some donors to institutions desire anonymity. Three of the principal donors to the Heritage Foundation in 1993 asked to remain anonymous.[9] But it is more normal for the giver to be acknowledged by the naming of a project, building, or endowment after the individual. The names that adorn buildings, libraries, and even rooms attest to this.

In my fund raising, I learned, also, about boards—those lists of prominent and not-so-prominent names that grace the margins of most organizations' letterheads. I assumed that such persons were appointed for their worth in providing advice and counsel to the institution on the basis of some related experience. Again, I was uninformed. After my arrival at the Institute for the Study of Diplomacy, I came to realize that boards were the means of giving recognition, not only to those who proffered advice, but, of even greater importance, to those who provided financial support.

Board appointments include individuals with an interest in the focus of the organization, those who may be expected to support it financially, and those whose names, it is believed, will lead others to give. The likelihood is that few of those listed as board members will be frequent attendees at meetings or will take an active part in the work. Many organizations now have two kinds of sponsoring groups: a board of trustees or directors who meet regularly and have corporate and fiduciary powers and responsibilities, and an advisory council that may never meet, has no decision-making powers, but may provide useful counsel and money and access to other potential donors.

Some donors prefer to make gifts in kind, including land. When items that require maintenance are provided, recipients sometimes have a greater burden than the gift may justify unless a maintenance endowment accompanies the gift. Land must be sold to benefit an institution, and this can create problems. In one case, the sale of land donated to a university was delayed for several years because of the presence of an eagles' nest. State regulations prohibited any activity on the land that would disturb the eagles.

Corporations

Corporations, a second major source of funding, give through their own foundations and directly from corporate funds. Some, such as the Exxon Foundation, have separate objectives somewhat apart from direct corporate interest. Exxon has provided extensive funds for initiatives in education. In other corporate cases, however, corporate foundations are little more than devices for funneling contributions seen as directly benefiting the company, its employees, and its community service image where it has significant operations. Like politics, much if not all corporate philanthropy is "local."

Corporations see various direct benefits in providing funds to nonprofit activities: institutional advertising, prestige, name recognition, access to policymakers and information, and support for policies friendly to private enterprise. In some cases, several objectives may be involved.

In the chart of contributions to think tanks shown above, corporations represented a major factor. Several, including Boeing Aircraft,

American Express, Amoco, Coca Cola, Philip Morris, and Chase Manhattan Bank, were on three or more of the donor lists.

At Georgetown, a major project was developed to bring young diplomats and officials from developing countries to the United States for training. The Coca Cola Company, both directly and through its foundation, provided substantial support. The company saw benefits in the association with those who would be future leaders in countries in which the corporation had facilities and sales. The selection of the candidates was made in cooperation with the local Coca Cola bottlers, bringing them into the process. Arrangements were made for the foreign visitors to go to Atlanta to visit company headquarters and, by so doing, to gain a favorable impression of the corporation.

The Institute at Georgetown received an annual donation from two oil companies. Shell based its donation on its interest in professional education. Mobil Oil's contribution came about through a personal friendship, justified by the company's interest in southern Africa and the possibility of Institute activities bearing on the issues of that region. Solicitations to other corporations were unsuccessful, primarily because a direct link between the work of the Institute and the commercial interests of the company could not be demonstrated.

Corporations have also been successfully approached on ideological bases. Ricci describes how William Simon, former secretary of the treasury, and Irving Kristol called on business leaders and corporations, as well as foundations, to "strengthen conservative think tanks and public interest groups and to create new ones."[10] He further wrote:

> Accordingly, Simon recommended that business people make contributions only to universities willing to hire conservative scholars to teach America's young people. Furthermore, he insisted that business money, presumably in corporate sponsorship and advertising, should be withdrawn from media outlets which are "anticapitalist" and given to media which are willing to treat "pro-capitalist" ideas fairly.[11]

Foundations

Probably the greatest sources of funds for nonprofit institutions result from large family foundations established with the benefit and encouragement of U.S. tax laws. Many reflect in their basic interests the religious backgrounds of the founders, others the family interest in regions, arts, science, or the U.S. role overseas. The result has been to turn some of the country's greatest fortunes into primary resources for research, teaching, the arts, and advocacy.[12]

The term "foundation" applies to several different types of entities. Some think tanks, such as the Heritage Foundation, use the term but depend entirely on external funding. Operating foundations such as Carnegie, Kettering, and Stanley give virtually no grants, but use their funds to initiate their own activities, generally in the form of conferences and publications. Carnegie has in recent years focused on the growing role of the new technologies, especially in the developing world. The Kettering Foundation emphasizes peace issues and has sponsored significant dialogues with the former Soviet Union. The Stanley Foundation holds periodic conferences on foreign policy subjects.

Grant-making foundations dealing with international issues can be roughly divided into two categories. One group, comprising in general those with the greatest assets (notably Ford and Rockefeller), pursues a broad range of social and political issues in the United States and abroad. A second group tends to focus on U.S. policy from a generally ideological point of view. The first is the mainstay of the more liberal think tanks, special interest organizations, university programs, and overseas development support. The second provides major support for conservative policy institutes. Whatever their orientation, the boards and executives of both clearly hope to use their assets to have an influence on significant, contemporary issues either by generating initiatives or by promoting ideas, ideologies, and causes.

The influence of these organizations on the existence and policies of the nonprofit institutional world in the United States cannot be exaggerated. The 100 largest total assets in excess of $200 billion. The largest, the Ford Foundation, in 1993 had assets of $6,253,006,737 and gave away $240,875,343 in its annual grant making program. (Since these resources are mostly in the securities market holdings, their total assets and annual "payout" can vary considerably from year to year.) Of the top ten foundations in terms of assets, those most identified with international issues and projects are Ford, the Rockefeller Foundation, the John D. and Catherine T. MacArthur Foundation, and the Pew Charitable Trusts.[13]

In general, foundations appear to favor private institutions and organizations over colleges and universities. A counting of the recipients of grants from the major foundations in 1993 showed fifty-six in the former category and thirty in the latter.[14]

The Ford Foundation played a key role in the establishment of one of the leading think tanks. Between 1955 and 1967, it contributed $39 million to the establishment of the Brookings Institution as "a private intelligence unit for government operations."[15] In 1994, its international grants program "seeks to promote a peaceful, stable, and just world order in which the potential for conflict is minimized and the possibilities for international cooperation and well-being are enhanced."[16]

Grants are made for research and training, policy development, and public education in several areas:

> regional and multilateral approaches to such international problems as security arrangements, arms control, and management of common resources; the international economic system and its effects on development patterns, migration, and international security; international human rights laws and practices; and U.S. foreign policy. In the former Soviet Union and Eastern Europe, the foundation supports the development of new economic and social policies and political and legal reform.[17]

Among the public policy institutes, Ford is listed as a donor to Brookings, CSIS, and the Joint Center. Ford is also a major contributor to the specialized advocacy organizations focusing on environmental protection and human rights.

The oldest of the major foundations, the Rockefeller Foundation (founded in 1913), is best known for its contributions to medicine, science, and development. Landrum Bolling, former president of the Council on Foundations, in his book *Private Foreign Aid,* comments, "The Rockefeller Foundation probably has had a more profound effect upon the lives of more people in the emerging lands of Asia, Africa, and Latin America than any other single private American institution."[18] In its policy-related international security grants program the foundation focuses on preventing the proliferation of weapons of mass destruction and "encouraging participation from the developing world in international security deliberations and related activities, and broadening the international security agenda to include the environment and other global issues."[19]

Rockefeller's grant-making in the United States goes largely to institutions focusing on these issues. Brookings is the only think tank that lists the Rockefeller Foundation as a donor.

The MacArthur Foundation, best known for its "genius" grants awarded annually to individuals for special accomplishments, is also important in support for public policy and special interest organizations and universities. Its contribution of $600,000 is the only publicly listed donation to the liberal Institute for Policy Studies (IPS). It contributes also to Helsinki Watch, the Joint Center for Political and Economic Studies, and to the Institute for International Economics. Special emphasis is placed through six-figure donations to population and environmental groups. In its program on Peace and International Cooperation it seeks to "expand and strengthen the field of international security studies and to increase public understanding of complex security issues."[20]

The Pew Charitable Trusts' international interests in the early years tended to be related to the overseas missionary activities of the family's church denomination. They too now have a broad agenda: "These trusts support nonprofit organizations and fund the specific areas of conservation and the environment, culture, education, health and human services, public policy and religion."[21] Their public policy grants program is more specific:

> Support is provided to tax-exempt organizations and public charities for collaborative efforts and U.S. and international partners to consolidate democratic, market-oriented transitions in East and Central Europe, Southeast Asia, and Latin America; and for projects to promote interdisciplinary approaches to understanding and responding to emerging threats to global peace and security.[22]

Bolling mentions the W. H. Kellogg Foundation, the Lilly Endowment, and the Rockefeller Brothers Fund as other important contributors to "relief, development, and other global purposes." He writes further, "Yet it must be made clear that at least another one hundred foundations play useful roles in international programs each year."[23] He also makes clear, however, that the vast majority of U.S. foundations, including some of the large ones, give nothing to international programs.

The tendency of major foundations to fund organizations perceived by conservatives to be liberal led to efforts, funded by conservative foundations, to establish conservative counterparts.

In the Nixon administration, leading foundations and think tanks were seen as enemies. Ricci describes how H. R. Haldeman, Nixon's chief of staff, issued an order that members of the administration were not to use the Brookings Institution. Consideration was even given to pressuring Brookings, the Ford Foundation, and the Institute for Policy Studies, through the Internal Revenue Service, although the idea was never carried out.[24]

The expansion of the think tanks in the latter part of the century has depended heavily on a group of foundations with generally conservative agendas.

The ideological agenda was illustrated to me when I approached a major foundation in southern California. The executive director of the company's foundation was a crusty elderly man who was retired from the position of general counsel. I explained that I was seeking money for the support of an institute to study and improve the practice of diplomacy. He replied, "We don't believe in diplomacy. If we are not going to fight the Russians, we sure as hell shouldn't talk to them."

Particularly identified with the growth of conservative institutions are the Lynde and Harry Bradley, Samuel Robert Noble, John M. Olin, and the Scaife family foundations (Sarah Scaife Foundation and Scaife Family Foundation). All are among the supporters of the rapidly growing Heritage Foundation (although two, Bradley and Olin, have also made contributions to Brookings). Founded in 1973, the Heritage Foundation had an annual income of $7 million by 1981. By April 1986, Heritage could invite President Ronald Reagan to preside over the celebration of raising its first $30 million. By 1990, its annual income had risen to $18 million;[25] by 1993, to $22.9 million.

The Scaife family has been particularly important in the founding of Heritage, CATO, and CSIS. The Sarah Scaife Foundation (assets $224,771,296) "supports public policy programs that address major domestic and international issues, as well as broader cultural issues, with a focus on strengthening traditional values."[26]

The Bradley Foundation supports projects that focus on "cultivating a renewed, healthier, and more vigorous sense of citizenship among the American people, and among the peoples of other nations as well."[27]

Despite the existence of Brookings and liberal institutions such as IPS, it is difficult in any survey of these institutes to avoid the conclusion that the largest and wealthiest are to the right of the political spectrum. Any survey of their reports reveals their emphasis on both the problems and areas of concern to U.S. business, a natural result of the sources of funding. Their annual incomes show the power of the conservative message in the raising of money:

TABLE 2: Think Tank Annual Incomes
(Based on 1993 Annual Reports)

Institutions (a)	Income (b)
Heritage Foundation	22.9
Brookings	20.1 (c)
CSIS	13.8
AEI	11.2
Joint Center	6.1
Cato Institute	4.9
IPS	1.5
CNP	.4

[Notes:
(a) The Carnegie Endowment has not been included since its programs are primarily financed by an endowment.
(b) In millions.
(c) Of this amount, 5.0 comes from endowment.]

Whatever the orientation of a foundation, the task of seeking grants is not simple, unless, as is sometimes the case, decisions are made by personal contact between the head of an organization and the president or a board member of a foundation. Even in these cases, extensive paper work must inevitably follow. Approaching any foundation in the normal way means the laborious preparation of project proposals and endless conferences with program officers. Such officers are under constant pressure from applicants. They are adept at saying "no." Rarely do they have the individual authority to make funding decisions that may be made by the president or the board of directors.

The preparation of proposals for foundations is in itself an art, requiring a careful reading of the foundation guidelines and an adaptation of an organization's objectives to those guidelines. Application packets frequently include biographies of all those participating, bibliographies, and, most important, budgets justifying the amount of the request. The successful proposal of the Institute for the Study of Diplomacy to the Pew Foundation for the case study project was twenty pages long, complete with pie charts. Approval took more than a year.

Such projects become exceedingly complicated if more than one element of an institution is involved. The Rockefeller Foundation once invited bids from universities for a project on the ethical aspects of international relations. At Georgetown, the proposal had to be coordinated with the departments of theology, philosophy, government, and economics. The multidiscipline negotiation took weeks and still did not result in a successful bid.

Although most foundations announce their objectives and the guidelines for making applications for grants, the politics of foundations play a role. It helps to know a board member or the president. Members of the original families continue to influence foundation policies in some cases. As in all fund raising, personal relationships with key figures are important.

In the case of the major foundations, this does not mean that decisions are capricious or based solely on favorites. Confidence that the recipient will meet the commitments of the grant is important to foundations. Grants are sometimes contingent on selected persons being chosen to implement a project. An application to the Ford Foundation for a grant on an arms control proposal, otherwise of interest to the board of the foundation, foundered because the individual the foundation desired to prepare the report was not available.

Personnel changes in foundation staffing can make a difference. When Franklin Thomas, an African American, became president of the Ford Foundation, the foundation adopted a major new emphasis on apartheid issues in South Africa. On one occasion Georgetown University had made progress in preparing a proposal—at the suggestion of a foundation project officer. That officer was replaced, and his successor, who was not interested in the issue, dropped the case.

In some instances, regional promotion enters the picture. The Hudson Institute was founded in Poughkeepsie, New York, by a prominent futurist, Herman Kahn. When he died, the Institute was lured to Indianapolis, Indiana, by an aggressive mayor, Richard Hudnut, and the Lilly Endowment, which agreed to be a major funder for Hudson when it moved to Indiana. When the American Academy of Diplomacy applied for a grant, it was told that the request would be considered if the Academy would move its activities to Indianapolis.

Government

The fourth source of funds for civic organizations is the government. Official funds are available either through legislative appropriations, direct grants, or contracts for specific projects. Development officers watch the congressional process for legislation that might authorize money for an institute or a university. They may encourage friendly members of Congress to specify their institutions as recipients. Dr. Hayden Williams, for many years president of the Asia Foundation, one of the most prominent of the institutes focusing on Asia, cultivated key senators who regularly added amounts to the State Department appropriation for the Foundation. He was subsequently successful in arranging for a congressional charter and annual line-item appropriation of $10 million.

Georgetown University had two Jesuit priests in the "Federal Relations" office to look for funds in legislation that might benefit the University. Known as the "Funding Fathers," they were often successful, but were frequently disappointed as other hawk-eyed members questioned why a designated sum should not be offered to all universities on a competitive basis.

Some private institutions depend heavily on contracts with government agencies. One of the earliest think tanks, the Rand Corporation (founded in 1948), was established with the encouragement of the U.S. Air Force primarily to retain civilian specialists who had worked on weapons research during World War II. Rand and two similar organizations, the Institute for Defense Analyses (1956) and the Mitre Corporation (1958), have been supported primarily by Department of Defense contracts. Each branched out from a strict focus on military development to issues of arms control, national strategy, and foreign policy.[28] Other public policy institutes are offered contracts for research projects by the Agency for International Development. More generally, however, funds are found through formal grant proposals to U.S. government agencies, usually an elaborate paper process. The National Endowment for the Humanities provides grants for some kinds of research. The Department of Education assists in language training and imaginative educational projects.

The one federally funded organization that concentrates solely on international and foreign policy issues is the U.S. Institute of Peace. Established by Congress under the Defense Authorization Act of 1985,[29] the Institute, in 1993, had an appropriation of $10,912,000. Of this, more than two-thirds goes to individuals, think tanks, and universities for projects related to conflict resolution and negotiation.[30] In the debate over its founding (discussed further in chapter 8), authority for the Institute to raise private funds was removed because of the opposition of universities and other institutions that feared the competition of a government-supported entity. In 1992, however, Congress authorized the creation of an Institute of Peace Endowment to receive "private gifts and contributions for a permanent headquarters and for program-related hospitality."[31] At a Tenth Anniversary conference in Washington on December 1, 1994, the Institute announced plans for a major capital campaign to finance a headquarters building. The Institute, although government supported, thus enters the institutional competition for private funds.

In recent years, foreign governments, individuals, and corporations have also become significant donors to nonprofit policy institutions in the United States. Motives are generally related to a desire for a positive image in America, trade issues, or an interest in access to U.S. policymakers. Japanese entities, both official and private, have been particularly active.[32]

The receipt of money from foreign sources sometimes raises both legal and political issues. As will be discussed in chapter 10, those receiving such funds may be subject to the Foreign Agents Registration Act. Others may not wish to be identified with the policies of the foreign donor. Georgetown University, in 1981, returned a donation of $600,000 to the government of Libya to avoid association with the policies of Muammar el-Qadafi.[33]

Most U.S. organizations wish to avoid identification with official work or policy, whether domestic or foreign, and turn to private sources.

Institutional Friction

Fund raising can be a source of friction within institutions and between them. Sources, whether foundations or individuals, are finite. Competition exists for each potential dollar. Development officials attempt to regulate approaches to potential donors to prevent multiple solicitations and confusion. In 1986, the Center for Strategic and International Studies, a prominent Washington think tank, ended its affiliation with Georgetown University. Although the report on which the separation was based cited differences over academic policy, the real issues related to funding. CSIS began a policy of establishing "chairs," to be occupied by scholars and to be named either after a donor or a prominent person (such as Henry Kissinger) whose name might bring contributions. The university faculty objected to what they considered the adaptation of an academic practice to a nonacademic institution. Negotiation over the possible joint appointment by CSIS and the university of a prominent scholar foundered because CSIS wanted the scholar to be available at any time to participate in meetings with important donors; the university wanted to give priority to teaching responsibilities. The issue was further aggravated because those appointed to these "chairs" were not subject to the normal university procedure for the selection of tenured faculty. Finally, there existed an inescapable conflict of objectives: CSIS was constrained in its fund raising by the need to coordinate with the financial appeals of other departments of the university;[34] the university felt its efforts were weakened because high-profile public policy projects are generally more attractive to potential donors than teaching or academic research.

It might be assumed that a natural mix existed between such institutes and universities. This has not been the case. The relationship between Stanford University and the Hoover Institution has frequently been troubled. Columbia University separated itself from Arden House.

The need for support also breeds a certain character in public policy institutions. It is one of continuing promotion of the institution, its activities, and products. Dropping prominent names, some with only a passing association with the organization, is an important tactic demonstrating the institution's worth and influence. Unquestioned loyalty of staff is essential to avoid differences of policy that could discourage donors.

The source of funds in large measure dictates the agenda of such institutions. The degree to which the funding source also determines the outcome of the research—and thus the view presented of events and issues—is a more complicated question. In the case of an ideologically oriented organization such as the Heritage Foundation, funding is sought and easily found for an acknowledged conservative view of the nation and the world. In the case of others, funding will determine the region and subject to be covered. Since project directors, often working with the donors, hire the researchers, the likelihood is that those working on a conference or publication will share the contributor's outlook and objective. Although serious and respected work is accomplished in think tanks, much of it is suspect outside precisely because donors are thought to dictate not only the subject but the result.

Inevitably, all funding, whether government, individual, foundation, or corporate, depends upon the economy. Changes in appropriations can reduce official funds. Individual contributions are particularly affected by recession. Foundations are vulnerable to changes in the value of securities portfolios. Corporations trim their generosity—even that associated with corporate benefit—when sales are down. A *Christian Science Monitor* article on May 23, 1994, quotes Tom Ingram, president of the Association of Governing Boards of Universities and Colleges, as saying, "The amount available for public and tax-supported or assisted universities has undergone substantial shrinkage. In private education, there is a strong resistance [from consumers] to pay more, and charitable contributions have leveled off to make up the difference between college tuition and costs."[35]

In the 1990s more and more questions are being raised about the future availability of funds for public interest and policy organizations. With the end of the Cold War, some of the issues that generated funding have faded. Recent changes in the tax laws are expected to reduce individual and corporate giving. Inevitably, many organizations will need to change the focus of their programs to meet the interests of donors in a changed environment.

At the same time, the press reports an increased cash flow into conservative coffers from galvanized opponents of the Clinton administration. An article on February 10, 1994, in the *Washington Post* quotes Bruce W. Eberle, a direct mail consultant for the Conservative Caucus and the Young America's Foundation: "When guys I don't like get into office, it's like the second coming. We are doing as well as we were doing a year after Jimmy Carter took office."[36]

The availability of money for public policy activities has made possible the unique proliferation of such activities in the United States in the last decades of the twentieth century. It remains now to examine what those activities have produced and how they influence the nation's foreign policy.

7 Academia

What is the role of the vast academic community in the United States in shaping images of international events for officials and the public? How do those associated with the numerous departments of political science, international relations, government, public policy, foreign service, history, and economics influence the policy-making process?

In any consideration of the public dimension of foreign policy in the United States, the role of academe—the 3,500 institutions of higher education and the individuals associated with them—is significant. It is natural to assume that, of all the institutions focusing on public policy, the free realm of the universities would have the most to offer in knowledge and insight. Challenges to conventional wisdom and provocative explorations of international issues not possible in the political world should be and are part of the domain of the scholar and teacher. Yet that realm, by virtue of practices and approaches that are part of its culture, is limited in its direct influence on public perceptions of events and on the formation of policy.

If foundations and donors provide the resources that support the public interest and pressures on foreign policy, the academic world provides much of the intellectual stimulus and talent. In the explosive years of the 1960s, both faculty and students crystallized opposition to the Vietnam War. In the final decades of the century, such mass manifestations on the less involved campuses have been rare; it has been left to individuals, faculty, and graduates to insert views refined in academia into national life. University presidents were once prominent figures in the national debate, but funding problems, campus turmoil, and the sensitivities of political dialogue have muted their voices.[1]

Communities of Individuals

The key to a comprehension of the role of universities in national life is to appreciate that they are communities of individuals. Each member survives and advances on the basis of individual accomplishments: writings, research, theories, prizes. Professors are trained and locked into disciplinary and subdisciplinary categories that they rarely leave; the institution, the university, is secondary. Their greater interest lies in the associations and the networking with colleagues in similar disciplines elsewhere. In a bureaucracy, a person blocked in a career may transfer to another part of government and assume a new identity. That privilege is seldom open to the academician, who is likely to carry permanently an identification with accomplishments or failures.

This individual character means that faculty members play a variety of roles, depending on interests, talents, and ambitions. A majority, fascinated by the searches for knowledge, are content to enjoy tenure, research, and students. Although their work may have implications for policy, influence on policy formulation is not a primary interest. Others desire influence beyond the campus and spend time in government, think tanks, national committees, and as experts on the op-ed pages of newspapers and TV talk shows. Disturbed by the direction of national policies, some become active in advocacy organizations.

The recruitment of prominent faculty members for high policy positions is a uniquely American phenomenon. Five of the national security advisers to presidents since John F. Kennedy were appointed from positions as university professors: McGeorge Bundy, Walt Rostow, Henry Kissinger, Zbigniew Brzezinski, and Anthony Lake. Three of the last four U.S. representatives to the United Nations, Donald McHenry, Jeane Kirkpatrick, and Madeleine Albright, have been from one university: Georgetown. Faculty members from numerous other institutions, and particularly the John F. Kennedy School of Government at Harvard, have been called to advise on foreign policy issues from arms control to economic development.

Those so recruited represent a class of academics who stay close to politicians and welcome an occasional immersion in governmental action. They tend to come largely from institutions such as the Kennedy School which have a primary emphasis on government. For some professors, the study of public policy is their primary interest and service in government helps their scholarship. In such cases, they bring the backgrounds and theories developed in their intellectual pursuits directly into the making of policy. Others are lured by the fascination and, perhaps, the prominence of official positions. Some move back and forth frequently between academia and government. Others, infected with "Potomac fever" or rejected by their former universities, do not return; for them the future lies in think tanks or another turn in government.

Most scholars in the social sciences, however, tend to remain critics rather than allies of official policy. They regard their colleagues who rotate in and out of government as a "breed apart," not truly members of the pure scholarly community.

Less bound by academic disciplines, such scholars publish in *Foreign Affairs* and *Foreign Policy* rather than the more theoretical *International Studies Quarterly* or *International Organization*. Scholars whose books are sold by major trade publishers and those who write for the more widely circulated journals are consciously trying to make an impact on opinion and policy. Their works frequently stimulate national debates on the nature of international issues and the position of the United States. The 1993 article by Harvard professor Samuel Huntington on "The Clash of Civilizations" generated more requests for reprints than any other article in the history of the journal, *Foreign Affairs*.[2] Yale professor Paul Kennedy's *Preparing for the Twenty-First Century*[3] has sparked wide discussion on the future role of the United States.

The seeds planted by teachers in the minds of each new generation are probably the most lasting contribution of the academic world. In the 1990s, professors are preparing another and less vociferous generation for an uncertain future. The questions raised and the attitudes expressed by these faculty members will have significant influences on how this next generation perceives the world.

Professors' views of past and contemporary policies, shaped by their own experience, have perhaps a more profound influence than is generally realized in creating, in the formative years of young peoples' lives, the perspectives through which those future citizens see world events. Faculty members of the World War II generation, especially those who were exiles from Europe, emphasized the significance of Neville Chamberlain's "appeasement" at Munich and of the Holocaust, creating the bases for drawing analogies to these events in future crises. Similarly, the Vietnam generation transferred to students the cynicism toward government and involvements abroad that grew out of the 1960s experience. The conventional wisdom about the failures of the Carter administration has been fed by international relations professors who found Jimmy Carter weak in the face of international challenges.

Different Worlds

The observations of this chapter are based on the author's twelve years in university positions—as an associate dean, director of an institute, and teacher. The overriding impression from this experience is that although the world of the professor and that of the policymaker meet in many ways, they are fundamentally very different. The differences have over the years been complicated by academic suspicion of government and opposition to policies, and not helped by the attitude of many in government that academia represents an irrelevant "ivory tower." During the late 1960s the State Department, to establish better relations with the academic community, began a series of scholar-diplomat programs. Young professors were brought in for a week of interaction with officials. What surprised many in the Department at that time was how many of these groups arrived deeply suspicious of the U.S. government and convinced that policy was dictated either by the CIA or big business. Such feelings have abated since then, but they are not entirely gone.

The frustration of scholars with policy and with the policy process is understandable, especially those who specialize in regional studies. They come to know countries well, speaking the languages and becoming acquainted with segments of society seldom seen by diplomats. Only with difficulty can officials be offered unsolicited outside advice, and scholars who seek to do so may not feel their observations are welcome.

Particularly during the period of the Cold War, scholars working abroad felt the full blast of those in other lands who resented U.S. support for authoritarian despots. Foreigners saw troubling inconsistencies between U.S. principles and U.S. actions. U.S. scholars, in their research, often focused on those in other lands opposed to U.S. policies. Academics could not understand why, when they expressed what they knew to be the genuine concerns of peoples abroad about the U.S. role, policies were not adapted to meet those concerns. They were generally unsympathetic toward official explanations of competing national goals or domestic politics that might dictate the U.S. approach.

Their writings painted a sharply different picture of circumstances and trends than did many official statements. They sought to influence the policy from outside by such writing and by testimony in Congress. In the long run, many of them were right. James Bill, a professor at William and Mary College, warned constantly in his articles and testimony about the risks of U.S. dependence on the shah of Iran.

Many leading African experts also were strongly critical of U.S. relations with South Africa and conservative regimes south of the Sahara. So tense were relations between the African specialists in the universities and the Department of State in the late 1960s that officials were not invited to speak at the annual meetings of the African Studies Association. Most scholars believed that long-range U.S. interests lay with support for liberation movements, such as the African National Congress and the South West African People's Organization, which came to power respectively in South Africa and Namibia.

Scholars found too often that bureaucracies are seldom open to information and assessments that cast doubt on current policies. Presidents and their principal associates have a vested interest in a policy; to reverse it can be politically embarrassing. The scholar or official who brings challenges to the policy and to conventional wisdom is unwelcome. In the Iran crisis of the late 1970s, warnings such as those of Professor James Bill were discounted because of senior officials' unwillingness to believe that the warnings might be correct. It is little wonder that professors sometimes despair of government.

It is not as if the officials turn a totally deaf ear to the views of the university communities. The Office of Research of the Bureau of Intelligence and Research in the Department of State has traditionally maintained links with the academic community on foreign policy issues. A brochure prepared by the Office in September 1994 noted that it had, in Fiscal Year 1994, funded and organized seventy-five seminars and conferences and published five studies which addressed Department priorities; in all, 300 participants from the university community had been reached. In addition, under the Soviet–Eastern European Research and Training Act of 1983, the State Department provided financial support for the creation of a cadre of experts on Eastern Europe and the independent states of the former Soviet Union.[4] Similar liaison branches exist in the Department of Defense and the CIA. Regional scholars are frequently invited in for discussions of crises. In one case, scholars on Iran dramatically illustrated an approach to the U.S. dilemma.

During the hostage crisis of 1979, a group of Iranian experts from various universities were invited to the Department of State. One issue was a question of how the United States could establish a negotiating dialogue with Tehran. Suddenly, during the meeting, two of the professors began to shout insults at one another. Finally one got up and left the room. A third rose and said to the somewhat shocked assembly that he would talk to the one who had walked out. Soon they both returned and explained to the startled bureaucrats that they had just demonstrated how one had to negotiate in Iran. A third party was needed who would bring the aggrieved parties together. Ultimately, when Algeria played that role in the resolution of the hostage crisis, the dramatic advice of the professors proved to be accurate. Another scholar, Richard Cottam, then a professor at the University of Pittsburgh with wide contacts in Iran, was able to provide assessments of the Iranian situation that filled in gaps in official knowledge at a time when Washington had no diplomatic relations with Tehran.

It is not surprising that academics and officials in their public presentations often present contradictory images of events and issues. For officials, the objective of action is to resolve or manage a problem. Their motives are operational, not intellectual. Often under intense pressures, they are endeavoring to reconcile domestic and foreign politics, resources, and realities abroad into a workable policy. They must make choices. They are vulnerable to the aftermath of failures. A *New Yorker* writer, Robert Shaplen, spent several weeks in the Department of State in 1979 writing a profile on the office of the Undersecretary of State for Political Affairs, which I then held.[5] He commented to me at one point, "I have been watching you. You make decisions every ten minutes on issues each one of which could merit a doctoral thesis." The scholar, less pressed by time, is basically an observer, endeavoring to discover in an event or a series of events verities that may apply to other situations.

The respective emphases on the experience of a practitioner versus the research of a scholar create a dividing line between the two and affect the perspectives each presents to a wider public. In analyzing international issues, both are subject to the same kind of limitations that impede informational efforts of government and the press. Conclusions often depend on access to and availability of sources. Although officials and diplomats today are able, in most countries, to go beyond the traditional foreign ministry sources, they still face practical and political limits in their approaches to populations. Traditionally, the relations of diplomats are with governments, not peoples. Scholars can move more widely, but may have difficulty reaching officials. Each to some extent sees only part of a picture. If officials, in their assessments, may be overly bound by the restrictions of politics, the scholar may depend excessively on intellectual counterparts in other lands who are instinctively negative toward policies of their government.

In research, scholars depend heavily on documents and, to a lesser extent, interviews. But documents as sources, too, have their weaknesses. To the official, documents can be misleading. To understand an action fully, one must know why the document was written. Memoranda for the president that appear to be suggesting options may be written for the record after a decision has already been made. Items that do not fully reflect internal debates may be prepared to establish a "paper trail" as protection against congressional inquiries. Memoranda of conversations may represent an effort by the writer or the principal speaker to put the best face possible on a difficult negotiation. Interviews may be equally misleading. Human nature dictates that those interviewed wish their role in history to be seen in a positive light. The interviewees may also be reluctant to contribute to a scholarly work critical of another colleague in government.

The scholar's task of recreating history is not an easy one. It is made even more difficult when, because of fears of leaks, officials more and more resort to conversations, directly or by telephone, without written records.

Because of this dependence on documents and interviews, much scholarly work is retrospective, looking back and seeking to draw lessons from what has happened. To look ahead and predict what may come is as daunting a challenge to the scholar as it is to the practitioner. As recent history has demonstrated, predictions of the collapse of the Soviet Union or of a handshake between Israeli Prime Minister Yitzhak Rabin and the chairman of the Palestine Liberation Organization (PLO) at the White House would have been dismissed as fantasy and damaged the credibility of the scholar. Yet even in regions such as the Gulf, where further Iraqi aggression was possible, a survey of literature on the period leading up to the 1991 Gulf War reveals little that predicted an Iraqi invasion of Kuwait. After the Gulf War, at least thirteen articles appeared in scholarly journals, both U.S. and foreign, analyzing the war and the steps leading up to it. These included attacks on U.S. policy toward Iraq, historical analogies, and speculation on a "new world order." Several sought to look to the future with valid but unrealizable recommendations—at least at that time—such as a Middle East arms control regime or a U.S. opening to Iran. Although there was general acknowledgment that the Gulf War had changed the political landscape in the region, none predicted with any accuracy how events would unfold on the Middle East peace process.

Not all scholars agree that predictions should be an expected goal of scholarship or that recommendations that appear unrealistic at the time are inappropriate. A more proper goal is the identification of underlying social forces, mismatches between regimes and peoples, and policies that may be doomed to fail. Each of these, to some extent, aids in looking at the future without precisely defining that future. Often recommendations that seem unrealistic at the moment may turn out, some years later, to be the basis for accomplishments. A number of scholars strongly recommended a dialogue between Israel and the PLO long before that took place.

Much research presumes or looks for failures and errors. This observation may not apply to all, but the practitioner is conscious of an emphasis in some academic work that seeks blame rather than an understanding of the forces and dilemmas behind an event or decision. I wrote a small volume on a bizarre episode in 1979 in which a Soviet brigade that had long been in Cuba was "discovered" by an intelligence satellite and believed to represent a new Soviet challenge.[6] When I spoke about it before some university audiences, the question posed by scholars almost invariably was, "Who was responsible for this policy embarrassment?" In one session at the London School of Economics, knowing of the academician's delight in theories, I replied, "The Shakespeare model applied. Every actor performed as position and inclination dictated and the result was tragedy."

Analogies to the past can be interesting but overstated and of little value in a full understanding of an event. One article on the Gulf saw similarities between George Bush and Winston Churchill in the former's handling of the Iraqi invasion.[7] At the same time, examinations of the past can lead to significant insights into the processes of government and diplomacy. On a positive note, they remind readers of aspects neglected in the euphoria of a crisis. One scholar, writing after the Gulf War in *International Affairs*, emphasized the gap between President Bush, the

Congress, and the public and cautioned about assumptions of further U.S. military action.[8]

Graham Allison of the Kennedy School of Government at Harvard University studied the Cuban missile crisis of 1962 and developed a series of theories about crisis management: rational actor, bureaucratic model, and organizational politics.[9] To the official, no one of these approaches is fully applicable to the management of a crisis. Aspects of each, however, can be found in nearly every crisis decision; they are thus valuable to a broader understanding of the process. Another scholar, I. M. Destler of the University of Maryland, studied the U.S. bureaucracy related to foreign policy and wrote an insightful book, *Presidents, Bureaucrats, and Foreign Policy.*[10] But accurate accounts of the policy process are rare. This was recognized in the 1988-89 annual report of the Social Science Research Council:

> Discontent with current analyses flowed from the dominance of research approaches to foreign policy that failed to capture the increasing complexity of the foreign policy process. One dominant approach emphasized the international sources and consequences of foreign policy; it tended to characterize the process of policy making as "black box," unknowable or unnecessary to know. A second approach built on classic decision-making analysis and focused on the interaction of a relatively small group of government officials—heads of state, cabinet ministers, and trusted advisors—to explain how a variety of organizational and cognitive factors influenced foreign policy outcomes. Broader political, economic, social and demographic influences on foreign policy making were excluded. Finally, a large share of foreign policy analysis was normative or prescriptive in character, analyzing an emerging agenda of issues and recommending policies that the United States (or some other government or institution) should adopt.[11]

Hans Morgenthau, the dominant theorist of international power politics, understood the limitations of scholarship applied to international relations:

> The first lesson the student of international politics must learn and never forget is that the complexities of international affairs make simple solutions and trustworthy prophecies impossible. Here the scholar and the charlatan part company. . . . The best the scholar can

do . . . is to trace the different tendencies that, as potentialities, are inherent in a certain international situation. He can point out the different conditions that make it more likely for one tendency to prevail than for another and, finally, assess the probabilities for the different conditions and tendencies to prevail in actuality.[12]

What seems most often to be missing in much scholarship relating to foreign policy is the relationship of primarily domestic agencies and politics to a foreign policy issue. Conventional academic wisdom seems generally to explain foreign policy making as largely confined to the National Security Council staff, the Department of State, and the Department of Defense. Other significant players, such as the Treasury Department and the Department of Agriculture, are rarely mentioned. In one commonly used textbook, *American Foreign Policy: Pattern and Process,* several references to the Treasury Department appear, but the description of its role and significance covers only two pages out of 560.[13]

Even an understanding of the non-official actors discussed elsewhere in this book seems lacking. The practitioner understands that, as a necessary part of stimulating the intellect of the students, the professor will advance theories and be critical of policies. What is surprising to a former official in an academic setting, however, is the degree to which oversimplified views of the process of decision making are conveyed. Once in a discussion of the influence of lobbying on foreign policy, a senior professor made the statement that lobbying does not have a great influence on foreign policy making because, in the last analysis, policy is what the State Department says it is. The professor seemed not to appreciate that what the State Department says publicly can be influenced by a variety of external factors, including the pressures of powerful lobbies.

Rigid Disciplines

Perhaps the core of the difference in perspective between the practitioner and the academic lies in the attachment to a discipline in the scholarly world. A government or political science department will focus on domestic affairs; international relations looks narrowly at the foreign policy process and abroad; the two seldom meet. In addition, the study of foreign affairs has confining subdisciplines: international relations (IR), regional studies (RS), comparative government (CG), and political theory (PT). *Items*, the publication of the Social Science Research Council, in its June–September 1993 issue had this to say after encouraging the formation of interdisciplinary research teams on Africa:

> Despite choosing themes that emerged from extended conversations with all relevant disciplines, in the main we found that the standard research agenda within institutions and of most scholars is rarely as flexible as this sort of collaboration requires.[14]

Another article in the same publication on preparing the colleges and universities for the twenty-first century had as its first recommendation: "We must reexamine the sufficiency of discipline-based training and the concept of disciplines as the basic building blocks of knowledge."[15]

To a practitioner who has spent years dealing with the role of Congress in the making of foreign policy, it is surprising to learn that only as late as 1989 did the Social Science Research Council believe that more attention should be paid to the role of Congress:

> The meeting explored what most participants believe to be the unique impact of the U.S. Congress on the content and process of policy making. This influence seems to have grown over the years with the increases in the number of Congressional staffs that focus on foreign policy, with the decline of the president's automatic majority on foreign affairs, and with political changes that have diminished the control of parties over their members. While there was a surge of research interest in this topic in the late 1960s and early 1970s when it became clear that Congressional influence vis-a-vis the "imperial presidency" was expanding in the wake of Vietnam and Watergate, there is clearly a need to view more recent developments in historical perspective and to compare the recent role of Congress in such issues as funding for the Contras to the role it has played in the last twenty years and before.[16]

The different perspectives of the practitioner and the scholar and their application to teaching are illustrated in an account of the Pew Initiative in Diplomatic Studies. In 1982, the board of the Pew Charitable Trusts became concerned at what it considered failures in U.S. diplomacy, particularly in U.S. negotiations with the Soviet Union. Two million dollars were set aside to improve the performance of U.S. diplomacy. A committee of retired diplomats and deans of schools of international affairs was convened to make recommendations to the foundation on how the money should be spent. The committee proposed that the resources be used to develop a series of case studies in the practice of diplomacy for classroom use.[17]

In the minds of the diplomats on the committee, much of the academic material relating to international relations and diplomacy failed to introduce the student adequately to the problems of decision making and representation abroad. Foreign policies tended to be critiqued as if the one chosen represented the only option open to the decision maker. From painful experience, the practitioner knows that policies result more often than not from selecting one course of action from among unappealing alternatives. Members of the committee felt that not enough attention was paid to the aspect of choice.

The diplomats on the committee also felt that in texts for students more attention should be given to the day-to-day issues in the conduct of relations with other countries. These include such matters as representing the interests of U.S. citizens, enlisting votes in the United Nations from the host nation, dealing with the opposition in an authoritarian country, reporting, and maintaining security in a hostile environment. Because available diplomatic documents focus on major negotiations, such negotiations also become the focus of the scholars writing on diplomacy. More mundane, but important, actions are neglected.

To meet the needs as it saw them, the committee recommended the development of a body of case studies, prepared by both scholars and diplomats. Such studies would ideally narrate events without indicating decisions or conclusions, leaving these for the student to determine.[18] The foundation accepted the committee's recommendation and added another element. Seeking a model for case-study preparation and a pattern that would guarantee its use in the classroom, the project directors turned to the Harvard Business School and Harvard's Kennedy School of Government. Case studies on matters of law and domestic policies had been used as the basis for instruction in both institutions for many years. The essence of these case-study teaching methods, in contrast to lectures, was to have the professors lead the students through discussion to a conclusion.

The implementation of the Pew project immediately encountered two obstacles in the academic community. Quite understandably, those faculty members invited to write cases wished to do so on the basis of their current research. Beyond that, however, they wanted to be certain that whatever they wrote was academically credible—that it would count for promotion or tenure: prepared articles should have clear conclusions and attachment to an accepted or original model or theory. Narratives without conclusions did not fit this pattern. Some professors resisted the concept of leaving the conclusions to the students.

These obstacles were, to a considerable extent, overcome. Special training seminars were established for case writing and for case teaching. More than 250 cases were prepared. They are widely used either as a basis for case-study teaching or as resource material.[19]

The Pew case-study project also illustrates the emphasis placed by scholars of international affairs on an understanding of negotiations as central to diplomacy. By far the bulk of the Pew cases deal with negotiations; most of the others relate to the development of policies at the national level. Few relate to the day-to-day practice of diplomacy in embassies abroad. The focus on diplomacy as negotiation in the Pew project is part of a larger national development of conflict resolution and peace studies. Behind this focus is the belief that a greater understanding of the process of negotiation can lead to greater success in the resolution of serious international conflicts. One of the principal proponents of theories of negotiation is Professor Roger Fisher, director of the Harvard Negotiation Project and author, with William L. Urey, of the book *Getting to Yes*.[20] To many practitioners, this approach is mechanistic. It places too little emphasis on the political and cultural factors or the uniqueness of any given international problem. It seeks to extrapolate from experiences in negotiating domestic issues, such as labor disputes, within the framework of a recognized system of law and practice to the international arena where no such framework exists. Fisher, in September 1990, after the Iraqi invasion of Kuwait, proposed "bargaining" with Saddam Hussein, starting with the condition that he "doesn't get anything he couldn't have gotten by peaceful means."[21] Although that approach may have had theoretical merit, it was unrealistic in light of the national attitudes toward the Gulf crisis at that time.

Fisher and others have sought to volunteer advice to officials during foreign policy crises. In general, however, busy officials, with a broader information base and pressures of time, politics, and diplomacy, have not been receptive. There have been exceptions in which those with an academic affiliation have played significant roles in the resolution of problems. Warring parties have been brought together in academic settings in which the review of the issues has been helpful in later peace efforts. One such case was that of Professor Yair Hirschfeld of Haifa

University in initiating the talks in 1993 between Israel and the PLO in Norway, which ultimately led to the inauguration of Palestinian autonomy in the Gaza Strip and Jericho.[22]

A very special case is that of former president Jimmy Carter whose Carter Center in Atlanta is affiliated with Emory University. Carter's interventions in North Korea, Haiti, and Bosnia in 1994 at the very least, postponed crises and brought parties in dispute together. His personal prestige undoubtedly played a role in his ability to intervene, but so did his application of a theory of conflict resolution popular among academic experts. That approach posits that what is important is to get sides in conflict in direct communication and to minimize confrontation by addressing, not each other, but the problem. No individual is a declared villain; ambiguity is essential for agreements.

Carter's methods illustrated both the possibilities and the difficulties of this theory. To gain the confidence of parties to a conflict, including those considered unredeemable villains by official and public opinion in the United States, he made positive statements about them. After meeting Kim Il Sung of North Korea, he described him as "vigorous, intelligent, surprisingly well informed about the technical issues and in charge of the decisions about his country."[23] In Haiti, he described the military leader Raoul Cedras as a man of honor.[24] In the case of Bosnia, he accepted the statement of the Serb leader, Radovan Karadzic, that the Serb side had not been understood in America.[25]

In addition, Carter felt the need, if he was to achieve his objective of preventing conflict in the case of Korea and Haiti or ending fighting in the case of Bosnia, to reopen positions that had been reached in official negotiations. He denounced sanctions against North Korea and opposed a forceful invasion of Haiti. In Bosnia, he inserted flexibility into a peace plan already accepted by one side. In each case, he left ambiguities to be resolved by further negotiations. The North Korean commitment to freeze its nuclear program was vague. In Haiti, it was not clear that the military leaders would need to leave the country. In Bosnia, the commitments to the existing peace plan of the two sides were separated by a serious semantic divide.

To those who had been working officially and in the context of political realities in Washington, Carter's actions were unwelcome. Only an independent negotiator with the standing of a former president could have made such statements without being totally discredited at home.

Yet, at the end of 1994, despite unexpected bumps along the way, each of the three issues was moving forward toward solutions. Whether any outside mediator could have acted as effectively in accordance with conflict resolution theory is questionable. Carter nevertheless demonstrated that, under certain circumstances, the approach favored by many academics will work.

To the practitioner, the most useful academic contributions to an understanding of negotiation are those based on effective interviews with participants in actual diplomatic negotiations that examine not only the techniques used but also the broader political and bureaucratic settings in which negotiations were conducted.[26] Many diplomats will state that negotiations with their own governments are often more difficult than with a foreign power.

In many cases, also, it is not the absence of negotiating techniques that dooms efforts at crisis resolution; it is the fact that parties will not come to the table to negotiate.

These differences over substance and approach inhibit to some extent full communication and reciprocal influence between the policy maker and the professor. The greatest barriers to any broad influence of the academic analyses of international affairs, however, today are the language and the patterns in which results are presented. There is no dearth of academic writing; publishing remains the key to tenure and promotion. One publication lists 88 political science journals; 20 deal exclusively with international affairs.[27] A favorable review of a book by the library magazine *Choice* and adoption as a classroom text can augment a professor's pay and reputation. Numerous presses, including university presses, exist to publish the works of scholars. Conferences generate academic papers that become chapters in multi-authored volumes. One recent catalogue of M. E. Sharpe, *Political Science and Social Policy,* listed 35 books on China alone.[28]

Much of what is written and published is clear and understandable to a wide audience. As previously noted, some works have made a significant contribution to an understanding of international events. Other works, however, disappear behind a curtain of jargon and scientific quantification of analysis that cannot but limit the readership and influence of much academic research.

Jargon is not exclusive to academia. In any profession, including government, the knowledge and use of specialized language signifies membership in a group. At the same time, such language erects an inhibiting barrier to those outside the group. David Ricci notes this problem in *The Transformation of American Politics*:

> In modern America, academic researchers amass many kinds of data relevant to policy issues, along with new theories about how such information bears on social [and presumably international] policies. Unfortunately, the technical jargon that scholars tend to use, and the fact that they often publish their findings in out-of-the-way journals, make many of their discoveries inaccessible to most policymakers.[29]

To the observer, much of the process of modern scholarship seems incestuous. Academicians often seem caught up in an exclusive culture in which labels, categories, and even humor have meaning only for "members." Their writings are filled with references to the writings of other scholars; they are talking to each other rather than to a wider public. All would be justified—and may be—as a means to the wider search for insights and truths. It is hard to escape the conclusion, however, that much of what is produced is for the purpose of gaining the kind of academic identification with a theory or equation that will lead to professional advancement. Little evidence exists in much scholarly writing of a direct effort to influence public policy.

Increasingly, scholars appear to be pressured by the academic culture to develop theories and paradigms within already established broad models identified with individual scholars or institutions. A professor visiting the University of Virginia from another institution once described to the faculty how certain universities would only hire new scholars who had studied under a recognized proponent of the *rational choice* theory.[30]

Game theory and the computer have added complexity to the research. In some cases, the scholarship explores and quantifies what has long been obvious to professionals in the field. The results, however, are sometimes stated in terms difficult for the non-academic reader to translate. The following is the summary of a paper designed to demonstrate the close correlation between foreign and domestic policies, a stark truism for the practitioner:

> Recent research on two-level game models emphasizes the close interaction between the domestic and foreign policies of states, but these states are usually interpreted as unitary rational actors and these

two policy arenas are usually kept separate. We develop integrated models of multi-level policy games in which the locus of strategic action remains at the individual (or group) level. Social choice theory identifies fundamental dilemmas associated with assuming that states have consistent preferences, yet empirical observation reveals that domestic political competition results in regularized patterns of behavior at the state and international levels. In our models the expectations of individual Bayesian policy actors converge to a "correlated equilibrium" that defines a probability distribution over domestic and foreign policy outcomes. We compare examples of correlated equilibria in a Chicken game between two unitary rational states, a voting game among three domestic groups, and a two-level game in which each state's foreign policy is determined by this voting game. By focusing on the collective consequences of the strategic interactions of Bayesian decision theories, this synthesis of game, social choice, and Bayesian decision theories highlights fundamental linkages among the regularities observed in domestic politics, foreign policy, and international relations.[31]

The patterns of modern scholarship on foreign affairs stem in large measure from efforts to create a science of international relations, searching for a "magic key" that will unlock the mysteries of how nations and their leaders behave and make decisions. Professor Stanley Hoffmann of Harvard has written,

> in political science . . . the fascination with economics has led scholars to pursue the chimera of the master key. They have believed that the study of a purposive activity aimed at a bewildering variety of ends, political action, could be treated like the study of instrumental action, economic behavior. They have tried in vain to make the concept of power play the same role as money in economics.[32]

Although, to the practitioner, it is difficult to see patterns in crises sufficiently common to lend themselves to the creation of scientific equations, this search for an understanding of international affairs is valid. The clear hope is that an understanding of one pattern will lead to theories that can not only be applied to understand others but can also predict changes in the global scene. Even recognized scholars, however, do not see this as a realizable objective. John Lewis Gaddis, writing about why scholars failed to predict the end of the Cold War, stated:

the "scientific" approach to the study of international relations appears to work no better, in forecasting the future, than do the old-fashioned methods it set out long ago to replace. Novelists and historians make forecasts all the time, but they do so more by analogy than by scientific theory. . . . For all of its insights into the nature of authoritarianism, George Orwell's 1948 vision of 1984 could hardly have been less accurate; and the historiographical landscape is now littered with the failed predictions of historians, my own included, who thought the Soviet Union would never peacefully tolerate its own collapse.[33]

The purpose of this chapter is not to question the validity of the pursuit of knowledge through the variety of means found on university campuses, but to explain why much of today's scholarship is either irrelevant or inaccessible to policy makers. Some of the more theoretical communications are filtered through think tanks or the research staffs of government departments or the Congress. But much remains locked within the circle of esoteric scholarly expression.

The growing withdrawal of university scholars behind curtains of theory and models would not have wider significance if it did not raise questions regarding the preparation of new generations and the future influence of the academic community on public and official perceptions of international issues and events.

Today the doctoral degree has become more and more important, not only for academic advancement, but for employment in many public policy positions as well. The scholar will point out that the preparation for a doctor's degree is not for professional purposes but to demonstrate the individual's capacity for intellectual initiatives and original research. The objective search for truth and patterns in society, including international relations, is essential in a democratic society, even if, at times, it may not meld easily with foreign policy. The person preparing for a teaching career may have a quite proper interest in a subject removed from the current scene. Nevertheless, both because of the emphasis on theories and models and the everlasting search for original dissertation topics, much of the research for the Ph.D. in international relations seems removed from application to contemporary issues.

The practitioner working in the graduate program of a university is struck by the narrow focus of much of the Ph.D. process. Dissertations that deal with very recent events are not encouraged because the necessary documentation is not available. Three to five years of a scholar's preparation for an academic career in the disciplines of government or international relations can be spent in the pursuit of answers to questions that seem irrelevant to a contemporary diplomatic agenda. One recent study presented in the context of international relations at the University of Virginia on the difference in colonial practices between "the British in India and the British in Brazil" was of obvious interest to the scholarly audience. The applicant, however, despite his extensive scholarship, lacked a full understanding of contemporary international issues.

The intellectual challenge presented by the study for a doctorate may be essential in the development of true scholars. The process, however, helps explain some of the gap in approaches to issues between the official and the academic and the limitations in the direct influence of university scholarship on foreign policy.

The world of the academic and that of the policy maker represent two significant elements of American society. The former contributes substantially in many ways to the work of the latter. Expectations, however, that harmony should exist between the two neglect the reality that the two are very different domains.

8 Think Tanks

I f talk and print could resolve problems, few would escape resolution in Washington. The nation's capital is a city of continuing conversations, many of them outside the formal settings of the executive and legislative branches of government.

On any given day, men and women can be found at breakfasts, conferences, study groups, luncheons, seminars, lectures, teas, receptions, and dinners engaged in serious discussions of foreign (as well as domestic) policy. In such meetings those both inside and outside the policy-making machinery mingle and create the networks that underlie pressures and actions at the center of the national government. The gatherings may take place in modern buildings on K Street, in old townhouses in Georgetown, or in one of the conference complexes outside of Washington, the Wye plantation in Maryland or Airlie House in Virginia. Such meetings will include officials, former officials, consultants, members of Congress and their staffs, scholars, business people, journalists, lobbyists, and proclaimed experts of various kinds. And the public beyond "the Beltway" looks in on these conversations through the op-ed pages of newspapers and talk shows on radio and TV.

Jay Collins, who headed a working group on Japan at the Center for Strategic and International Studies, explained how the process worked through his description of a meeting of congressional staff, executive branch officials, and businessmen:

We had the Defense experts listening to the trade types. We had former Governor Lamar Alexander come up and talk to the group about his efforts to promote Japanese investment in Tennessee, a very different perspective from what members of Congress normally hear. We did things like have Ed Artzt, the chairman of Procter and Gamble, come in and explain how companies like P&G managed to succeed in penetrating the Japanese market. We would have officials go up and brief the group on strategy, without Japanese embassy officials, without reporters, without trade associations, and without any lobbyists, all off the record in a way that facilitated policymaking between the two branches.[1]

At the heart of this process is an array of organizations under a variety of names—centers, institutes, councils—made possible by the funding phenomenon described in chapter 6. Under the general appellation of "think tanks," they provide the administrative structure for numerous events and the source of the hundreds of reports, monographs, newsletters, and books that daily fill the incoming mail of the Washington community and beyond. From them come the myriad experts who frame national perceptions by means of their comments in print, radio, and television.

Some of the conversations take place in restricted membership environments such as the Metropolitan Club, Cosmos Club, International Club, and University Club. The Council on Foreign Relations, with headquarters in New York, shares an office in Washington with the Carnegie Endowment for International Peace and hosts membership meetings in the nation's capital and other cities with speakers from the U.S. government, the private sector, and abroad. The ground rules of Council meetings prohibit attribution of specific remarks to speakers, but the general thrust, especially of anything startling, quickly becomes known. Members, including journalists, can be seen feverishly taking notes in what are off-the-record sessions.

Some have the broader public as the audience. The Foreign Policy Association in New York is an example. Its "Great Decisions" program annually provides essays and guidelines on international issues to affiliates throughout the country. In Washington, its affiliate, the World Affairs Council, is perhaps the largest open public forum in the city. One of its most popular annual programs brings together the information media and the public through a presentation by the foreign correspondents of the *Washington Post*.

The interactive conversation in the capital is most assiduously promoted, however, by think tanks. James Allen Smith, in *The Idea Brokers,* lists thirty "Leading Think Tanks." Of these, twenty-two are in Washington, and, of these, seventeen deal wholly or partially with international issues, including defense, foreign policy, economics, and the environment.[2] The oldest of the Washington institutes is the Carnegie Endowment, dating from 1910. The Brookings Institution was founded in its current form in 1927, but all others date from World War II and the postwar decades. This chapter will concentrate on eight of the postwar institutions: American Enterprise Institute (AEI), Center for Strategic and International Studies (CSIS), Institute for Policy Studies (IPS), Heritage Foundation, Cato Institute, Joint Center for Political and Economic Studies, Center for National Policy (CNP), and the congressionally funded U.S. Institute of Peace (USIP).

Although these institutions, together with Carnegie and Brookings, are the most prominent, this list touches only the surface of the organizations in Washington that contribute to the policy dialogue. The list of such institutions changes constantly. While some are long-standing and virtually permanent, others rise and fall with the political fortunes of individuals or parties; money and important people flow to the successful and the influential institutions. Few organizations in Washington can resist the temptation to hold meetings and conferences and publish monographs on current issues, reflecting either the interests of the director or the wishes of donors. Meridian House, in an old mansion on Sixteenth Street, in cooperation with the Smithsonian Institution, has added to its traditional student exchange and diplomatic-briefing functions regular conferences on foreign affairs. Regional issues preoccupy groups such as the Institute for Near East Policy, the Asia Society, and the Council on Hemispheric Affairs. The National Endowment for Democracy, founded to promote democracy overseas, also promotes discussions in Washington. At least two, the Institute of International Economics and the Overseas Development Council, concentrate on economics.

Why Think Tanks?

Public policy institutes have grown significantly in the last half of the twentieth century. This development can be attributed to several factors, most related to the expansion of U.S. responsibilities around the world after World War II. Demands for more information on unfamiliar areas and subjects and the need for a greater dialogue between the private sector and government are among the reasons for the increased numbers. Think tanks became important because they met these needs.

The end of World War II confronted officials, legislators, journalists, and scholars with an imposing set of new issues. The confrontation with the Soviet Union and the organization of the United Nations raised new questions of world order and conflict management. The nuclear age and efforts at arms control brought technology and strategy issues. With decolonization, the Vietnams, Zaires, Kashmirs, and Palestines of the world, which had been behind colonial curtains, suddenly became strategically important; policymakers and those who followed policy needed to know more about them. The conflicts of the postwar world created new dimensions of terrorism and threat; American citizens became involved as never before.

The foreign policy areas of government have not been able to cope with the new demands. Politics and policy decisions have limited the degree to which conventional wisdom could be challenged within official circles. The need for confidentiality limited formal discussions with nongovernmental sources. Long-range planning has always been an objective of presidents and secretaries of state and defense. Policy planning staffs and contingency groups have been established for this purpose. Such hopes have been dashed in every recent administration. Personnel originally assigned to "think" have been diverted to deal with crises or to write speeches. Leaks of contingency papers have created premature and often unnecessary problems for officials, thus discouraging further forward looking.

Congress became more involved in foreign policy. The congressional reforms of the early 1970s diminished the power of the old committee chairs, and far more legislators than ever before became potentially influential—and ambitious. They wanted information to support their new role. They increased staffs. The Congressional Research Service responded to short-term and special needs, but was less able to meet long-range and unusual requests. Staffs found welcome sources in the new think tanks. The think tanks, in turn, found the openings to Congress ideal for entry into the policy process.

Although a large number of the fellows and researchers came from the universities of the nation, the academic community, even with its abundant resources, was not able to meet the new demand. Much of academic research lacked the brevity, timeliness, and clarity necessary for policy institutes. The think tanks became "research brokers," putting academic research into readable forms for policymakers.[3]

Business organizations suddenly found the need to follow foreign policy to determine opportunities abroad, assess risks, and influence decisions. Many in the private sector find direct approaches to executive branch officials difficult. They will be open to an individual business representative to discuss a specific problem affecting that business. They will be more reluctant to meet with such a representative to discuss policy issues. Questions of conflict of interest, of favoritism, and of how their actions will appear to the public are always in the official's mind. Even the journalist or scholar seeking long-range information on policy may have a difficult time gaining access unless the official sees the interview as fitting some immediate official purpose. Think tanks have provided opportunities for officials and those prominent in public life to meet without the inhibitions of formal visits. These networks enable contacts to take place outside of the formality and spotlight of government offices. As pressure mounts against the entertainment of officials by non-officials and the business lunch or dinner becomes less frequent, sessions over coffee and danish that precede conferences, lectures, and briefings become even more important as occasions for exchanges with policymakers.

The Institutions

Perhaps more than anything else, however, the rapid growth of the think tanks was a manifestation of an intensified ideological division in national politics. Conservatives in particular felt their views on national and international issues needed to be heard. At the beginning of World War II, the Brookings Institution was the most significant policy institute in Washington. Although it drew experts from both political parties, it had fed ideas into Democratic administrations and was considered by conservatives to be left of center. It remains, in 1994, the least ideological of the major policy institutes. It defines its mission, in the post–Cold War world, to formulate "thought-provoking questions to focus global debate" on new security strategy.[4]

The American Enterprise Association was founded in 1943 primarily to provide a business point of view in the nation's capital. The Association became the American Enterprise Institute for Public Policy Research in 1960 "to counter the influence of the liberal intellectual establishment"[5]—to which, in the view of the founders, Brookings belonged.

In 1962, the Center for Strategic and International Studies was founded specifically to deal with a new set of issues, those of national strategy. The founders, Admiral Arleigh Burke, retired chief of Naval Operations, and David Abshire, a West Point graduate with experience as a congressional staffer and scholar at AEI, saw their model in the Institute of Strategic Studies in London. Reacting to the problems exhibited in the Bay of Pigs, the Cuban missile crisis of 1962, and the "systems analysis" approach of Secretary of Defense Robert McNamara, they envisioned an institution, somewhat right of center, that would feed ideas relating to the nation's reaction to the Soviet threat into the policy-making machinery. In the initial phases of CSIS, many of its personnel were drawn from the military academies.[6]

The ideological spectrum was further widened with the organization of the Institute for Policy Studies, founded by Marcus Raskin and Richard Barnet in 1963. Both had left the Kennedy administration, critical of American foreign policy and the social science research institutions that sustained those policies.[7] In its thirtieth anniversary report, published in 1993, IPS states that its objective is to provide "progressive politicians, policymakers, and activists with practical recommendations for reform."

The first African American think tank began in 1970 as the Joint Center for Political Studies; economic studies was added to the title in 1990. It describes itself in its 1993 report as "one of the nation's handful of preeminent research institutions that bring unique insight into public policy issues from an African American perspective."[8]

The 1970s also saw the rise of determined conservative groups that believed older institutions, even AEI, lacked the purity, tactics, and focus needed to promote conservative ideas. At the same time, AEI, with the death of its founder, William Baroody, suffered both administrative and funding problems and its influence declined. To fill that niche, the Heritage Foundation was established in 1973 to "formulate and promote conservative public policies based on the principles of free enterprise, limited government, individual freedom, traditional American values, and a strong national defense."[9] By 1981 it had become the most aggressive of the think tanks. Unlike other institutes, it made no pretense of seeking answers through research; its activities were directed at promoting preordained ideas, what Ricci calls "principled consistency."[10]

The founding of Heritage was followed in 1976 by the establishment of the Cato Institute, a Libertarian institution whose 1993 annual report emphasized Cato's promotion of "civil society through public policies consistent with a market-liberal worldview." The political spectrum was rounded out with the establishment in 1982 of the Center for National Policy, representing a moderate Democratic point of view and with former secretary of state Edmund S. Muskie as chairman of the board.

The Policies

The orientation of these institutions was further reflected in their statements of policy and in the individuals they attracted as fellows and researchers.

The Heritage Foundation's 1,093-page *Mandate for Leadership* (1980) became a guidebook on many issues, both domestic and foreign, for the Reagan administration. Heritage published, among other "Blueprints," *A Safe and Prosperous America: A U.S. Foreign and Defense Policy,* calling for a strong nation militarily, supporting NATO and traditional defense arrangements, and wary of involvement where clear interests are not at stake.

> The central thesis of this report is that U.S. foreign and defense policy should be designed to promote and defend the freedom, security, and prosperity of the American nation. . . . Some Americans believe that the U.S. needs some loftier moral goal, such as promoting democracy or human rights abroad. Others argue that American democracy is not safe unless democracy everywhere is secure. . . . Both of these viewpoints, however well-intentioned, miss a fundamental point: The first and most important obligation of the U.S. government to its citizens is to promote and defend the lives, liberties, and prosperity of the American people.[11]

Other Heritage studies concentrated on trade ("Encouraging Yankee Traders"), the North American Free Trade Agreement (NAFTA), and free market principles in the former Soviet Union.

In addition to its traditional focus on international economic issues, AEI is also prominently oriented toward defense and arms control issues. Its studies embrace, as well, developments in Eastern Europe and Russia. Like Heritage, it is critical of Clinton administration foreign policy, as this quote from Jeane Kirkpatrick in the annual report demonstrates:

America is no longer the military power it was at the end of the cold war, and still deeper defense cuts are inevitable. Meanwhile, the United States has floundered from problem to problem abroad, failing to devise a strategy remotely equal to the complexities of the post–cold war world. What we need, in effect, are new rules of engagement that suggest where we must be involved and where we can safely afford to stand aside.[12]

The Cato Institute promotes a foreign policy of minimal involvement:

The foreign policy program published a Policy Analysis by former British diplomat and Cato adjunct scholar Jonathan G. Clarke calling for a "rebirth of American foreign policy" that could keep the United States out of foreign quarrels and save $150 billion a year. A Foreign Policy Briefing by [Ted Galen] Carpenter called for an armistice in the international drug war. . . . Another Carpenter paper said that intervention in Somalia sets a bad precedent for the United States. Foreign Policy analyst Barbara Conry contributed a paper documenting the harm done by the National Endowment for Democracy.

Other studies published in 1993 proposed the downsizing of the navy in the post–Cold War era, argued against a military response to North Korea's nuclear program, urged asylum for Yugoslav refugees, opposed the use of the CIA for economic espionage, and endorsed the Eurocorps as a way of reducing U.S. military commitments to Europe.[13]

The CSIS annual report, unlike those mentioned above, does not espouse a particular point of view on foreign policy. With its eighty to one hundred research projects in both regional and functional areas, it is the most eclectic of the institutions. Among the "eight main issue areas of the Center's research agenda" as of 1993, however, were clues to the emphasis and the philosophy:

Strengthening the Americas, through our new commission on "NAFTA and Beyond," which . . . gives special attention to the enlargement of the free trade zone in the Americas;
Bringing business experience to the problems of emerging markets and job creation, through projects such as our U.S.-Poland Action Commission, U.S.-Thai Leadership Council, U.S.-Korean

Wiseman's Group, and our Working Groups on South Africa, Angola, and Nigeria;

Facilitating the transition of Russia and other former Communist states to democratic political systems and free market structures; . . .

Formulating a coherent strategy that maintains global alliances, open markets, and economic order.[14]

The foreign policy emphasis of the Joint Center relates to gathering experience on multiracial issues elsewhere and on areas of possible opportunities for African Americans. This includes six forums in cooperation with the Japan Society of New York, helping African American leaders to build communications bridges across the Pacific Ocean to Japanese business leaders, government officials, journalists, and scholars. The main international focus, understandably, has been on determining opportunities to assist in the transition in South Africa.

The Center for National Policy conducted two missions to Cambodia and Vietnam. These missions illustrated the role that think tanks can play in opening up contacts with nations without diplomatic relations with the United States. The mission to Cambodia, led by former secretary of state Edmund Muskie in 1989, was the first significant visit to that country by prominent Americans in a decade. Its report was widely circulated in Congress and the executive branch.[15] A similar mission, sent to Vietnam in April 1993, recommended lifting the embargo on that country. Although the CNP report was not the only voice making such recommendations, its observations added to the pressures that led President Clinton shortly thereafter to remove restrictions on bank loans to Hanoi.

The Institute for Policy Studies had a distinctly different approach from the others in its Global Security Program:

> The challenge now is to push harder for the following: a 50 percent additional cut in the U.S. military budget; gradual disassembly of the U.S. nuclear arsenal, as part of an international disarmament regime mandating that all nations, strong and weak, foreswear nuclear, biological, and chemical weapons; strong U.S. support for United Nations peacekeeping; dismantlement of most of the CIA and other parts of the now obsolete "national security state"; . . . nonviolent promotion of democracy in every nation, whether friend or foe, or a totalitarian or authoritarian regime. . . .[16]

In creating the agendas for action and research, these institutions, to survive, need to stay in step with events and national concerns. Whether the issues were terrorism and the Soviet threat in the 1980s or trade and the environment in the 1990s, relevance leads to listeners, readers, and, above all, donors.

Personalities

Institutional leadership also makes statements about the direction of policy and research. As prominent personalities move in and out of government, think tanks gain prestige both from those individuals they contribute to administrations and from the recruitment of well-known former officials awaiting a political change that might take them back into government. These policy institutes may be the nearest parallel in the United States to the shadow cabinets of European parliamentary governments.

AEI was able to boast that twenty of its staff went into the Reagan White House. CSIS has contributed officials to each administration since that of Lyndon Johnson. James Woolsey, co-chair of a committee to examine the Center's future, became director of the CIA; Robert Hunter, former head of the Center's European Studies program, became Clinton's ambassador to NATO. Madeleine Albright, president of the Center for National Policy, was appointed ambassador to the United Nations in the Clinton administration.

Former officials are prominent in nearly every institution. The American Enterprise Institute was, in 1994, the home of twelve members of the Reagan and Bush administrations under a variety of titles: resident scholar, visiting scholar, and senior fellow. Their list included Reagan's U.N. ambassador, Jeane Kirkpatrick, Assistant Secretary of Defense Richard Perle, and Bush's secretary of defense, Richard Cheney. The Heritage Foundation in 1994 boasted seven former officials as "Heritage Fellows," including Reagan's attorney general, Edwin Meese III, and Jack Kemp, secretary of housing and urban development in the Bush administration.

CSIS boasts that "five groups of outstanding men and women guide CSIS in its intellectual and managerial pursuits: the Board of Trustees, the Advisory Board, the International Councillors, the International Research Council, and the 2020 Committee [to examine the Center's future]."[17] Of this group of nearly 200, more than 40 have served in administrations, both Republican and Democratic, and eight have served in cabinet-level positions. Prominent among them are Henry Kissinger who was national security adviser in the Nixon administration and secretary of state under both Nixon and Ford; James Schlesinger, who served under Reagan and Ford as secretary of defense and head of the CIA; Zbigniew Brzezinski, national security adviser under Carter; Harold Brown, secretary of defense in the Carter administration; and James A. Baker III, secretary of state under President George Bush. Other names are mobilized by CSIS for special projects: four former presidents—Bush, Carter, Ford, and Reagan—were presidential chairmen of the Center's "NAFTA and Beyond" commission.

The Joint Center for Political and Economic Studies, primarily directed to the interests of the African American community, had ten former officials from both parties on its multiracial International Affairs Advisory Council. Richard J. Barnet and Marcus Raskin, founders of the liberal Institute for Policy Studies, served in government under President John F. Kennedy, but IPS today puts less emphasis than other organizations on enlisting those from recent administrations. Its emphasis is on activists: "Our fellows played key roles in the civil rights and anti-war movements of the 1960s, in the women's and environmental movements of the 1970s, and in the peace, anti-apartheid, and anti-intervention movements of the 1980s."[18]

In this realm of public policy, where competition for funds and influence is intense, leadership becomes critical to success. Those who have effectively developed and led the successful and influential institutions have been individuals with a strong sense of a mission. Sensitive to the Washington political climate, they have recognized key personalities in the power structure and know how to gain their participation and support. Through astute selections of staff personnel and fellows, they have been capable of generating and advancing ideas that have captured the attention of policymakers in both branches of government. Their understanding of the character and problems of the business community has enabled them to gain not only financial support but the active respect and cooperation of business leaders. To a remarkable degree the most effective of them have been able to shift the focus of their institutions to meet changing national and world conditions, thus ensuring continued attention and funding. The most successful have been adept at self-promotion, dropping important names and conceiving dramatic ways to further the agendas of their organizations.

AEI prospered under the presidency of William Baroody, an energetic and imaginative Lebanese-American who saw the possibilities of support in the concern of American business with an increasing government role in domestic affairs and growing problems abroad. Under his direction, AEI's budget rose from $1 million in 1970 to $10.4 million in 1980, while the staff expanded from 19 to 135.[19]

David Abshire has been the inspiring force at CSIS. Although he twice left the Center to serve in government, his vision continued to influence the organization during his absence. He has been particularly adept at leading the organization into new fields as interest—and support—in old fields declined. Originally established to examine primarily strategic and military issues, the Center today conducts research in regional affairs, trade, energy, and the environment. With a strong sense of public relations, Abshire assures that whatever the activity, the role of his organization will be known and appreciated.[20]

The Heritage president, Edward Feulner, Jr., brought not only a strong sense of the conservative message, but skill in the techniques of marketing that message. He developed hundreds of succinct and timely "backgrounders" and "bulletins" annually on individual issues for busy Washington policymakers and observers. He recruited a mainly young staff who shared his vision and shaped research to fit that vision. More than any other think tank leader, Feulner also has demonstrated by his direct mail efforts a sense of the importance of individuals in the country beyond the Beltway.[21]

The Joint Center has for many years been synonymous with the influence of its president, Eddie N. Williams, who saw the need for a focal point for the interests of African Americans and demonstrated the skills that found friends, resources, and prestige.

The driving objective of all these organizations is to influence national policy, either through providing information or promoting ideas. The appearance of influence is essential to survival. The Heritage Foundation undoubtedly gained prestige—and funds—because of reports that its publication, "Blueprint for a Nation," was widely used by the Reagan transition team. CSIS gained in stature when its study on the Defense Department organization led to legislative changes in the authority and responsibilities of the Joint Chiefs of Staff.

Peace

The ideological factor common to Heritage and AEI has also been present in the development and initial programs of the congressionally chartered and federally funded United States Institute of Peace (USIP). Although not normally listed among the Washington think tanks, USIP, with its programs, conferences, resident fellows, and publications, parallels virtually all the activities of the privately funded organizations, including, since 1992, public fund raising.

Because the nation had so many official elements dedicated to war—the Department of Defense, armed services, National Defense University, and the military academies—the concept of an official organization dedicated to peace developed in the Congress in 1935. Two related movements gave the idea more prominence in the late 1970s and early 1980s—the aftermath of the Vietnam War and a growing peace movement advocating greater detente with the Soviet Union. At the same time, a new discipline, called either peace studies or conflict resolution, was developing in some of the nation's universities. Drawing on experience in the domestic resolution of disputes through arbitration and mediation, proponents of the approach believed such experience could be transferred to the resolution of international disputes.

Three concepts behind the USIP legislation were very American:

First, the hope that creating such an institution could lead to world peace. In 1980, a national committee was formed to press Congress to legislate the establishment of a U.S. Peace Academy. One statement of the committee reflected the purpose:

> Last year Congress authorized $190 billion for military spending, while balking at a mere $20 million to create the United States Academy of Peace.
>
> Now legislation to create such an Academy has been reintroduced, sponsored by over 50 senators and 150 representatives. *If it passes, it could be the beginning of the end of armed conflict around the world.*[22] [Emphasis added]

Second, the assumption that the government would be active in pursuing peace in troubled areas of the world. Subparagraph (a)(1) of the Declaration of Findings and Purposes in the final legislation states:

> a living institution embodying the heritage, ideals, and concerns of the American people for peace would be a significant response to the deep

public need for the Nation to develop fully a range of effective options, in addition to armed capacity, that can leash international violence and manage international conflict.[23]

Third, the perception that peace is elusive in the world because of a lack of problem-solving techniques. Sub-paragraph (a)(2) states:

people throughout the world are fearful of nuclear war, are divided by war and threats of war, are experiencing social and cultural hostilities from rapid international change and real and perceived conflicts over interests and are diverted from peace by *the lack of problem-solving skills for dealing with such conflicts.*[24] [Emphasis added]

When the legislation was introduced in 1983, it immediately sparked debate. Representatives of schools of international affairs questioned whether a federally funded institution duplicating their work was necessary. Diplomats doubted whether conflict resolution techniques could overcome obstacles of cultural differences, history, and politics and whether outside experts, however well trained, would be called upon by pressured policymakers. Conservatives considered the premises naive and feared that the establishment of a peace institution would show the world a lack of American resolve; they equated "peace" with detente with the Soviet Union.[25]

Ultimately, the reluctance of members of Congress to appear "against peace," the interest of the academic community in a new grant-making source for the nation's scholars, and the need for a tribute to the chief sponsor, retiring Senator Jennings Randolph of West Virginia, overcame opposition and the legislation passed and was signed into law on October 19, 1984, as an amendment to the Department of Defense appropriations act. In the process, significant changes were made that reflected currents of the debate. "Institute" was substituted for "Academy." Authorization to grant degrees and to raise private funds was dropped. (The latter was revived in 1992.) The secretary of defense, the director of the Arms Control and Disarmament Agency, and the president of the National Defense University were made ex-officio members of the board.

Ideological influence did not end with the passage of the legislation. The Reagan administration, although at first hesitant to implement the authority, apparently decided that the Institute, under proper direction, could be an antidote to the peace movement. A conservative board was appointed that saw peace more in terms of victory over the Soviet Union than in the resolution of regional conflicts.

Especially during the early years, the activities of the Institute showed the influence of that tendency. Although a broad range of external studies related to conflict resolution and peace were funded, the activities directly sponsored by the Institute concentrated on the study of war and the confrontation with the Soviet Union and its surrogates. The keynote speaker at the first major conference of the Institute, in June 1988, was Edward Luttwak, a military historian. USIP at a session on July 24, 1989, sponsored the first public presentation of Francis Fukuyama's book *The End of History and the Last Man*,[26] which announced the total victory of democracy over communism. The subjects of the Institute's early working groups and studies further illustrated this tendency: Peace and Deterrence after the Intermediate-Range Nuclear Forces Agreement; Strengthening World Order and the United Nations Charter System Against Secret Warfare and Low-Intensity Conflict; The Sarajevo Fallacy: A Discussion on the Historical and Intellectual Origins of Thinking on Arms Control (also based on an article in *The National Interest*[27]); The Meaning of Munich, Fifty Years Later.

In 1994, USIP existed primarily as a major source of funding and stimulus for conferences and research, frequently in cooperation with other think tanks, congressional committees, and executive agencies. The emphasis of its conference in November 1994 shifted from strategic concerns to peacekeeping and the role of nongovernmental organizations in a chaotic world. Congress increased its appropriation from $8,393,000 in fiscal year 1991 to $11 million in FY 1992. Appropriations for FY 1994 were $10,912,000, according to its tenth anniversary report, *Building Peace*. Approximately one- fourth of its budget, by statute, goes for grants to individual scholars and educational institutions. A portion was allocated toward reaching out to secondary school teachers through workshops and conferences and the preparation of curriculum materials.

As do similar documents of other think tanks, the biennial report of USIP emphasizes the organization's relevance to current events and to policy making by frequent references to the briefing of officials and to their participation in USIP events. An example was a special report on "Sudan: Ending the War, Moving Talks Forward":

> On October 20, 1993, the Institute and the U.S. House of Representatives Subcommittee on Africa held a two-day symposium

that led to negotiations between the two principal southern factions. Rep. Harry Johnston (D-Fl), subcommittee chairman, mediated the negotiations.[28]

Despite a few such cases of direct involvement in current conflict issues, the possibilities of direct influence on peace in the world have clearly been inhibited by the complexities of international problems and the reluctance of the United States to be officially involved. Although the education and research may widen the nation's understanding of world conflict, the high hopes of the USIP's sponsors that the development of problem-solving skills would lead to an end of war have yet to be realized.

Activities

In all the think tanks, whether privately or officially funded, meetings large and small bring together prominent personalities, staffs, and the public. The Heritage Foundation held 120 lectures, seminars, and debates in 1993; CSIS held a similar number of events. The smaller Joint Center reported sixteen forums and conferences in 1993. The USIP biennial report of 1991 lists twenty-one major conferences and countless other working group and study-group meetings.

Study groups under one name or another crowd the think tank landscape. The Cato Institute in 1993 held several Policy Forums on Somalia, the expansion of NATO into Central and Eastern Europe, and the crisis in the Balkans. The CSIS annual report for 1993 lists nearly fifty ongoing round tables, forums, working groups, committees, and commissions ranging in subject from U.S.-Polish relations to AIDS. The Center for National Policy, in a variation, sponsored three "squaretables" in 1993.

One particularly influential approach sought by most of the think tanks is the congressional study group bringing together members of the legislative branch, congressional staffs, and outside experts to examine a particular issue. One such group, sponsored by CSIS, laid the foundations for the revisions in the Defense Department ultimately incorporated in the Goldwater-Nichols Act.[29]

After the congressional elections of 1994, the Heritage Foundation scored a coup when 73 new Republican members of Congress decided to attend the Foundation's briefing rather than one traditionally staged by the Kennedy School of Government at Harvard. The Heritage briefing was clearly partisan; no Democrats were invited. Speakers included Newt Gingrich, the new House Speaker, conservative stalwarts such as William Bennett and former U.N. ambassador Jeane Kirkpatrick, and talk show host Rush Limbaugh.[30]

The most elaborate gatherings are conferences. AEI's 1993 report notes, "Major AEI research conferences in the past year included a three-day session on the future of Sino-American relations, a two-day meeting on health care expenditure controls, and a series of meetings of the AEI-Brookings Institution Renewing Congress Project."[31] Not all sessions are held in Washington. CSIS held a series of Williamsburg Conferences between 1974 and 1991, funded by *Reader's Digest,* that surveyed global issues. A history of the Center notes that "over the nearly twenty years of the annual conferences, several hundred legislators have traveled to Williamsburg, Virginia for two or three days of off-the-record sessions with academic specialists, journalists, and government officials."[32] CSIS holds regular Roundtable meetings in Dallas and Houston. CSIS has held conferences in Brussels, Istanbul, London, Morocco, Tokyo, and Mexico City. The Cato Institute's annual Benefactor Summit was held at the Ritz Carlton, Rancho Mirage, California. Over many years of the Cold War, the Kettering Foundation kept the door open to Soviet scholars through their Dartmouth Conferences in the United States and the Soviet Union. The primary emphasis of the Stanley Foundation is on small conferences on specific issues, mainly conducted at the Wye plantation outside of Washington.

The impact of the conferences does not stop with the participants—or so the organizers hope. The publications that follow such meetings, based on the proceedings and papers prepared in advance, form the most significant output of the editorial staff of these institutes. Beyond these books are journals, newsletters, monographs, and reports. In some cases, such as the Brookings Institution, which specializes in long-range research, books are the mainstay. Others, like the Heritage Foundation, which wish to have an immediate, targeted impact on policy, depend on shorter issues papers and newsletters. Although publications are considered a necessary part and, for some, are useful in raising revenue, most observers of these institutions agree that their greater impact is through the conversations that take place during the programmed events. The published or printed conversations are less influential by-products.

The public presentation of research results, however, is important to these institutions both for reasons of funding and to establish reputations that will lead to increased influence. Such institutes encourage their fellows and researchers to appear on television and write for op-ed pages. Many distribute directories of experts to media outlets. Press conferences are regarded as an important technique, generally marking a high-profile presentation to announce significant findings. The leaders are alert to anniversaries and other special occasions that may form the basis for special appeals and events. The promotional tone of their annual reports reflects the importance of new and continuing support: "CSIS has never been so well positioned to have an impact on key policy issues"; "AEI has become one of America's most respected and influential policy research organizations"; "the Cato building has become an important center for policy discussion"; "Heritage has become the most broadly supported public policy research foundation in the United States." Increasingly, also, think tanks are employing new methods of presentation and research to project their findings such as simulations and the creation of specialized computer networks. In 1984, CSIS, in cooperation with the University of Arizona Management Information System, set up SOVSET, an international computer network linking 750 scholars in the former Soviet Union and Eastern Europe. The Heritage Foundation operates Town Hall, "a 24-hour-a-day interactive computer network for conservatives,"[33] jointly owned with the magazine *National Review*.

The activities of the think tanks are supported by staffs recruited largely from academia, journalism, non-governmental organizations, and retirees from government, both civilian and military. Except in USIP, where employees have civil service status, staff tenures vary according to funds available for a project and career objectives.[34] They represent, in a sense, a new class of professionals. Ricci refers to them as "policy professionals who use expertise to operate in issue networks where they deal with matters formerly handled by amateurs, by people who used to advance in Washington through bureaucratic promotion or political appointment."[35]

Ricci also believes that, despite the pressures of the various interests involved in think tanks, the professionals maintain their integrity:

> All professionals know that their academic disciplines permit a certain latitude of speculation, whose boundaries are real if not precise. And thus various think-tankers may select different facts and, after considering them, recommend diverse policies. Still, ethical

standards in scholarly fields are not infinitely elastic, and that is where professionalism becomes an important force in Washington. It is considered somewhat disreputable, for example, for serious scholars to write a research report where, in common parlance, the verdict was reached before conducting a trial, even though many partisan forces in the city would like to operate exactly that way.[36]

Another view of the limitations on the professional comes from Stephen Sestanovich, former director of Russian and East European Studies at CSIS:

> Too much of the think tank world's work may reflect an attempt simply to replicate what happens in government; we cannot do that. We do not have the same kind of information. We do not really know in a daily way what questions are of interest to policymakers. If I simply try to play out the hour-by-hour concerns that the director of Soviet affairs in the State Department has on his mind, I won't get anything useful done. I will not do anything that is of interest to him or his colleagues, and I won't really do anything that will help others outside the government understand what needs to be done. We have to find some way of framing questions that is a bit more general, more conceptual. In our distance from what bureaucrats have on their minds, we help bureaucrats to change their minds.[37]

Influence

The exact influence on foreign policy of this continuing process of information and persuasion is difficult to assess. There can be little doubt, however, that whatever the ultimate impact on policy, the process creates and refines perceptions of international events and the American responses to those events with influence on publics well beyond the Beltway. The process is one more significant link in the interlocking chain that binds the two branches of government and interested constituencies in the American democracy.

As one surveys the array of private and quasi-official institutes in the Washington area, an inevitable question arises: How do these institutions influence policy? A few examples, such as CSIS and the Goldwater-Nichols legislation reforming the Department of Defense, and the Heritage Foundation and the policies of the early Reagan years, demonstrate that such organizations can make a direct contribution to policy. The process of research and information-gathering has become an important resource for the Congress and the private sector. In this function, think tanks serve as bridges between academia and government. Although each of the various institutes and centers has its particular ideological focus, most attempt to preserve a reputation for professionalism and objectivity; the Heritage Foundation is perhaps the most notable exception.

More general influences on policy come through the rotation of individuals between these institutes and the government, through adding topics to the national agenda that focus on neglected issues, and by providing locales away from government where the multiple conversations of the nation's capital can take place. Think tanks serve a wider public when their experts and scholars appear on television and write for newspapers and journals, and their publications are frequently used in classrooms throughout the country.

At the same time, limitations exist on their effectiveness, and questions arise concerning their disinterestedness in issues.

One assumed value of the think tanks is that they permit an exploration of contingencies and policy options not possible in government where discussions are generally limited to what is possible at the moment. Even the public policy organizations, however, are constrained by what the general policy community and the public consider possible. A researcher's conclusions in 1983 that the Berlin Wall would fall in five years or that, in ten years, the Israeli Prime Minister and leader of the Palestine Liberation Organization would shake hands in the White House Rose Garden would have been discarded as fantasy. Even think tanks are limited to what is considered currently realistic.

Although an openness to the products of these organizations exists in the Congress, the executive branch is a different matter. Think tank products can exert some influence on planning at the time of transition, but once officials are in office, the pressures on them permit little time for the consideration of outside ideas and opinions. At one point in the debate over a peace academy, proponents suggested that a cadre of experts in negotiation could be created who could be called upon by officials in time of crisis to assist them with resolutions. The idea was subsequently dropped. Those familiar with government could explain the difficulties of inserting someone from outside suddenly into the conflicting pressures and constant flow of information that face the policymaker.

Officials do participate in a think tank's meetings and study groups. For all but the most daring official, however, participation is limited to explaining official policy and responding—often carefully—to questions. The policymaker who is cautious in speaking to any large group in the bureaucracy will be even more so in a public forum. Think tank conversations involving officials are important for public information and guidance to researchers, but no one should assume that they have the full character of an official policy discussion.

In general, the scope of these organizations is also limited by the audience. Obviously, the outreach of experts on TV and in print is wide. Meetings and conferences, however, tend to bring together sets of people already in tune with the basic thrust of the sponsoring organization. A scientific survey would probably show little crossover between the audiences at the American Enterprise Institute and those at the Institute for Policy Studies. Washington audiences generally go where they are likely to agree with what they hear.

The most serious question concerning think tank products and their influence relates to funding. To what extent do the donors' ideologies and attitudes influence research? In general, the products reflect professionalism on the part of the scholars and experts who work in the institutions. Their own reputations are at stake. They will not be staying forever in a particular center or institute; they will have in mind future employment, possibly in academe or government. The reputation of the institution itself is also at stake. The many alternate sources of inquiry in Washington mean that each work is challenged by others; that which is clearly biased or without foundation will suffer.

At the same time, the interests of the donors cannot be ignored. Grants to institutions, whether by foundations, individuals, or corporations, are almost always dedicated to a particular project. Those seeking grants must outline the project and, often, the conclusions they anticipate. Researchers cannot wander too far from those conclusions. Most grant-giving foundations, responsible to their boards, keep a close eye on the products they fund; if such products are too far from their guidelines, future funding will be in doubt. Corporate and individual sponsors may be even more capricious in withdrawing funding if the results of research are not to their liking. A think tank scholar must walk a tight rope between integrity and the continuation of support.

The problem is to some extent mitigated by the natural tendency of think tanks to hire those who seem ideologically compatible. The problem is also minimal in research that is primarily technical or scientific in nature; research into political and policy issues carries the greatest peril.

Another threat to objectivity gets little attention in the current literature on think tanks: the role of fellows and researchers as consultants to business organizations and foreign governments. The head of the Middle East Studies program at CSIS until 1993 was also a consultant to the Saudi Arabian government. The head of the energy project also consults for oil companies. The pattern is repeated in nearly every think tank. Little evidence exists that these connections affect the products of the institutions, but they certainly raise a potential conflict of interest.

The think tank world of Washington is an important contributor to the conversations of the capital. With all its limitations, it plays an indispensable role in assuring a wide and democratic exchange among all of the disparate elements that ultimately contribute to the creation and support of the nation's foreign policy.

9   Advocacy

The Center for International Policy (CIP) occupies a crowded set of offices next to the Brookings Institution on Massachusetts Avenue in Washington. The name and some of its activities would suggest that it is another think tank. It issues publications, conducts conferences, and approaches Congress. Its president is Robert White, a former U.S. ambassador. Yet this center is different. It not only studies policies; it works actively to implement them. In 1994 when other public policy groups were studying the issue of Haiti, the CIP was directly involved in efforts to negotiate the return of President Jean-Bertrand Aristide to the island.

CIP is one of a vast array of organizations in the United States and abroad dedicated to action and the advocacy of specific issues. One estimate places the number of national nonprofit organizations that devote a significant amount of their funds and energies to transnational issues at "about 1,950."[1] Such organizations not only serve to alert the public and policymakers to problems and possible solutions, but many become formal consultants to the United Nations and to major international conferences, aggressively pressing their concerns and ideas upon official delegates. They are often at odds with both governments and multilateral organizations. Private-organization delegations to two major international conferences, the U.N. Conference on the Environment and Development in Rio de Janeiro in 1992 and the U.N. Conference on

Human Rights in Vienna in 1993, complained at both that they were shut out of official proceedings. At Rio, many nongovernmental organizations joined in a parallel conference to draw attention to their agendas.

Their impact on foreign policy in individual nations can be substantial. Information is their weapon. Through mail, the press, TV, and computer services such information often is a major influence in shaping the public perception of situations abroad. Directed to governments, it is intended to force action. Directed to the citizen, it is designed to mobilize support and pressure and to raise money. It has proven difficult for either audience to ignore the more dramatic appeals of these advocacy groups.

Such organizations may range from one person working part time out of a university office to major global institutions with million dollar budgets and large staffs. More than in any other set of institutions, dedicated and earnest volunteers play a significant role. Individual professions will develop their own units: "Doctors for ——" or "The Lawyers' Committee for ——." They can be found in nearly every state in the Union and in most democratic societies overseas. Some have existed for many decades; others have lived only so long as financial support lasted or the public concern remained. Unlike lobbyists, paid— sometimes handsomely—by special interests, advocacy groups must raise their support from private individuals and foundations. In many instances they combine activism on issues with overseas development and humanitarian assistance. They represent the fullest manifestation of the civic society that sets democracy apart from authoritarianism.

Citizen activism has long been a feature of American society. In 1915, Henry Ford chartered a Peace Ship and sailed to Europe with a group of ministers, college professors, social reformers, journalists, business people, and professionals in an effort to stop the Great War.[2] The last part of the twentieth century saw a major expansion in the number and influence of advocacy organizations, especially those concentrating on international issues. In its greater role and responsibilities after World War II the United States became not only involved in the affairs of other countries, but judgmental about those affairs. The way the president of Zaire treated his people, the management of the rain forests of Brazil, and the family planning policies of Kenya became U.S. concerns. The interest was spurred by communications that became faster and more vivid, bringing foreign problems into American living rooms. Organizing to promote responses to those problems became possible as major foundations shifted their priorities to international concerns.

These citizen groups feel little obligation to follow or support an official line. Opposition to U.S. policy is inherent in their mission, since they are in large measure seeking radically to change aspects of foreign policy. In many cases, their activism defies government approaches and even laws. During the height of the controversy over policy in El Salvador in the 1980s, the Sanctuary movement openly defied the government by providing shelter in churches for illegal immigrants from Central America. Greenpeace, the most militant of the environmental groups, seeks physically to impede governmental actions.

Advocacy or special interest groups concentrating on international issues are active in many fields: refugees, health, AIDS, womens' rights, arms control, peace, regional and ethnic problems. Each represents a sufficient constituency to provide the funds and force for civic action. No single chapter of a book can cover them all. To illustrate the role of such groups, I have chosen to discuss three sets of organizations dealing with issues of special prominence in the last half of the twentieth century: human rights, the environment, and population. These issues share not only wide public attention but also the disputes that arise from deep divisions over how to bring about improvements in the human condition.

Human Rights

Advocacy organizations in the field of human rights operate against a backdrop of tradition and controversy.

Throughout the history of the American republic, its people have been concerned at the plight of the oppressed in other lands. Much of this concern, before the 1960s, was directed at relief for victims of famine, ethnic slaughter, and war. War relief associations were organized during World War I to assist Belgians, French, Serbs, Persians, Romanians, Russians, Armenians, Syrians, Poles, and Jews.[3] In 1917, despite wide opposition to the revolutionary government in Moscow, Congress appropriated funds for famine relief in Russia, administered through the American Red Cross and other private organizations.

Two well-established groups of institutions, the trade unions and the churches, were especially active in such relief efforts. The basis of labor organization interest lay originally in the fact that in the garment, furrier, and hat-making trades many members came from Russian-Jewish immigrant families. That interest subsequently expanded to efforts to protect free trade unions and human rights generally in authoritarian countries. Church groups became conscious of privation in other lands through their missionary efforts. During World War I, the Mennonites, Quakers, Brethren, Unitarians, Lutherans, and Catholics established international service agencies that subsequently became the bases for relief and activism. They were joined by other denominations operating independently or through the National Council of Churches in drawing attention increasingly to political and developmental as well as disaster problems abroad.[4] Organizations that had concentrated solely on relief efforts came to feel that they needed not only to provide assistance but to oppose and seek to change official policies that lay at the root of privation.

Although the American people had throughout their history demonstrated an interest in human rights, it took several developments after World War II to galvanize that interest into private and, ultimately, official activism. These included, first, the revelations of atrocities against peoples during the war and, especially, the Holocaust and, second, the Cold War and subsequent public opposition to the support of dictatorial regimes allied to the United States in that ideological confrontation. Public attention to these events was furthered by the interest of major foundations, particularly the Ford Foundation, in promoting human rights organizations.

Even as the war raged, citizen groups considered how peoples could be protected in the future against the rise of Nazi and Fascist regimes. The International League for the Rights of Man (which in 1976 became the International League for Human Rights) was organized in 1942.[5]

With the end of the war came the revelation of the massacre of the Jews by Hitler. Citizens, Jewish and non-Jewish, were shocked into a realization of what a government could do to a people. A network of Jewish organizations developed to protect the rights of Jews still living under oppression and to work for emigration to the new state of Israel.

The organization of the United Nations in 1945 resulted in further attention to the rights of peoples; three years later, in 1948, the General Assembly adopted the Universal Declaration of Human Rights, establishing for the first time an international standard by which national actions could be judged. A Covenant on Civil and Political Rights, more binding than the declaration, was adopted in 1966. (It was finally ratified by the United States in 1992.)

The 1960s saw two further developments that pushed human rights issues forward: the experience of the civil rights movement in the U.S.

and the Vietnam War. The first awakened activists who had marched in Mississippi to comparable human rights violations in other countries. In the second, the controversy over the nature of the South Vietnamese regimes with which the U.S. was allied called attention generally to the dilemma of support for and identification with nondemocratic, oppressive allies. The two currents came together in pressure for attention to the internal policies of nations friendly to the U.S., not only in Asia but in Central and South America.

At the same time, with the Cold War and the incorporation of Eastern European countries into the communist orbit, immigrants from those countries led efforts to awaken the American people to the plight of individuals under Soviet control. Violations of human rights were used to demonstrate to the world the evils of the Soviet system. In 1975, the Helsinki Final Act was signed between the United States, the Western European powers, and the Soviet Union and its eastern European satellites. The provisions of that Act calling for the monitoring of human rights in the signatory countries provided the basis for the organization of Helsinki Watch, established in 1978 "in response to the persecution of citizens in the USSR and Czechoslovakia for their attempts to organize Helsinki monitoring groups in their countries."[6]

In the coming together of these various currents and in subsequent congressional actions, new opportunities were opened for influential actions by the private advocacy organizations.

In 1973, Congressman Donald Fraser of Minnesota, chairman of the international organizations subcommittee of the House of Representatives, began a series of hearings on the consideration of human rights in U.S. foreign policy. By 1978, more than 150 hearings had been held with more than 500 witnesses. Reacting to opposition from the Nixon administration to what was considered an inappropriate probing of internal conditions in friendly countries, Fraser pushed through laws requiring that human rights be considered in foreign military and economic assistance, export credits, and the U.S. position on loans by the World Bank.[7] Some of the laws were general in nature, some were directed at curtailing U.S. relations with specific countries considered gross violators of human rights. A compilation of U.S. legislation relating to human rights and U.S. foreign policy lists 19 general acts, 13 amendments to foreign assistance acts, and 144 specific restrictions on relations with individual countries considered to be violators of human rights.[8]

Congress also enacted legislation establishing an assistant secretary of state for humanitarian affairs and requiring that the executive branch submit annually to the Congress reports on human rights conditions in countries receiving American aid. When Brazil rejected assistance in protest against such reports, the legislation was amended to require reports on all the member countries of the United Nations.[9]

The administration of President Jimmy Carter generally supported an active official interest in human rights. Staff members from the Fraser subcommittee were appointed to positions in the administration and became internal advocates for strong support of human rights actions. Secretary of State Cyrus Vance emphasized the importance of the administration's policy in a 1977 speech in Athens, Georgia, and defined what was meant by human rights:

> First, there is the right to be free from governmental violation of the integrity of the person. Such violations include torture; cruel, inhuman, or degrading treatment or punishment; and arbitrary arrest or imprisonment. And they include denial of fair public trial and invasion of the home.
>
> Second, there is the right to the fulfillment of such vital needs as food, shelter, health care, and education. . . .
>
> Third, there is the right to enjoy civil and political liberties: freedom of thought, of religion, of assembly; freedom of speech; freedom of the press; freedom of movement both within and outside one's own country; freedom to take part in government.[10]

If doubt existed about the broad public support in the United States for attention to human rights in other countries, it was dispelled with the advent of the Reagan administration in 1981. In the election campaign, Reagan had voiced strong opposition to criticism of friendly allies on human rights grounds. The transition team proposed abolishing the assistant secretary of state for humanitarian affairs position. When they were reminded that the position had been mandated by Congress, they nominated Ernest Lefever, an opponent of the human rights policy, to fill the position. Lefever was subsequently rejected by a Republican-dominated Senate Foreign Relations Committee.[11] The Reagan administration, too, was required to pay attention to human rights issues, although it placed the greater emphasis on the promotion of democracy and on violations in countries in the Soviet orbit.

As is the case in every cause, the advocacy of a human rights emphasis in U.S. diplomacy sparked debate in Washington, mirroring that which went on around the world. Few in the United States questioned the correctness of both private and official actions directed at improving human rights in the Soviet Union and Eastern Europe. During the Cold War period, however, divisions arose over whether it was appropriate to be seeking reforms in human rights in non-communist countries and especially those that shared security interests with the United States. Even Carter was required in a number of cases, such as Pakistan after the Soviet invasion of Afghanistan, to modify pressures on rights in the light of geopolitical concerns.

A related issue was whether different standards should be applied to communist and non-communist countries. Jeane Kirkpatrick, U.S. Permanent Representative to the U.N. in the Reagan administration, drew a distinction in an article between "totalitarian" (communist) and "authoritarian" (non-communist) regimes.[12]

A third debate arose over whether the U.S. definition of rights was in conflict with the cultural patterns and economic and political needs of other societies. Was the U.S. seeking to impose its unique way of life on others? Human rights advocates argued that the rights specified in the Universal Declaration of Human Rights established a standard by which all countries could be judged. Opponents of an emphasis on human rights in diplomacy, both in the United States and abroad, argued that the United States needed to recognize cultural differences; it could not impose its views of society on others. The arguments arose especially in relation to efforts to promote rights in Asia and in the Muslim world where proponents of a hands-off policy insisted not only that concepts of rights and customs were different, but that centralized and firmly controlled regimes were essential to internal stability and economic progress. This debate superseded the issue of striking a balance between rights and security. In the 1990s, especially in Asia, the question was whether trade should take priority over rights considerations. The decision in 1994 to grant most-favored-nation status to China without any marked improvement in its human rights record demonstrated the power of commerce over principle.

Finally, the issue arose of which rights should be promoted and protected. Human rights organizations and the Congress have put the emphasis on personal rights and, in particular, those outlined in the U.N. Universal Declaration of Human Rights. Even the promotion of democracy has been outside the scope of concern of leading advocacy organizations. Aryeh Neier, executive director of Human Rights Watch, noted in

1993 that "there is division within the [human rights] movement about whether human rights organizations should promote democracy." He explained:

> Some fear that associating themselves with the espousal of democracy would align them with the political opponents of nondemocratic governments and, thereby, diminish their credibility in criticizing violations of core human rights. Others consider that support for the right of citizens to take part in self-government is legitimate and that it is analogous to, and an extension of their efforts on behalf of, the freedom of expression recognized in international law. Even those within the movement who fall into the latter camp readily agree, however, that promoting democracy is far less central than stopping torture, murder, and disappearances.[13]

Human rights organizations have been even less involved in the promotion of economic and social rights. The U.S. officially has been reluctant to recognize the existence of economic rights. Although Congress in 1992 ratified (after twenty-five years) the U.N. Convention on Civil and Political Rights, it had not, as of 1994, ratified the parallel Convention on Economic, Social, and Cultural Rights.

The continuing national debate has been stimulated by the human rights advocacy organizations that were established in the last half of the century, financed primarily by private donations and foundation grants. These private organizations played a pivotal role in the stimulation of legislation. The testimony of their representatives before Congress provided both a body of information and pressure in support of congressional action. John Salzberg, a staff member of the Fraser subcommittee, in his discussion of the committee action, noted,

> The subcommittee received testimony from international human rights nongovernmental organizations, representatives of religious organizations and others with expertise in the country concerned. Frequently the public witnesses had recently returned from the country under study and had direct knowledge of the human rights conditions.[14]

Later, after the mandating of the country reports, the information from such organizations formed a benchmark against which to judge the accuracy of official reports—and created pressures for honesty in the latter. These actions were augmented by close personal relations with members of Congress and their staffs. Relations were also formed with press and TV journalists. They mobilized private citizens' groups to attend, as observers, the U.N. Convention on Human Rights in Vienna in 1993, extending awareness of the issues among the American public and increasing pressures on the official U.S. delegation to take positions favorable to the objectives of the human rights community.

Although many in Congress and the public were skeptical at first about the reliability of the reports of such organizations, revelations that human rights groups were uncovering what governments were trying to hide gave these groups credibility, especially regarding events in Central America. With site visits and interviews with local officials, local human rights monitors, victims, families, and representatives of churches and labor, the private organizations were able to reach individuals not willing to talk to diplomats or the press. As the result of their established reliability, their relationship with Congress, officials in the executive branch, and the media was two-way; they became both the purveyors and recipients of information related to their tasks.

The *Encyclopedia of Associations* in 1994 listed 253 active organizations worldwide focusing on human rights, of which 96 were in the United States.[15]

Three of these organizations have been of special significance in bringing human rights concerns to the attention of the Congress, administrations, and the American people: Human Rights Watch, Amnesty International, and the International Commission of Jurists.

Helsinki Watch activities were extended to all 35 countries that had signed the Helsinki Accords. As the spotlight fell on problems in non-Soviet areas, other Watch organizations were formed for the Americas (1981), Asia (1985), Africa (1988), and the Middle East (1989). In 1987, Human Rights Watch was formed as an umbrella organization to oversee and coordinate the work of the five regional divisions and the four thematic projects, covering arms, free expression, prisons, and women's rights.[16] For many years, units of Human Rights Watch have been active in documenting human rights violations and death squad activities by the armed forces in El Salvador. U.S. officials, particularly during the Reagan and Bush administrations, which supported the elected government in that country, discounted the facts of the Watch reports and of other reports, such as those of the Center for International Policy. The credibility of those reports, however, was established fully when the report of the United Nations Commission on Truth for El Salvador was issued in March 1993.[17]

Amnesty International (U.S.A.) concentrates solely on individual cases of prisoners of conscience, seeking trials and release of "individuals imprisoned for the exercise of their human rights whose imprisonment cannot be reasonably attributed to the use or advocacy of violence." It strongly opposes torture and the death penalty.[18] Its impact on opinion and policy comes through generating letters and telephone calls to officials in the United States and abroad. An Amnesty International report gives this quote from a released prisoner of conscience in the Dominican Republic:

> When the first two hundred letters came, the guards gave me back my clothes. Then the next two hundred letters came, and the prison director came to see me. When the next pile of letters arrived, the director got in touch with his superior. The letters kept coming and coming; three thousand of them. The President was informed. The letters still kept arriving, and the President called the prison and told them to let me go.[19]

The International Commission of Jurists, composed of jurists and academics in international law, human rights, and international affairs, mounts inquiries into the human rights conditions in countries where violations are suspected. These inquiries are often at the request of the suspect country as a means of beginning a credible response to external pressures. Such a report on the Philippines under President Ferdinand Marcos in 1984 highlighted for U.S. policymakers the problems of that regime.[20]

Other organizations in the Encyclopedia list a variety of services and interests, including legal services abroad and in the U.S. for victims of human rights abuses, assistance to teachers and scholars in the field, and special problems of psychiatrists, scientists, health care professionals, musicians, and parliamentarians. Several groups focus only on countries or regions: South Africa, the Balkans, Central America, Colombia, India, Nicaragua, and Hungary. Specific interests are represented in organizations concentrating on Jewish and religious concerns. One New York–based institution, the Research Center for Religion and Human Rights in Closed Societies, "translates and analyzes official and underground documents and other articles regarding religious life in communist, formerly communist, and other totalitarian societies."[21] The Center of Concern in Washington promotes the concept that every individual should have "access to nutrition and shelter, basic education, and minimum health services, and that each person should be guaranteed participation in the decisions affecting his or her life opportunities."[22] The USA section of the International Society for Human Rights in Toms River, New Jersey, undertakes special campaigns such as that to free Andrei Sakharov, the Soviet dissident. Bringing the human rights campaigns into cyberspace, the International Studies Association has established Internet: International Human Rights Documentation Network based at the University of Ottawa in Canada.

Population

Paralleling the case of human rights, the post–World War II period also saw a marked expansion in the number of organizations concentrating on population issues. Several trends combined to stimulate this interest. The emergence of new nations in the process of decolonization attracted the world's attention to problems of economic development. The creation of the United Nations and its specialized agencies and of foreign aid agencies in major countries provided further impetus to concern over the conditions in the newly independent nations. It was not long before those involved in assisting these countries became aware of the inescapable relationship of development to the growth of population.

A headline in the World Population News Service's *Popline* dramatizes the issue: "Earth Count: 5.6 Billion and Growing." The lead gives further specifics:

> World population stands at 5.6 billion in mid-1994, with 4.4 billion in the developing countries and 1.2 billion in the industrialized world, according to the Population Reference Bureau.
>
> Each year approximately 90 million more people are added to the world, with developing countries accounting for 97 percent of the growth.[23]

Thomas Malthus, in "An Essay on the Principle of Population," in 1798 first called the world's attention to the potential problem of the expansion of population and global economic health. A century and a half later in 1915, the National Birth Control League, the first U.S. birth control organization, was founded in New York. Margaret Sanger organized the Birth Control League of New York in 1917, and in 1927 organized the first World Population Conference. These precursor activities led eventually to the founding in 1938 of the Birth Control Federation of America, which later changed its name to Planned Parenthood Federation of America (PPFA). In 1923 Sanger established the National Committee on Federal Legislation for Birth Control, the first private organization in the United States that sought to provide assistance in controlling population and to alert legislators and the public to the implications of growth.[24] In 1961 PPFA absorbed the World Population Emergency Campaign and in 1994, with a budget of $405 million, it was the largest of the privately supported groups focusing both on the delivery of services at home and education on birth control abroad.[25]

Again, the major foundations have played significant roles. The Rockefeller Foundation took an early interest in the issue. In 1948, a team of scientists it sent to Asia concluded that population control was one of the most important problems facing the countries surveyed. Recognizing the complexity of the problem, the Foundation moved cautiously, beginning with a grant to the Office of Population Research at Princeton University. In 1952, the Foundation provided support for the organization of the Population Council.[26] In 1992, Steven W. Sinding of the Foundation was among the experts working directly with the United Nations on population policies and programs.[27]

The United Nations further stimulated international attention to the population issue by organizing a series of world conferences. In 1994, the U.N. Conference on Population and Development in Cairo, Egypt, was the focus of the work of both governments and private organizations in the field. Delegations of private groups not only provided information and pressed their perspectives on official delegates, but also submitted drafts of amendments to be officially adopted by the conference.

In 1994, the *Encyclopedia of Associations* listed 28 organizations in the United States concentrating on population issues. The Population Council, with a budget of $42 million in 1994, is the largest organization in the U.S. targeted primarily on population issues in developing countries. Its location across the street from the United Nations headquarters in New York is symbolic of its global audience; at the same time, through its dissemination of information, conferences, seminars, and workshops it seeks to influence American public attitudes. Three others concentrate on seeking to influence U.S. official policy. The Population Crisis Committee "informs policymakers, opinion leaders, and the public on world population issues."[28] Zero Population Growth, established in 1968, seeks "to mobilize support for the adoption of policies and programs necessary to stop global population growth."[29] The most active in efforts to influence U.S. policy is the Population Institute, founded in 1969 and, in 1994, located within a brief walking distance of the U.S. Congress. It lists as its objective to "marshall public opinion on global overpopulation problems" and urges its members to "convey their views on global population issues to their elected representatives on matters of major legislation."[30] The Institute publishes *Popline,* mentioned above. A further sampling of its publications demonstrates its focus:

> *No Matter What Your Cause—It's a Lost Cause—If We Don't Come to Grips with Overpopulation,* a special appeal from Werner Fornos, the president.
>
> *How You Can Help Solve the Global Population Crisis,* a flier urging members to call their members of Congress to support an enhanced budget for international population assistance and explaining how to contact members of the House and Senate. The same flier gives advice on how to approach the media.
>
> *We Can Balance the Scale: World Population Awareness Week Manual.*
>
> *The Road to Cairo,* a brochure urging members to attend the World Conference on Population and Development in Cairo in September 1994. (By July, the Institute anticipated that 60 of its members would join its delegation.)

Like each of the issues discussed in this chapter, population is controversial. The controversy begins with those who question whether a crisis exists. The Population Renewal Office in Kansas City, Missouri, "advocates population growth and stands opposed to population control, since . . . the hazards of a declining population far outnumber the hazards of an over-populated planet."[31] The Catholic Church and some conservative religious groups, including Muslims, oppose all artificial birth control measures and wage especially strong campaigns against abortion. Private voluntary groups opposed to contraception and abortion developed and paralleled activities of the groups less restricted in their approach to the problem. Their target in 1994 was to discourage U.S. attendance at the Cairo World Population Conference. A full page advertisement in the *Washington Post* on June 29, 1994, signed by nearly 300 persons, clergy and laity from around the world, was headed: "Stop the U.N.'s Killer Conference."[32]

Many of the private population agencies receive funds from the U.S. Agency for International Development to support contraceptive and womens' health programs overseas. During the Reagan administration, with its strong support from those opposed to abortion, this support became a matter of intense controversy in both the Congress and the executive. In 1984, Representative Jack Kemp, acting in furtherance of Reagan administration policy, gained the passage of an amendment to the Foreign Assistance Act that prohibited U.S. assistance to any organization that "supports or participates in the management of a program of coercive abortion or involuntarily sterilization."[33] This was specifically aimed at ending U.S. contributions to the United Nations Population Fund. The U.S. delegation to the U.N. Conference on Population in Mexico City in 1984 took a strong stand against abortion and sterilization, putting it at odds with many in the developing countries and with some of the U.S. private organizations. U.S. official assistance to the International Planned Parenthood Federation was terminated in 1984 and not resumed until the Clinton administration rescinded the policy in 1993.

The controversy over funding for the population groups highlights the problems associated with receiving government money, problems that apply in some measure to most private organizations. Many groups refuse to do so because of a fear that such dependence will be used to blunt opposition to official policy. As a Stanley Foundation conference summary notes,

> While governments may be relieved when NGOs [non-govern-mental organizations] can step in and effectively deal with crisis situations, these ad hoc organizations may not be so welcome in government circles when they're lobbying for policy changes or opposing government practices.[34]

As the 1960s dramatized the link between population and develop-ment, the 1980s saw a growing realization of the tie between population and the increasing global concern over the environment. The Environ-mental Fund established in 1973 became, in 1985, the Population-Environment Balance; its purpose is "to educate and impress upon the American public and policymakers the 'adverse effects' of population growth on the environment."[35] Population organizations were present at the Rio Conference on Environment and Development in 1992. In preparing for the Cairo meeting in 1994, they insisted that the environ-ment, as well as development, needed to be part of the agenda. A statement by the International Planned Parenthood Federation stressed the relationships:

> Non-governmental organizations have a long history and wide experience in advocacy and action on behalf of poor and marginalized people and in working for women, whose role as child-bearers and resource managers places them in a crucial position in relation to population, environment, and true human development.
>
> But like government ministries and international agencies, nongovernmental organizations have to overcome a tendency to limit their focus to specific development sectors and sometimes, to surmount ideological barriers, which can inhibit advocacy and educational activities and make cooperation and networking difficult.[36]

Environment

In 1892, a group of citizens, concerned about preserving the beauties of the American West, formed the Sierra Club, the first private organization focusing on issues of the environment.

Seven decades later, in 1962, a Maine writer, Rachel Carson, caught the attention of the nation with her book *The Silent Spring,* alerting the public to the threats from chemical pesticides. Slowly thereafter isolated scientists and seers introduced into the world's vocabulary terms such as "the greenhouse effect," and "global warming." Scientists in the Antarctic discovered a hole in something called the ozone layer. People became aware that the very existence of life on the planet might be at stake. The environmental movement was born.

In 1969, the environment received more attention when NASA landed men on the moon and, for the first time, people saw the earth as a small blue sphere in vast empty space. The celebration of Earth Day began shortly thereafter.

To a greater extent than either human rights or population—as intimately concerned with human life as these issues are—the environment touches the most basic aspects of living: food, water, and livelihood. At issue are how people will heat their homes, power their industries, dispose of their waste, raise their crops, move from place to place. As peoples became increasingly alarmed and as governments considered how to respond, civic action became inevitable. And with such action came intense differences.

If the threats were as real as many insisted, fundamental changes in lifestyles and policies would be required. Estimates of the cost of necessary changes in energy, transportation, agriculture, and conservation were enormous. Those who would be affected in business and industry challenged the data: the world was not really getting warmer; estimates of disaster failed to appreciate the recuperative power of the planet.

As the scientific data proved more and more correct, opponents of substantial action acknowledged that problems existed but insisted that corrective measures must be balanced with other needs—for employment, for recreation, for economically viable industry and agriculture.

Internationally, as the danger was more and more accepted, the argument erupted over responsibility—both for past actions and for future corrections. The first U.N. conference on the environment took place in Stockholm in 1972. The decisions largely were dictated by the industrialized nations. When plans were laid for the next U.N. conference, in Rio de Janeiro in 1992, the situation had changed. Like the conferences on human rights and population, the Rio conference brought differences between groups of nations into sharp focus. Developing nations, under pressures to improve their environmental practices, insisted that the developed nations were the largest polluters and should bear the major responsibilities and costs of change. As in the case of population, new policies had to take into account the needs of development. The concept of "sustained development"—balancing environmental change with economic progress—was born.

Throughout the past thirty years in which the issues of official responses to the pressures on the global environment have arisen, advocacy organizations have played substantial roles in shaping policies—on both sides. Two, in particular, have been active on international aspects of the issues: the Environmental Defense Fund (EDF) and Greenpeace U.S.A. Although a long list exists of private environmental groups in the United States, most are primarily concerned with conditions in the U.S.

The EDF, founded in 1967, describes itself as a "public interest organization of lawyers, scientists, and economists dedicated to the protection and improvement of environmental quality and public health."[37] In 1993, according to its annual report, it had revenues from foundations and individual gifts of $19,488,655. Although the bulk of the organization's work relates to problems within the continental United

States, it has undertaken actions that relate to areas beyond U.S. borders. Its 1993 yearly review mentions a successful lawsuit mounted to extend the application of the National Environmental Policy Act to U.S. government activities abroad; efforts to shut down a polluting incinerator at a U.S. base in the Antarctic were involved. Emphasizing the importance of rain forests in the global environment, the EDF encouraged the World Bank and other multilateral banks to cease financing projects destructive of forests.[38]

Greenpeace U.S.A., associated with Greenpeace International, headquartered in Amsterdam, is the most militant of the environmental organizations. Established in 1971, it has undertaken to block nuclear tests, dumping of toxic waste, whaling, and drift netting. It established a base in the Antarctic and successfully lobbied worldwide against mining in that continent. It gained special attention in 1985 when its ship, the *Rainbow Warrior,* was bombed by French agents in New Zealand. The ship had been attempting to block French nuclear testing in the South Pacific. An article in the twentieth anniversary edition describes its activities as "Twenty Years of Raising Hell."[39] Greenpeace, through films and videos and other publicity of its actions, has done much to bring international environmental problems to the attention of the American public. Within the United States, it has targeted corporations producing products dangerous to the environment. Its annual report for 1992 describes a campaign of post cards, phone calls, and faxes to the Du Pont Corporation, which was about to produce a new generation of ozone-threatening gases.[40] In a direct campaign to influence legislation, Greenpeace, according to the same annual report, worked successfully to defeat the Montana National Forest Management Act and save 6 million acres of unroaded public wilderness.[41] Greenpeace also seeks to sponsor research and development of alternative environmentally safe products; one recent emphasis has been on developing paper processing that will not lead to pollution of rivers by pulp manufacturers.

Quite understandably, the opposition of environmental groups to actions of industry has sparked counter efforts by industry-backed organizations, which question the basis for environmental actions by dramatizing the costs and loss of jobs. Conservative think tanks, such as the Heritage Foundation, have been active in such efforts, generally couched in terms of a "balanced approach." The National Environmental Development Association in Washington, founded in 1972, believes that both public and private interests benefit from a credible approach to the challenges of the environmental-economic interrelationship. Seeks practical means of assuring continued development of industrial, agricultural, transportation, land and water resources, while solving environmental problems.[42]

In some cases, the environmental groups seek to work directly with industry to resolve problems. The *Washington Post* of July 9, 1992, reported that EDF and General Motors were starting a dialogue about strategies for reducing air pollution.[43]

As in the case of the other issues covered in this chapter, the international U.N. conference on the environment triggered major activities on the part of the environmental organizations. They were credited, for example, with pressures that led a reluctant President George Bush to decide at the last minute to attend the conference in Rio.[44] Among the more than 500 private organizations that applied for accreditation to the conference, more than 150 were from the United States. They represented not only environmental groups, but scientists, churches, urban planners, lawyers, physicians, public utilities, industries, economists, fisheries, and loggers. Four delegations were from states. Others were from the peace movement. Some concentrated solely on creating support for the U.N. conference in various parts of the United States. One, from San Francisco, wanted to lure an international organization to move its headquarters to the Presidio, a recently closed military base.

In the mid-1990s, the United States was environmentally conscious, emphasizing recycling, curbing of emissions and waste, placing environmentally related conditions on its trade and relations with others. These efforts were a result, in large measure, of the aggressive actions of the advocacy organizations.

10 Lobbies

With the coming into prominence—and dominance—of the United States as the world power after 1945, every nation in conflict saw its future in Washington. Those in office in other countries, and their opposition, realized that understanding and influencing the processes of government and opinion in the U.S. capital could lead to substantial military and economic aid, the opportunity to buy weapons, and support in the United Nations and multilateral lending agencies. Undemocratic regimes learned that failure to gain sympathy from American official and public audiences could mean unwanted criticism and outside probing into one's internal affairs.

For representatives of the new nations flooding into the nation's capital in the late 1960s, Washington was not an easy place to understand. How could a diplomat make effective contact with a vast bureaucracy, a divided Congress, and the host of private persons and organizations that seemed to influence policy? One could see officials at the State Department, although rarely the secretary of state. Seeing the president was virtually impossible. How could foreign envoys learn what was going on and, beyond that, have some say in the U.S. capital on issues of importance to their governments?

The think tanks provided forums, but their agendas were broad and most sought to avoid direct lobbying to preserve both their tax status and their image as impartial research institutions. Moreover, only those sympathetic to the institute's general political or ideological tendency were welcome. Advocacy organizations would at times carry the torch for the cause of a particular regime or nation, but their agendas also were broad. To maintain their status as a charitable or educational entity, they too were required to avoid the pressured approaches and manipulation associated with lobbying. Admittedly, the line between advocacy and lobbying was often thin, but, for the Internal Revenue Service, it existed.

Direct lobbying was essential, however, for those pressing their case in the legislative and executive branches in Washington. The American Constitution, in the "right to petition" clause of the First Amendment, provided the legal basis for such activity. A whole industry came to be based on the process of crafting and promoting a favorable image of another country or its leader. Lobbyists also performed invaluable services for the foreigner new to Washington in advising on speeches and statements, on whom to see, and what to do and not do.

Lobbying is not without restrictions. The Foreign Agents Registration Act of 1938 (revised 1966) requires all those, except for accredited diplomatic and consular officials, receiving funds from a foreign country to register with the Department of Justice and file with the Attorney General copies of "political propaganda."[1] In 1994, 741 persons and firms were registered under this act.[2] Loopholes, however, exist. Lawyers are exempted. Those organizations that may press the interests of a foreign country but receive all their funds from domestic U.S. sources also fall outside the scope of the law.

In addition, the Federal Registration of Lobbying Act of 1946[3] requires that all persons lobbying the Congress—not just those employed by foreign entities—report detailed accounts of contributions, including sources, to the Clerk of the House of Representatives and register with the Clerk and the Secretary of the Senate. As of July 1994, there were 6,308 active registrants.[4]

Increasingly, in recent years, additional restrictions have been added in laws and congressional ethics procedures restricting gifts, entertainment, favors, conflicts of interest, and the "revolving door."[5] The latter means that officials who leave government for the private sector may not for a designated period of time approach the government on issues for which they were responsible while in office. Neither set of laws and regulations, however, has prevented former government officials from serving private clients using the knowledge of how the policy machinery works and the personal access bred in political campaigns and experience in office.

The emphasis of this book is on the institutes and individuals in Washington that help shape the public's perceptions of foreign issues and events and, through those perceptions, seek to influence policy. This chapter concentrates on those that work fundamentally from a political or ideological agenda. Any full assessment of the impact of lobbying must nevertheless acknowledge that a substantial number of others beyond these primarily political actors are involved in creating pressures on trade, financial, and economic issues which also inevitably bear on the wider foreign policy images and concerns.

In the foreign policy field, those lobbies of greatest significance are those that seek to promote or block policies in the interest of another country or group of countries. For some countries, the problem is eased by the presence in the U.S. of large ethnic groups already predisposed to a nation's cause and prepared actively to support a lobbying effort. Those without such group support pay professionals in Washington to do their work.

At least five ethnic groups have mounted lobbies with some influence on U.S. foreign policy. The Greek lobby, working through the American Hellenic Institute of Public Affairs (AHIPAC), working primarily by pressures on Congress, has preserved a 7:10 ratio of aid to Greece to aid to Turkey. After the Turkish invasion of Cyprus in 1974, the Greek lobby was successful in gaining legislation to impose an arms embargo on Turkey, despite Turkey's strong position as a NATO member and ally of the United States. In 1994, the lobby's influence resulted in legislation that limited U.S. relations with the new state of Macedonia.

Those of Irish descent, primarily in New England, formed an Irish National Caucus to collect aid for the Irish Republican Army (IRA) in its fight with the British in Northern Ireland. In the 96th Congress (1979-81) 130 members constituted an Ad Hoc Committee for Irish Affairs and pressed unsuccessfully for hearings on the issue. As former Senator Charles Mathias points out in an article, "Ethnic Groups and Foreign Policy,"[6] however, the leadership of the Congress, including Speaker Thomas O'Neill, resisted, not wishing to provide a forum for IRA propaganda. In 1994, the Irish lobby was more successful and was able to get the Clinton administration to grant a temporary visa to Gerry

Adams, spokesman for the Irish Republican Army. The Clinton administration took credit for the subsequent declaration of a cease-fire by the IRA and the opening of peace talks with the British.

Immigrants and their descendants from Eastern European countries behind the Iron Curtain formed an Assembly of Captive European Nations that lobbied Congress for attention during the Cold War. The result was the unanimous passage in 1959 of a congressional resolution calling for a "Captive Nations Week." Congress repeated the ritual each year thereafter, even though the possibility of U.S. action to liberate those nations was remote. Individual lobbies of these nations were active, although at times divided. The Polish community, for example, was deeply divided when martial law was declared in December 1981 during the Jaruzelski government between those who saw the regime as an improvement over the past and those who urged Washington not to deal with any communist government in Warsaw.

Cuban-Americans, and especially the exile community in Florida, have been effective in promoting legislation and other official acts to preserve and strengthen the embargo against Fidel Castro's Cuba. They have worked through the Cuban-American Foundation, based in Miami, to oppose any concessions to Castro and to identify and threaten those in their community who favor a softening of the embargo. In 1979 they were able to curtail efforts by authorities in Washington to curb the Mariel boat lift in which Castro encouraged Cubans to set sail for the Florida coast. Radio and TV Marti, federally financed programs aimed at Cuba, came about largely through the pressures of this lobby.

African Americans have adopted as their causes foreign policy issues in Africa and especially the ending of apartheid in South Africa and, more recently, problems of those of African descent in the Caribbean. For many years, they lacked the resources and the political influence to achieve this goal. Moreover, the grave domestic issues that plagued their community had priority over foreign policy concerns. As more and more of their number were elected to Congress and formed the Black Caucus, their influence expanded. It was further strengthened with the organization in 1977 of TransAfrica. This lobbying group concentrated primarily on the problem of apartheid in South Africa, pressing for sanctions against the white regime and disinvestment by U.S. firms in that country. As the power of black constituencies grew in U.S. politics, African Americans were able to find allies even among conservative Republicans and pass the Comprehensive Anti-Apartheid Act over President Ronald Reagan's veto in October 1986. With the ending of apartheid in South Africa, TransAfrica has redirected its attention to problems of democracy in West Africa, particularly Nigeria.

In 1992, Haiti became a major issue in U.S. politics. African Americans had long resented the automatic asylum given to Cubans fleeing their country when Haitians fleeing were turned back. The matter came to a head when, on September 30, 1991, the elected president of Haiti, Jean-Bertrand Aristide, was overthrown in a coup and a flood of refugees took to unsafe boats trying to reach U.S. shores. The Black Caucus in Congress and TransAfrica pressed for the return of President Aristide to Haiti and for a different policy on repatriation. Their efforts were dramatized when Randall Robinson, TransAfrica's president, protesting a policy of returning Haitian refugees, went on a hunger strike. The Clinton administration in 1994 sent troops to Haiti to support the reinstatement of Aristide as president. It is doubtful that any administration would have given as much attention to the situation in Haiti without the strenuous efforts of the Caucus and TransAfrica.

AIPAC

No group has been more successful in making its influence felt on national policy than the American Jewish community. Although many Jewish organizations exist in the United States, the force of the community's political activity has, since 1959, centered in the American Israel Public Affairs Committee (AIPAC),[7] the only Jewish lobby registered under the Federal Registration of Lobbying Act.

The story of AIPAC demonstrates both the possibilities and the limitations of a well-organized, well-financed group in the U.S. political system.[8] Admittedly, the circumstances within which AIPAC has worked are unique and unlikely to be duplicated by any other ethnic lobby. The Holocaust created in the United States a strong feeling of sympathy for what had happened to the Jewish people and, to some extent, a sense of guilt that Americans had done too little to stop Hitler's actions. In addition to personal recollections, memory of the massacre of the Jews has been kept alive by books such as *Exodus,* films such as *Schindler's List,* and exhibits at the Holocaust Museum, which opened in Washington in 1992. Among non-Jews these reminders have created a broad sympathetic audience for the lobby's activities. The Jewish community in the U.S. saw in the creation of the state of Israel the ultimate security for the

Jewish people and believes fervently that Israel's future depends on strong, continuing support from Washington; Europe, from where so many had come, was not to be trusted. The lobby would be the instrument that would guarantee American support.

The community, moreover, is wealthy, well educated, and active. The percentage of Jews who vote in U.S. elections is the highest of any ethnic group. Many in the community believe Israel's interests and those of the United States are identical. This has led in extreme cases to espionage, as in the case of Jonathan Pollard, convicted of spying for Israel and sentenced to life imprisonment in March 1987. In less extreme cases, U.S. civil servants sympathetic to the cause of Israel have shared official information with Israeli officials. It is not uncommon in the Department of State for officials to be told by Israeli diplomats the exact status of internal documents relating to Israeli requests.

The fear of open dissent within the community is another positive factor for any lobby. Although differences exist in politics and ideology among American Jews, few are prepared to voice dissent publicly for fear that such divisions might be exploited by enemies.

AIPAC has benefited also from a lack of competition. Although an Arab lobbying group, the National Association of Arab Americans, was organized in 1972, it has never matched the power of the Jewish lobby. The Arab world is itself divided, and those divisions are reflected in the Arab American community. Arab countries, such as Saudi Arabia and Egypt, however important to U.S. interests, are seen in the United States as undemocratic. Saudi Arabian kings, however, believing they enjoy a special relationship with American presidents, have not seen the need for active lobbying. Saudi Arabia, in addition, faces another handicap; their principal asset is oil, but, in the U.S. Congress, where many of the battles are fought, it is believed inappropriate if not immoral to place access to oil above support for Israel.

Finally, AIPAC has had the advantage of strong sympathy for Israel among fundamentalist Christians in the United States who see the establishment of the Jewish state as a fulfillment of biblical prophecy. This factor has too often been discounted by those who assume that support for Israel comes almost exclusively from the Jewish community.

AIPAC espouses clear objectives: (1) to secure continuing aid to Israel on the most favorable possible terms; (2) to obtain the most advanced U.S. weapons possible; (3) to move the U.S. embassy from Tel

Aviv to Jerusalem; (4) to preserve tax-exempt status for Jewish fund raising in the U.S.; and (5) to oppose strongly any U.S. measures or proposals seen as a threat to the security of Israel, including arms for Arab countries and peace proposals that might require Israeli concessions. In 1995, AIPAC added an aggressive interest in promoting restrictions on U.S. relations with Iran, primarily because of Iran's presumed role in support of anti-Israel terrorist movements in Lebanon and the Gaza strip.

The concentration of AIPAC's efforts has been mainly, but not exclusively, on the Congress. When AIPAC in 1980 appointed a new executive director, it chose Tom Dine, from the staff of Senator Edward Kennedy; Dine's knowledge of Congress was a major asset to the organization. The leaders of the lobby early realized that senators and representatives were vulnerable in two ways. Given the broad sympathy for Israel in many parts of the country, they were sensitive to charges of being "anti-Israel," or, worse, "antisemitic." Beyond that, and more important, they required substantial funds to be elected and to remain in office. When a prominent member of Congress was once asked the reason for the power of AIPAC in the legislature, he replied, "Money. It's as simple as that."[9]

The influence comes both from contributions to candidates and contributions to opponents of those who have voted contrary to the positions of the lobby. AIPAC itself does not contribute to candidates, but it prepares the information for voters on the records and positions of members of Congress. The contributions are made through political action committees (PACs); according to an analysis of the Federal Election Commission's figures for 1984, quoted in Edward Tivnan's *The Lobby,* pro-Israel PACS contributed nearly $3.6 million that year to candidates for the House, Senate, and presidency.[10] One of the best known cases of AIPAC targeting was that of Senator Charles Percy of Illinois, defeated in the race for Senate by Paul Simon in 1984. A factor in that defeat was the campaign AIPAC waged against Percy, then chairman of the Senate Foreign Relations Committee, for statements made urging Israel to talk to the Palestine Liberation Organization (PLO) and for votes in favor of arms for Saudi Arabia. The "Percy case" became thereafter a lesson observed by other members of Congress: opposing AIPAC runs serious political risks.[11]

The reach of AIPAC is not confined to those members of Congress with substantial Jewish constituencies. The lobby has the capacity to encourage the raising of funds outside a member's district to support those who demonstrate strong support for Israel. Members of the House and Senate from areas with few Jewish constituents are thus sensitive to AIPAC's views.

The political strategy of AIPAC embraces more than Congress. The organization has worked effectively to include items in national party platforms favoring, for example, the move of the U.S. embassy from Tel Aviv to Jerusalem. The general efforts of the friends of Israel also have benefited from personal ties of prominent members of the Jewish community with U.S. presidents. President Harry Truman was influenced in his decision to recognize the new state of Israel, over objections from his State Department advisers, by the intervention of his former haberdashery partner, Edward Jacobson.[12] After a period of cooler relations between Israel and its friends in Washington and the Eisenhower administration, Philip Klutznick, a liberal Jewish businessman from Chicago, influenced the new president, John F. Kennedy, to be more sympathetic toward Israel.[13] Lyndon Johnson, with many Jewish friends from his Senate days, was personally sympathetic to Israel.[14] Richard Nixon developed a close relationship with Israeli Prime Minister Golda Meir; their conversations included not only the Middle East, but U.S. policy on Vietnam.[15] Relations between the U.S. and Israel were strained again during the presidency of Jimmy Carter and the prime ministership of Menachim Begin, but grew closer in the time of Ronald Reagan. In that administration, Tom Dine, the executive director of AIPAC, developed a personal friendship with Secretary of State George Shultz and frequently conferred privately with him.[16]

The tactics of AIPAC involve more than threats and promises of money. Sympathy toward Israel is generated by carefully orchestrated visits for elected officials and candidates.[17] When an issue is before Congress, the lobby generates letters, telegrams, and telephone calls to members on the fence by circulating information on the issue to Jewish communities and sympathizers throughout the country; the flood of mail alone causes some legislators to cave on an issue. Senators have been encouraged to sign letters to the president. When President Ford announced his intention to "reasses" U.S. policy in the Middle East, AIPAC generated a letter signed by 76 Senators opposing such a move, effectively killing the "reassessment."[18]

The lobby operates, also, by defining the issues and the limits of dissent within the community. This has been done generally—but not always—in close coordination with the government of Israel. In some cases, so effective has AIPAC been in conditioning the supporters of Israel within the United States Congress that it has acted without Israeli bidding or guidance. This became especially true in the time of national unity governments in Israel in the late 1980s when the signals from that nation's governments were not always clear. The lobby's supporters in Congress in 1981 moved to oppose the sale of airborne warning and command systems (AWACS) aircraft to Saudi Arabia at a time when Israel was silent on the issue.

To define the issues and to highlight Israel's opponents in the United States, AIPAC began in 1982 to issue a series of "position papers," including one, *The Campaign to Discredit Israel.*[19] AIPAC sought not only to label individuals as opponents, but groups; the assertion that U.S. Middle East policy was dictated by "Arabists" in the State Department sympathetic to the Arab cause has been widely circulated. At the same time, AIPAC supporters organized a think tank, the Institute for Near East Policy. In 1992, with the election of Bill Clinton, Martin Indyk, then head of the institute, became the Middle East specialist on the National Security Council staff and, later, ambassador to Israel. The lobby considered its strength lay not only in its pressure but in stressing certain themes that might gain wider support in the U.S. public: Israel is the only democracy in the Middle East; in the confrontation with the Soviet Union, Israel was a "strategic asset," and, on international issues, Israel is a reliable ally. It is to AIPAC's advantage in fund raising to stress that Israel is a beleaguered country surrounded by implacable enemies—even though the military balance is much in Israel's favor.

AIPAC has not been without its problems. Its opposition to U.S. policies in the Arab world brought it into direct confrontation with other powerful interests in the U.S. government and outside. In the 1980s, in particular, actions of the government of Israel, such as the invasion of Lebanon in 1982, created serious criticism in the U.S., even among many American Jews. More and more, also, in the latter years of the century, the reality of Israel and its politics differed from the often out-of-date views of the community in America—a circumstance not unusual in ethnic communities.

Nevertheless, by the 1990s, although AIPAC had not achieved all of its stated objectives, it could look back on a series of accomplishments. It lobbied effectively after the 1967 war to supply Israel with sophisticated U.S. aircraft, the F-4 Phantom. Its pressures brought increases in U.S. aid to Israel and betterment of terms to the point that, by 1990, most assistance was on a grant basis. Although it did not defeat proposals to sell arms to Saudi Arabia, it was successful in two instances—the sale of AWACs and of F-15s—in gaining legislative restrictions on the use of the aircraft. Its actions effectively blocked aid and arms to Jordan until King Hussein agreed to participate in a peace process. Up to the end of the Reagan administration, AIPAC was one important element standing in the way of direct talks between the United States and the PLO. Although some critics charge AIPAC blocked earlier Arab-Israeli peace proposals, the record is less clear. In some instances, support for such proposals within the United States was weak; in others, rejection by the Arabs made AIPAC's opposition unnecessary.

By 1994, however, AIPAC's fortunes seemed to be changing. It lost the battle in the Bush administration against tying housing loan guarantees to restrictions on settlement building. It was rebuffed in its continued opposition to direct dealing with the PLO by changes in Israel itself. It found itself facing divisions within the Jewish community between those sympathetic to the policies of the Israeli Labor Party and the more conservative elements still supportive of Likud policies. Internal squabbles resulted in the departure of Tom Dine, through the 1980s its most effective leader.[20] In an unprecedented event in 1992, Prime Minister Yitzhak Rabin publicly criticized AIPAC for needlessly inflaming U.S.-Israeli relations.[21] An article in the *Wall Street Journal* in April, 1994, called AIPAC in a "state of drift."[22]

Ethnic lobbies, however, represent only part of the picture of pressures brought upon the U.S. government by those supporting particular interests or positions in foreign policy. The larger part may, in fact, be represented by lobbyists hired by foreigners to influence the U.S. Congress and the public. In several cases, effective lobbying efforts brought to the forefront individuals and issues that would not normally have gained substantial public attention or sympathy.

China

Although the hiring of public relations firms and lobbyists to promote the interests of a foreign power or movement has long been a feature of American public discourse, the prominence and the amounts paid increased after World War II and the onset of the Cold War. Very large sums were spent in the last decades of the twentieth century to create images of individuals, movements, and nations to win the moral and financial support of the American public and the Congress. Such was the case of the efforts mounted to maintain U.S. support for the regime of Chiang Kai Shek when that regime was forced by the Chinese Communists to flee the mainland. A Kuomintang government was established in Taiwan claiming to represent all of China. In the United States, former missionaries to China and conservatives organized the Committee of One Million to pressure Washington to continue its recognition of the government on Taiwan as the government of China. They mobilized rallies and pressures on Congress, primarily around the figure of Madame Chiang.

For more than twenty years, until President Richard Nixon visited the People's Republic of China in 1972, these pressures succeeded in retaining recognition for the Republic of China on Taiwan and keeping the Beijing regime out of the United Nations. The resistance to relations with Beijing, created in large part by the efforts of this lobby, continued even after Nixon's visit; he felt he could not yet extend full diplomatic relations. When Jimmy Carter in 1978 decided to proceed with full relations, he felt it necessary to do so in secret. The friends of Taiwan, still mobilized by a strong lobby, were able to blunt the new relationship even then by forcing passage of the Taiwan Relations Act.

The China lobby case had features that set patterns for other later efforts. The problem for the lobbyists was to overcome a perception of a corrupt regime that had lost a war. That image was countered by emphasizing the loyalty to an anti-communist ally. The tactics centered, at the beginning at least, around a charismatic figure—in this case, Madame Chiang. Although some contributions to the cause were raised in the United States, much of the campaign money came from the Chiangs themselves, for the effort was carried on without the appreciable participation of the majority of the Chinese-American community, ambivalent about both Taiwan and Beijing.

By 1995, conservatives in Congress still urged the U.S. to restore formal ties with Taiwan, but, otherwise, the issue of the recognition of China had largely been settled. New issues arose as human rights organizations fought awarding China most-favored-nation trade status. In this battle, China did little direct lobbying; the burden was carried by American business groups interested in China's market potential. The power of the trade argument prevailed.

Biafra

Africa became the focus of several intense lobbying efforts unrelated to apartheid. As in the case of Taiwan, these efforts had little support from the ethnic community most concerned, the African Americans. When the eastern Ibo provinces of Nigeria broke away in 1969 to form Biafra and civil war with the Federal Military Government ensued, a combination of Biafran supporters mounted a major lobbying effort to gain recognition and humanitarian support for the break-away provinces. They included Americans who had been Peace Corps volunteers in the Biafran area, members of a Catholic missionary order, and a small community of Ibos, many of them in universities in the United States. A public relations firm in Switzerland, Marks Press, supplied material and mobilized action in Britain and the United States. The emphasis was placed on the starvation being caused in Biafra by the blockade and military assaults of the government in Lagos. The objective was to gain official U.S. support for an air-lift into Enugu, the capital of Biafra, over the opposition of the Nigerian government. The campaign's centerpiece was a picture of a child with a bloated belly resulting from kwashiorkor, a disease of malnutrition.

When I paid a visit to my family in San Francisco before becoming Assistant Secretary of State for African Affairs in 1969, I was greeted by a full-page advertisement in the *San Francisco Examiner* with the picture of the child and a caption, "If you want to save this child, write to David D. Newsom." When I reached Washington I had several stacks of vituperative mail.

So well had the Biafran lobby infiltrated both the executive and the Congress that, when I appeared as a witness before Senator Edward Kennedy, chairman of the Senate Judiciary Committee, examining human rights violations of the Nigerians, I was presented with a classified cable on conditions in Biafra from the U.S. embassy in Lagos that had come into the Department of State only hours before.

The lobby was effective, in part, because it operated without serious opposition. The Nigerian government took the position that its cause was just; therefore, there was no need for a lobbying campaign.

In the Biafran case, as in other African issues, another element was also at work—race. Although the Ibos are African, their separatist effort was seen by some of the conservative supporters of Biafra as an indication that Africans cannot hold together a major nation and as a welcome blow to African nationalism, represented by Nigeria, the largest nation in Africa. African Americans, conscious of this, strongly supported the Federal Military Government in Lagos. The Biafran lobby was effective, however. The Nixon administration, despite objections from the State Department, was leaning toward recognition; had the war not come to an end with a Lagos victory in 1970, recognition might have happened.

Race, kinship, and the Cold War were present in major efforts mounted on behalf of the regimes in Rhodesia and South Africa.

Rhodesia

The white minority regime in Rhodesia, fending off pressures for majority rule, declared its independence in 1965. Conservatives in the U.S. Congress came to the immediate support of the Rhodesian action. The late senator S. I. Hayakawa of California became a special sponsor of Ian Smith, the Rhodesian leader, and pressed the State Department to receive him. Under pressure from sympathizers and members of Congress, the Rhodesian Information Service was permitted to retain an office in Washington, in contravention of U.N. sanctions against the Rhodesian regime. That office, and paid lobbyists, circulated material to sympathetic groups throughout the United States; when Department of State officers spoke at public meetings on U.S. policy in Africa, individuals in the audience, primed with material from the lobby, would rise to challenge the speakers. Their themes stressed that the Rhodesians were doing no more than the founders of the U.S.A. had done—throwing off the yoke of British imperialism. In the most effective theme, they pointed out that, because of U.N. sanctions, the United States had been required to cut off its supply of a vital mineral, chrome, and depend instead on the Soviet Union. Under the pressure of the lobby and mining companies, the Byrd amendment, passed by the Congress in 1971, unilaterally exempted the U.S. from restrictions on the U.N. sanctions, permitting the purchase of Rhodesian chrome.

South Africa

Lobbyists for the white regime in South Africa used similar themes. The African National Congress (ANC) and other liberation groups were pictured, as in the Rhodesian case, as leading the way for communist influence. Lurid maps showed red arrows of Chinese and Soviet influence pointed at South Africa. Glossy publications stressed the dependence of the United States and the Free World on the minerals of South Africa. The Cape Route and Simonstown Naval Base were pictured as vital to the oil supplies of Western Europe and the U.S.

When Frederik W. de Klerk became president of South Africa and moved toward negotiations with the ANC, the emphasis shifted to the pressure to lift sanctions. A *Washington Post* article in 1991 reported that $2 million was spent in the campaign, including a $352 lunch, services such as speech writing for de Klerk when he first visited Washington, and campaign contributions to political candidates favorable to the de Klerk regime.[23] Eleven firms, according to the article, were registered on South Africa's behalf.

Angola

One of the most elaborate efforts to create a positive image of an African leader was that on behalf of Jonas Savimbi. When the Portuguese withdrew from Angola in 1974, Savimbi led the Uniao Nacional pro Independencia Total de Angola (UNITA), one of four liberation movements contesting for power in the former colony. Most African nations and many outside the continent recognized the government of the Movimento Popular de Libertacao de Angola (MPLA) installed in the capital, Luanda, as the legitimate successor to the Portuguese. Because the MPLA was Marxist in orientation, had received help from the Soviet Union during the fight against the Portuguese, and subsequently requested the help of Cuban troops, it was anathema to many in the U.S. capital. Although Savimbi had a questionable past, including a Maoist period, and was receiving assistance from the government in South Africa, he emerged as a "freedom fighter," resisting Soviet and Cuban incursions in Africa.

Not everyone in the U.S. was enthusiastic, either about Savimbi or about U.S. involvement in the Angolan civil war. The African American community, in particular, favored following the African lead in recognizing the government in Luanda and was strongly opposed to supporting a movement also working with South Africa. In 1975 opponents of U.S. involvement succeeded in passing an amendment to the Defense Authorization Bill, proposed by Senator Richard D. Clark of Iowa, that prohibited U.S. assistance to forces opposed to the government in Luanda.[24]

When Ronald Reagan became president in 1981, the climate for

Savimbi and his movement changed and, with the sympathetic endorsement of the administration, a major lobbying effort was mounted to blunt any move by the U.S. to recognize the government in Luanda, to gain support for the repeal of the Clark amendment, and to sanction covert assistance to UNITA. Those objectives, achieved in 1985, illustrate more aspects of the tactics and power of a concerted lobbying effort.[25]

The image creation on behalf of Savimbi was the product of many elements: conservative think tanks such as the Heritage Foundation; sympathetic publications like the *Washington Times, National Review, American Spectator, Human Events,* and *Commentary*; South African lobbyists; Cuban-American lobbyists; and individuals friendly to the cause in the White House and the Congress. Chester Crocker, the assistant secretary of state for African Affairs in the Reagan administration, who negotiated the successful withdrawal of Cuban troops from Angola and independence for Namibia, writes that "this lobbying campaign was directed by Americans working for the military intelligence directorate of the SADF [South African Defense Force]."[26] In the latter stages of the campaign, even the services of Morris Amitay, former head of AIPAC, were enlisted. The strands were pulled together by one of Washington's principal lobbying firms, Black, Manafort, Stone and Kelly, reportedly paid $600,000 per year by Savimbi and his supporters. The contract was arranged by Christopher Lehman, who joined the firm after leaving the Reagan National Security Council staff and immediately thereafter went to Jamba, Angola, to offer the firm's services.[27]

Against the backdrop of the Cuban presence in Angola and the Reagan doctrine of helping anti-communist forces around the world, a picture was created of an effective leader and, by implication, at least, a democrat. The cause was aided by Savimbi's commanding personal presence and his control of sources of information in Africa. The Luandan government was, in the beginning, at least, inhospitable to the foreign press; the side of the conflict journalists witnessed and wrote about was that presented in carefully arranged trips and briefings at Savimbi's headquarters at Jamba.

The campaign included high-profile events designed to stimulate press and TV coverage and to solidify U.S. commitments to Savimbi. In March 1985, conservative supporters sponsored a "Democratic International" conference in Jamba with representatives of the contra forces in Nicaragua and anti-communist guerrillas in Afghanistan and Laos.[28] In January 1986, Savimbi came to Washington on a visit orchestrated by the

Black, Manafort firm. He met with the president, the secretaries of state and defense, and spoke at the National Press Club. He appeared on every TV network and the PBS MacNeil-Lehrer News Hour. He was feted by conservative organizations. In a ceremony presenting him with an award from the American Conservative Union and Young Americans for Freedom, Reagan's ambassador to the United Nations, Jeane Kirkpatrick, called him "one of the few authentic heroes of our time."[29]

The UNITA leader and his lieutenants were carefully coached to speak the language that appeals to American audiences, to talk of freedom, democracy, and elections. Lobbyists assisted with his speeches and even drafted congressional resolutions of support. The lobby was a constant obstacle to Assistant Secretary Crocker's negotiations in the region. He writes:

> In early 1983—just as a promising chapter opened in our talks with the Angolan regime—we became aware of a shadowy activity called "the UNITA project." Its apparent goal was to undercut the U.S.-led negotiations on Namibian independence and Cuban withdrawal from Angola. Instead, the United States should support an interim, South African-controlled arrangement in Namibia and a UNITA victory in Angola. The "project" was inconsistent not only with presidentially approved U.S. policy but also with official South African policy.[30]

Only toward the end of the decade did a different picture of Savimbi begin to emerge. Dissidents from his movement began to describe him as a ruthless dictator responsible for serious human rights deprivations. Similar reports that had appeared earlier in the European press began to be picked up in the United States. A memorandum the lobby had prepared for Savimbi on how to deal with Congress leaked to the *Washington Post* and caused some embarrassment.[31] The lobby continued nevertheless to be strong, switching from the theme of military assistance to assurances that Savimbi would be included in any peace negotiations with Luanda and urging economic assistance. Only with the end of the Cold War did the covert assistance end. The image of a democratic Savimbi was finally tarnished when, in 1992, he lost the election in Angola and, refusing to concede, started another military campaign.

The Savimbi campaign was the last major effort in the Cold War context to create an image of a "freedom fighter." Lobbying on foreign affairs issues by no means ended with the Cold War, but emphases changed. One of the major lobbying firms, Hill and Knowlton, achieved some success and notoriety in its efforts on behalf of Citizens for a Free Kuwait during the Gulf War.[32] Lobbying efforts in the 1990s concentrated more on creating the images necessary for effective trade relations, especially on the part of Asian clients.[33]

Influence

What is the impact of lobbies on foreign policy? Can it be measured? The U.S. system of government lends itself to lobbying; not only does the constitution sanction it, but the multiple elements of politics and bureaucracy create endless opportunities for the injection of influence. Those lobbies are most effective that have a message credible to a sizeable constituency and access to a friendly administration. The latter, as the case of Savimbi demonstrated, not only increases the possibility of influence but the fact of being received by the president of the United States gives the leader of a cause both national and international stature.

There is little doubt that, to some extent, lobbying distorts policy making. The cases of the Greek opposition to arms for Turkey after the invasion of Cyprus and of the AIPAC campaign against arms for Saudi Arabia can be cited as examples of policy initiatives apparently thwarted by lobbies. In both cases, however, the lobbies had legitimate issues relating to the Turkish actions and the security of Israel that could not be ignored by the policy makers. The ultimate decisions may be in the U.S. national interest, but lobbying efforts marked by money and political threats diminish the degree to which foreign policy issues are considered solely on their merits. To the outside world, the results of such efforts convey a picture of national leadership at the mercy of single-interest pressures.

It is nevertheless difficult to make a case that lobbying pressures create serious damage to foreign policy initiatives. Washington has remained sufficiently important to the world that policies unpopular in significant areas of the world and promoted by lobbies at home have not appeared to damage permanently American prestige abroad. Support for Rhodesia was largely forgotten as relations with Zimbabwe later developed. Turkish-U.S. friendship remains despite the Greek lobby. U.S. relations with Saudi Arabia have remained close despite the efforts of AIPAC to hinder that relationship; more basic common interests between the two countries have prevailed. The Israeli lobby opposed several of the peace plans put forward by U.S. administrations, yet it was never clear in these cases that, given opposition by both sides in the region, any of the plans would have succeeded. Chester Crocker was concerned that the efforts on behalf of Savimbi might undermine his negotiations to gain independence for Namibia and the removal of Cuban troops from Angola. As it turned out, however, he was able successfully to work out an agreement on Namibia and the Cuban troops in Angola. It was signed in New York on December 22, 1988.

What is more worrisome in any analysis of lobbying efforts is the demonstrated vulnerability of the American press and public to images of individuals and causes created by pressure groups. The desire of such groups to paint a picture in black and white and to link an image to popular patriotic emotions or fears is understandable. As the case of Savimbi demonstrated, however, little is done to challenge the perspective built by money and clever public relations. Even the mainstream press failed to notice contrary images in the European press; few journalists made concentrated attempts to gain different views by visiting Luanda or neighboring areas.

AIPAC for many years was able to portray the Arab world in general as enemies of the United States, protectors and instigators of terrorism, and dedicated to the destruction of the Jewish state. All these elements were present in the Arab world, but other positive tendencies were also there; these received less attention. In the case of AIPAC—as well as the Biafran lobby—both benefited from the unwillingness or inability of opponents to mount effective competing lobbying campaigns.

The look at lobbies illustrates the power of the momentum of images created. The process is aided by the cohesion of enthusiastic supporters and by a polarizing ideological environment that admits no contrary views. For many years, the pictures of South Africa and Rhodesia as important sources of minerals and potential allies had wide acceptance. Labels such as "pro-communist," leveled at opponents of such views, discouraged dissent. With individual leaders, the positive picture of a Savimbi or the negative one of Yasser Arafat become conventional wisdom in the press and the Congress. The climate of opinion is not open to balanced pictures of a personality or nations considered as adversaries. When circumstances begin to bring a more complete picture into focus, it takes many months to change public perceptions.

Lobbies have existed on both sides of the political spectrum, even if at times the battle was unequal. In the later years of the twentieth century, Arab lobbies have challenged the dominance of AIPAC. African American lobbies gained power through the Black Caucus in Congress to challenge the voices of Rhodesia and white South Africa. But none ever matched their opponents in money or effectiveness. The supreme irony of this story of lobbies, however, is that by the mid-1990s nearly all the causes on which these lobbies spent so much time and money were, by circumstances beyond their control, lost. Israel recognized and was negotiating with the PLO. South Africa was ruled by the ANC. Rhodesia was Zimbabwe. And with the collapse of the Soviet Union, the acute interest demonstrated in the clients of the Reagan doctrine—Afghanistan, Nicaragua, and Angola—disappeared. Those who ardently supported the Reagan doctrine insist that this support for anti-communist movements helped bring about the demise of the Soviet empire. Perhaps they played a role. Perhaps the dire predictions of what might happen if the PLO or ANC came to power may, in the long run, have some merit. The most effective of the lobby organizations, however, could not stand in the way of peoples who wanted a say in their destinies. The movements and their leaders, no longer "freedom fighters," and the countries in which they operated were left to deal, largely unassisted, with the destruction left behind by the ideological warfare so fervently defended and promoted in the corridors of Washington.

11 The Congress

In the preceding chapters, one theme is constant. When citizen organizations, whether think tanks, advocacy groups, or lobbies, wish to influence policy, they look primarily to the Congress. The executive branch is not neglected, but approaching officials at the White House end of Pennsylvania Avenue is not easy. The legislative branch, on the other hand, provides infinite opportunities for access to those who make policy through legislation. It is not by chance that at least four of the leading policy institutes have their headquarters on Capitol Hill.[1]

Presidents retain significant power in foreign policy, particularly in crises. Statements by administration officials remain the most significant policy declarations. Legislators, however, especially in matters of budget, can be the ultimate arbiters of policy. With the advent of a Republican majority in both houses in 1994, the influence of the Congress became heavy in foreign as well as domestic matters.

Since the decade of the 1970s, Congress has more and more asserted its role of constraining and qualifying presidential power. Executive branch representatives recognize this through their consultations, testimony in hearings, and required reports. The congressional role has been enhanced, also, by opportunities the Senate and the House provide to public interest groups to give their views and present information on international events, countries, personalities, and policies.

This process of influencing the Congress includes both quiet contacts in the corridors and offices of the Capitol and highly publicized hearings. Both contribute to congressional and, ultimately, to public attitudes. The conflicting views presented in the Congress are more than debates over policy options. They are often over the nature of issues, the facts "on the ground," the place of U.S. interests, and assessments of the intentions and capacities of adversaries. Conclusions reached in Congress regarding the risks to Americans in Somalia, for example, were a major influence in the decision to pull U.S. troops from that country in 1993. The growth of opinion in Congress that the Vietnam War could not be won at an acceptable cost led to the U.S. decision to leave that country.

Congress speaks with many voices and listens to many more. The pictures members paint are not necessarily complete or accurate and are often marred by the simplicity of sound bites and the tendency to use analogies and stereotypes. Partisanship, obligations to pressure groups, and occasional xenophobia get in the way of objectivity. The ambitions and separate agendas of individual members add more distortion, but out of all those voices often comes a consensus that can, to the policymaker, spell caution or retreat on a significant issue. "The sense of Congress" thus portrayed does not carry the legal obligations of legislation, but nevertheless is taken seriously. Although the president makes the final decisions in foreign affairs, only in rare circumstances are those decisions outside the boundaries of politically acceptable versions of events and issues articulated in the Congress. Even Ronald Reagan could not win legislative support for all his Central American policies in the face of strong congressional opposition.

The media feed information and opinion into the body politic, but the policymaker generally becomes alert to the constraints of a common picture of events only when that picture becomes important to Congress. For many years journalists portrayed the South Vietnamese regime as corrupt and the North Vietnamese as skilled and determined fighters, in contrast to the picture of loyal allies versus communist puppets that dominated the policy establishment. But not until the journalists' view permeated Congress did the Johnson administration realize that public support for the war had vanished. As one Senate staff member put it, "the Senate hearings made dissent respectable."

Both houses of Congress also bring issues to public attention. The role of the House subcommittee in the matter of human rights has already been mentioned. In 1970 the press began carrying stories of a severe drought in the southern Sahara region of Africa—the Sahel. As assistant secretary of state for African affairs at the time, I was able to get little interest at the higher levels of government. But when Senator Hubert Humphrey, then chair of the African subcommittee of the Senate, held hearings and the picture was laid out in that context, the Nixon administration began to respond. In some cases, Congress has been responsible for new ideas and strategies that create constituencies for important legislation. Senator Humphrey conceived the idea of university contracts to implement overseas aid projects, thus generating strong support for foreign aid on university campuses. Members of the Senate Foreign Relations Committee, aware of the opposition to the Panama Canal treaties in 1979, assisted in devising a strategy that would make it possible for members to support the ratification.[2]

At times congressional committees uncover and exploit differences within an administration. No other forum gives such open splits more exposure. During the contentious events surrounding the fall of Anastasio Somoza in Nicaragua in 1979, the House Committee on Foreign Affairs held a series of public hearings. One of the issues was the nature of the Sandinistas who were at that time threatening to gain power. James Cheek, the deputy assistant secretary for American Republic affairs, seeking to maintain the maximum flexibility for the administration, declined to characterize the Nicaraguan opposition as communist. The very next witness, Frank Carlucci, then deputy director of the CIA, did just that. Years later, in hearings on Haiti, Congress uncovered a similar division between the State Department and the CIA over the character of Jean-Bertrand Aristide, the president of Haiti.

Washington works through networks. Nowhere is this more clearly demonstrated than in the Congress. The Rolodex becomes an instrument of influence. Skillful representatives of interest groups find members interested in their cause, often starting with congressional staffs. Such contacts provide names of others on the "Hill" who share the same concern and to whom further approaches can be made and information given. The term "iron triangle" has been applied to the links between the Department of Defense, defense contractors, and congressional committees. The alert agent of a special interest may also assist with arrangements and advice when members of Congress go on trips and may even draft the trip report and actual legislative proposals. The ultimate objective is to become so valuable that members of Congress will call these advocates as often as the advocates call them. Where political action committees exist, private organizations will encourage gifts to legislators sympathetic to their cause. Those seeking friends and influence in the Congress keep in mind a legislator's number one priority: campaign financing.

Study groups and conferences provide other opportunities to meet members informally. Such meetings may be especially helpful to new members of Congress unfamiliar with major issues. In the 1960s, when African issues were emerging in the aftermath of decolonization and the Black Caucus was beginning to be a force in Washington, the Ford Foundation and the African American Institute arranged for a series of Anglo-American Parliamentary Conferences on Africa in such isolated spots as Jackson Hole, Wyoming, St. Croix, and Jersey in the Channel Islands. The meetings generated a common interest—if not always agreement—in African issues and long standing friendships between legislators, officials, and those members of public organizations interested in Africa.

CSIS, with strong regional programs, seizes the occasion to brief Congress when a relatively unknown country, area, or issue suddenly emerges in the news. A particularly striking example of how a private group can bring together representatives from varied institutions, both official and unofficial, occurred in 1969 when CSIS held a conference on the Nigerian-Biafran conflict. The day-long meeting was opened, not only by CSIS officials, but also by Senator Claiborne Pell, a member of the Senate Foreign Relations Committee. Panelists included academicians, members of Congress, journalists, and executive branch officials. Foreign diplomats, congressional staff, and business representatives were among the seventy-five attendees. The conference proceedings were printed in full in the report of the hearing. They were an important step in defining the U.S. policy options in that conflict.[3] Chapter 8 noted how the Heritage Foundation undertook the briefing of new Republican congressmen in 1994.

These private contacts in the Congress are essential to the day-to-day effectiveness of public policy groups. They form, also, an essential backdrop to the higher-profile events—congressional hearings. Whether hearings are part of the normal cycle of authorizing and appropriating legislation or are called to review particular developments, they are the most potent congressional instrument for highlighting international issues. In theory, hearings are held only as a prelude to legislation. In fact, however, they are generated by a variety of motives—politics, investigations, a desire of members for prominence. Looking down from their circular daises in committee rooms, members of Congress and their staffers eagerly seek the limelight of public conversation to promote themselves and their agendas. They regard these functions as within the natural mandate of elected representatives to interpret the views of constituents and establish the effective limits of national action.

Hearings are preceded by congressional travel to areas of concern and by staff investigations and interviews. Staffs prepare lists of prospective witnesses and advance questions. They sit behind members during hearings and feed them additional questions. With the growth of staffs, the congressional capacity to gather information and take issue with official policies and assessments has grown. This process is often fed by the ambitions of individual staff members who see in their uncovering of an issue or discrepancies in official statements a route to prominence.

I observed an example of this in 1970 when a Senate committee asked me, as a former ambassador to Libya, whether I was aware of extra payments U.S. companies may have made to secure oil concessions in that country. I said I had no knowledge and pointed out that embassies had no jurisdiction in such cases. A Senate staff member, however, found a disgruntled accountant from one of the companies who gave detailed information on its payments. The result of the staff initiative was a series of hearings and, ultimately, the passage of the Corrupt Practices Act making such actions illegal.

Publicized extensively in press and TV, congressional hearings give representatives of unofficial groups opportunities that could only be duplicated by large expenditures in advertising and public relations. Every promoter of a cause dreams that it will be possible to participate in televised hearings that will give an issue the exposure of a major Capitol Hill event. Such events provide not only the opportunity to appear and testify but also the chance to submit papers, publications, and reports that get the wider circulation of hearing records.

For some private organizations, the exposure and publicity arising from the hearing is the objective, but for others success is determined by the legislation that may ultimately result. The process, however, is unpredictable; the influence is often hard to measure.

Hearings can be chaotic affairs, with members and staff coming and going. Multiple conversations may be going on in the hearing room, making it difficult to focus on the formal testimony. In the movement of members, the very one a witness may wish to impress may be absent at just the wrong time.

Such appearances risk both disappointments and surprises. As much as those from private institutions may value the time spent on Capitol Hill, the actual opportunity for influence may be limited. Members may have made up their minds on an issue, either because of political leanings or on-site observation—or both. In such cases, hearings become exercises in window dressing. The policy institute witness may not be prepared for all the questions posed, especially hostile ones. Even those who are passionate about a cause may need to be prudent in their comments; donors, supporters, and critics are listening. Those seeking publicity for a cause may discover that the press has a tendency not to cover unofficial witnesses unless they are personally prominent or their testimony creates a sensation.

Most committees will give a brief hearing (usually five minutes) to anyone who wants to appear. In many cases, however, a pre-screening of witnesses will be conducted by staff to determine whether the witness will bring to the session that which the committee wants. Hearings are time consuming; the members want to be sure they are of some benefit to them personally and politically. In selecting witnesses, committees look for those who can contribute knowledge on an issue, but they are also looking for those who will give prominence to the hearing. A George Kennan may be selected over a lesser-known but more currently knowledgeable Russian expert. Committee chairs wish to give the appearance of impartiality and seek witnesses giving more than one side. At the same time, they wish to be sure that the majority opinion is given prominence and, in doing so, may pass over some favored by the minority members. Those with knowledge and a strong position to put forward may not necessarily be invited. If an administration's party is in the majority and seeks only to support official policy and the official view of events, the minority party will find witnesses with a different perspective. Those from the government do their best to present and defend official policy; they do so often to be immediately challenged by other witnesses summoned by the committee.

If, as is sometimes the case, the chair of a committee has a private agenda and chooses witnesses to support a point of view, hearings can distort issues. In other cases, however, the Senate and the House may force into the open aspects of an issue being concealed or obscured by the executive branch.

During the Cold War, the hearing rooms of the major committees were the scene of primary battles over the perception of the Soviet Union and its threat, including Third World areas considered East-West battlegrounds. Hearing agendas were also dictated by international issues with a strong domestic interest, especially those relating to Africa. With the end of the Cold War, the congressional role has remained significant as the forum of debate on Bosnia, Somalia, and Haiti.

The following four case studies illustrate the congressional role in bringing together various strands of opinion on foreign policy issues that were significant during the Cold War years: the second Strategic Arms Limitation Treaty (SALT II); Nicaragua after the fall of Somoza; apartheid in South Africa; and the civil war in Angola.

SALT II

One of the longest and bitterest set of hearings during the Cold War years was that in 1979 on Senate ratification of the second Strategic Arms Limitation Treaty. The treaty with the Soviet Union was intended to supplement the first SALT agreement of 1972 by placing additional limitations on launchers for intercontinental missiles and on multiple warheads (MIRVs) on such missiles. Its approval was widely opposed by groups that believed it did not go far enough in limiting Soviet arms buildup and in providing adequate verification.

The SALT II ratification involved three Senate committees: Foreign Relations, Armed Services, and the Select Committee on Intelligence. In 1979, the Senate Foreign Relations Committee alone held 30 days of public hearings and 13 days of executive session from July 9 through October 12. About 100 witnesses were heard, resulting in more than 2,000 pages of printed public record and 1,200 pages of executive session transcript.[4]

The public committee sessions illustrated dramatically the role of the Congress as a catalyst in bringing together official and unofficial witnesses in a highly publicized debate. The more famous the witness, the more attention given to the hearings. Press and TV attention focused particularly on the appearances of former secretary of state Henry Kissinger.

The hearings, moreover, demonstrated the power of well-organized groups in such debates and also the importance of prominent personalities in the leadership. Much of the testimony against the treaty came from members of the Committee on the Present Danger, headed by Paul Nitze, veteran public official and arms control negotiator.

The testimony of witnesses in the Senate committee meetings not only dealt with the technical aspects and alleged inadequacies of the treaty, but also changed the nature of the debate. It was not, in the final consideration, the provisions of the agreement that were at issue but the basic trustworthiness and character of the Soviet Union.

The 1979 issue of *Congress and Foreign Policy* describes the process:

> One broad function in foreign policy that Congress serves is to bring about the public discussion of issues on which there are fundamental differences of opinion. . . . Perhaps the primary impact of Congress on foreign policy during 1979 was to force into the open a major debate on the adequacy of U.S. strategic and defense posture. While the controversy had been underway for several years within the national security community in both the legislative and executive branches and outside the Government, it was Senate consideration of the SALT II treaty, and the raising of doubts as to whether it should be ratified, that brought the strategic issue to the forefront of public discussion. At first the debate was centered on the terms of the treaty and the question of whether U.S. national security would best be served with or without the treaty. By the end of the year, the announcement of a Soviet combat brigade in Cuba, the Iranian crisis, and the Soviet invasion of Afghanistan had broadened the public debate to include conventional as well as strategic weapons and a basic reassessment of policy toward the Soviet Union and detente.[5]

Three aspects of the relationship with the Soviet Union dominated the debate: whether arms control should be linked to other Soviet actions, whether, given the nature of the Soviet system, Moscow could be trusted in any agreement, and whether the U.S. was at a strategic disadvantage vis-à-vis the Russians.

Secretary Kissinger raised the "linkage" issue by suggesting that SALT ratification should be accompanied by a warning that failure of the Soviet Union to restrain its allies such as Cuba "would seriously jeopardize continuation of the SALT process."[6]

Paul Warnke, director of the Arms Control and Disarmament Agency and a key government witness, in the session of October 16, 1979, addressed the "misconceptions" of the opponents:

> I should like to deal first with the challenge to SALT presented by those who argue that it should be linked directly to the intermittent ups-and-downs in United States/Soviet relations. Some carry this argument about linkage to the extreme and contend that our two countries are so different in world view and internal organization as to make any useful agreements impossible.[7]

Richard Pipes, a professor at Harvard University and a prominent member of the Committee on the Present Danger, took a different view:

> Soviet thinking is imbedded in a network of linkages connecting history, economics, politics, ideology, and military hardware. The very idea that one can separate nuclear weapons from the broad range of political-military instrumentalities, and the latter from the historic conflict between socialism and capitalism would appall any person even superficially versed in the theories of Marxism-Leninism.[8]

The other question related to the strategic balance, as illustrated by this exchange between Senator Joseph Biden and Paul Nitze:

> **Nitze:** I think it is important to deny the Soviet Union effective strategic military superiority. Many people in the executive branch have said that nuclear superiority is impossible because neither side would permit the other side to attain it. That is exactly what this debate is about. The debate is precisely about that, as to whether we or not we, in the face of incipient Soviet strategic nuclear superiority, are going to do those things which are necessary to keep the Soviets from getting it. That is what this debate is about.
> **Biden:** With all due respect, that is not what the SALT debate is about.
> **Nitze:** I believe it to be about that because I believe the SALT debate is a broader debate than just a debate about the treaty. I believe it is a debate about the treaty, our defense policy, and also the broad thrust of our foreign policy.[9]

Secretary of Defense Harold Brown, in the same hearing, had addressed the imbalance question:

The trends in the strategic balance have been adverse to the United States . . . and that is a matter of concern. In fact, it is this trend which causes some people to assert—incorrectly, in my view—that the United States is now strategically inferior. It is not. But people tend to project trends and with some reason. . . . I believe that by pursuing the strategic programs that this administration has decided upon, and by pursuing them vigorously, we will be able to prevent the Soviets from gaining strategic superiority through the period of the treaty, that is, through 1985.[10]

But Nitze came back to the subject again:

When one takes all factors into account, including that the initiative is apt to be theirs, that their command control and wartime intelligence facilities are substantially harder and more diverse, that they have more and harder hard targets, that their active defense and their civil defense preparations are substantially greater than ours, it is quite evident that strategic parity is slipping away from us and that the Soviets can be expected to achieve meaningful strategic superiority by 1982, and most certainly by 1985, unless we take the most urgent and prompt steps to reverse current trends.[11]

And, in the October hearings, another member of the Committee on the Present Danger, Fred Ikle, returned to the charge:

During the 10 to 12 years that the SALT process has been going on we have witnessed a massive strategic buildup by our adversary, a buildup that will continue unhindered even with the SALT II Treaty. During the SALT process our strategic position has drastically deteriorated, our ICBM force is becoming vulnerable, the theatre nuclear balance is being wrenched apart.[12]

The highly publicized statements raised doubts both in the Senate and in the country regarding the trustworthiness of the Soviet Union and the strategic imbalance. Against this background, the Soviet invasion of Afghanistan was merely confirming evidence of what had been spelled out in the hearings. Little support remained for the treaty, whatever technical advantages it might have had. The concerted coalescence of negative views in the Senate committee sessions was a major factor in a serious foreign policy defeat for the Carter administration.

With the hindsight of 1994, these predictions of ultimate Soviet superiority sound strange. Yet, in 1979, it would have been outside the bounds of reality to have predicted an early collapse of the U.S. adversary. The nearest that anyone came in the hearings was in a statement by Pipes, intended primarily at the time to argue for a greater U.S. defense posture:

> Historical experience indicates in the case of Russia that when you blunt her external drive she begins to experience domestic problems and turns inward. All the major reforms in Russia have been the result of fiascoes in foreign policy: the Crimean War, the Russo-Japanese War, World War I. Each one led to major internal changes. The only way you can accomplish major internal changes in the Soviet Union, which I think is most necessary, is by blunting Soviet external expansion.[13]

Nicaragua

The Reagan administration's determined efforts to win congressional support for renewed aid to the Nicaraguan resistance forces, the "contras," became a major issue of public debate in 1985 and 1986. In mid-1984, Congress cut off a two-and-a-half-year program of covert assistance to the contras in response to revelations that the CIA had directly participated in the mining of Nicaraguan harbors. Despite the aid cutoff, legislators left open the possibility of renewing $14 million in military aid "after February 28, 1985, if both Houses of Congress should approve a presidential request to release it."[14]

Although there were deep divisions within Congress on the aid issue, mainly along party lines, many legislators had not yet made up their minds on the aid renewal request. Between 1985 and 1986, Congress held a minimum of thirteen hearings, many over the course of several days, to debate the issue further. Six full committees of the House and Senate as well as five subcommittees heard testimony from administration officials, congressional representatives, advocacy groups, church organizations, and influential individuals concerned about military aid to the contras.[15] Rather than serving to create a national consensus, the hearings became a picturesque war of words producing widely contrasting images of the "facts on the ground." The highly publicized debate created greater divisions in public opinion about the country's involvement in Nicaragua.

The fierce debate over the president's contra aid request sparked a vigorous lobbying effort by the Reagan administration and its supporters. Calling the contras "the moral equal of our Founding Fathers,"[16] President Reagan kicked off his 1985 contra aid campaign with a speech to 180 Central Americans visiting Washington to lobby on behalf of the contras. This address, arranged by a special five-member Central America unit of the White House Office of Public Liaison, was but one part of an ongoing administration effort to gain public support for the president's policy. From May 1983 to early 1985, the committee had put on 96 seminars and arranged 225 speeches in 75 cities backing the administration's support for the contras.[17]

The administration's campaign blitz was stepped up in the spring of 1985 by mobilizing the support of conservative groups concerned about Central America. These organizations encouraged support for the contras by bringing "freedom fighters" to Washington. "Receiving substantial press attention, the contra fighters and Sandinista victims told their stories in meetings with Members of Congress and staff, and at various events, including a $250-$500 a plate dinner," attended by the president and sponsored by the Nicaraguan Refugee Fund.[18]

The conservative groups also enlisted a variety of other tactics. The American Conservative Union sent out 100,000 pieces of mail to solicit public support for contra aid and escorted Nicaraguan refugees around Capitol Hill to persuade undecided members to vote with the president. Citizens for Reagan spearheaded the administration's lobbying campaign by mobilizing 100,000 members nationwide to contact about seventy-five members of Congress considered to be "fence sitters" with letters, postcards, and phone calls. Not to be outdone, the conservative group Center for Inter-American Security (CIS) aired a half-hour TV documentary entitled "Central America Before It's Too Late." The film depicted Nicaragua as a Soviet stooge bent on subverting its democratic neighbors.[19]

The administration's vigorous lobbying effort was not unchallenged in its campaign to win the hearts and minds of the Congress or the American people. Opposition to contra aid was widespread. Opponents of the aid request engaged in an all-out blitz to block the proposal. Congress began its official policy debate in mid-April amidst tremendous fanfare and media attention:

Congress this week begins a Nicaragua policy extravaganza—a high-stakes battle over aid to "contra" rebels that will combine deadly purpose with pin stripes and clown acts.

. . . The pageantry involves computers and postcards, sit-ins and videotapes, clown shows and photos of bloody corpses, Nobel laureates and Hollywood actors. Mountains of paper, thousands of speeches and probably millions of telephone calls are involved, as well as a technique of direct contact with members of Congress.[20]

Churches and religious organizations formed the backbone of the domestic opposition to Reagan's Nicaraguan policy. They defined the contra aid program as immoral, illegal, and largely ineffective. Those opposing contra aid seldom refuted the undemocratic nature of the Sandinista regime. Instead, they sought to focus the debate on the character and deficiencies of the rebel forces and on their human rights abuses. The National Conference of Catholic Bishops, the National Council of Churches, and Witness for Peace were primarily responsible for organizing the grass-roots religious opposition to contra aid. They employed tactics similar to those of their opponents, including TV documentaries, letter-writing campaigns, direct lobbying on Capitol Hill, and public demonstrations. Witness for Peace engaged in the controversial effort of arranging for more than 1,200 clerical and lay leaders to visit the war zones in Nicaragua.[21]

Human rights groups joined the churches in opposing contra aid. Three separate human rights organizations accused the contras of widespread abuses. Americas Watch Committee released a strategically timed, 98-page report "charging the contras with killing unarmed soldiers, kidnapping women and children to Honduras and selectively murdering civilians." Two days later, the Washington Office on Latin America published a similar 141-page report and the International Human Rights Law Group echoed the abuse charges as well.[22] The influential Americas Watch report, titled "Violations of the Laws of War by Both Sides in Nicaragua, 1981-1985," was circulated widely on Capitol Hill and its findings reported in the press.[23] Contra supporters attacked the credibility of the reports with Elliott Abrams, assistant secretary of state for human rights, charging that the Washington Office on Latin America was "bought and paid for by the government of Nicaragua."[24]

Congressional hearings reviewing President Reagan's request for new contra aid began in the spring of 1985 and continued throughout

1986. These official forums brought together the many discordant voices concerned with the aid request and produced contrasting pictures of the Nicaraguan situation. Two key questions dominated the debate: Who are the contras? and Do they participate in widespread human rights abuses? While other issues emerged, these two concerns monopolized the testimony. According to Representative Gerry Studds, the war of words that ensued over these questions transformed the debate "into a wonderfully simple world of heroes and villains."[25]

Archbishop James A. Hickey's congressional testimony summarized poignantly the nature of the debate about the contras:

> Radically different perspectives on the Contras exist. Some see them primarily as fighters for the ideals of the Nicaraguan revolution now coopted by the Sandinistas. Some see them chiefly as holdovers from the Somoza regime seeking to regain power. Some in political opposition to the Nicaraguan Government see the Contras as providing a threat which deflects government attention from other political opponents.[26]

Whereas the Reagan administration preferred to depict the contras as "freedom fighters" and "democratic resistance forces," others saw them differently. Representative Ted Weiss put it bluntly: "The Contras used to be freedom fighters, now you call them resistance forces. They are, in fact, counterrevolutionaries."[27]

Critics of the contras tried to discredit the administration's claims with allegations that former Somoza officers comprised the bulk of the rebel forces' leadership. Representative Peter Kostmayer joined the issue early on:

> The fact is that of the military command [of the FDN], of the most important key people, the overwhelming majority are former Somoza National Guardsmen, and the administration comes here time and time again and tells us that 2 percent of the Contras were associated with the Somoza regime. . . . The administration very well knows that the overwhelming portion of the military leadership are associated with the former Somoza National Guardsmen.[28]

Representative John McCain's exchange with former CIA deputy director Ray Cline presented a different perspective:

> **McCain:** It seems a bit ludicrous to me to assume that the make-up of the freedom fighters or Contras is a bunch of ex-Somocistas.

Now, I would like to ask you, what is your knowledge of the make up of the so-called Contra movement as far as the individuals who not only compose that leadership but the rank and file?

Mr. Cline: I think the most prominent leaders to the best of my knowledge are, in fact, ex-Sandinistas who became disillusioned with the totalitarian turn of the present Sandinista Government.

There are indeed some former Somocista officers and enlisted men in the Contra force. There are many ex-Somocistas in the Sandinista armed forces, too.

Nicaragua is full of people who worked for Somoza. So this is not a very damaging charge in my view. The leadership and the policy of the Contra movement, it seems to me, very clear from the public record is not conditioned in any way by their previous participation in the Somoza regime.[29]

In response to allegations that the CIA "created" the rebel forces, including McGeorge Bundy's charge that the contras were "CIA-backed, CIA paid-for, CIA-managed," Jeane Kirkpatrick offered the following retort:

I should like to begin by noting a bit about who the Contras are. And I should like to say that I regard it as profoundly offensive to them to describe them as "bought and paid for by the CIA," "forces open to purchase by the CIA," "instruments," if you will, "of American intelligence agencies," and so forth.

. . . I think it is clear to anyone who knows the leadership of the democratic resistance forces in Nicaragua—that of the Nicaraguan resistance forces in and out of Nicaragua, that they are overwhelmingly committed democrats who are fighting for democracy and liberalization in exactly the same way that they did against Somoza; and to exactly the same ends that they did against Somoza. They exist. They did not come into existence because the CIA attempted to bring them into existence.[30]

The second controversy surrounding the contra aid proposal focused on alleged human rights abuses. Americas Watch circulated its report on Nicaraguan human rights violations in early March 1985. Aryeh Neier, vice chairman of Americas Watch, admitted that the report's release was strategically timed to influence Congress as it began debate on the contra aid issue.[31] Neier summarized the report's principal findings in congressional testimony. He acknowledged that both sides had participated in gross violations of human rights; however, Neier argued that the Sandinista regime was improving its performance while the contras were not. In his testimony, he focused on contra atrocities:

> We found that the Contras had attacked civilians both selectively and indiscriminately, that they have tortured and mutilated prisoners, that they have murdered those placed *hors de combat* by their wounds, they have taken hostages and committed outrages against personal dignity. Moreover, we believe that the role of the United States in acting as the vigorous public relations advocate of the Contras on top of the earlier role in organizing, supplying, training, financing the Contras and publishing the CIA manual soliciting such abuses by the Contras makes the United States significantly responsible for the systematic abuses that were committed by the Contras.[32]

Congressman Robert Lagomarsino, who had just returned from a field trip to Nicaragua, joined administration officials in questioning the accuracy of the Americas Watch report. Before the House Subcommittee on Western Hemisphere Affairs, Lagomarsino suggested that Americas Watch had not spent sufficient time in Nicaragua and that it had refused to examine documentation of Sandinista rights abuses. He concluded with the criticism that "their motive was not to do an investigation but that they already had a predetermined objective."[33]

Representative John McCain lamented the contras' critics refusal to distinguish the differing nature of contra and Sandinista abuses.

> There is a great deal of difference between the atrocities, between those committed by the Sandinistas and the FDN. . . . One is a calculated, organized, orchestrated government action such as the treatment of the Miskito Indians, such as the stripping of a priest and driving him down the street naked, such as the repression of the freedom of the press, and all of the other typical Marxist-Leninist oppression, repression, and atrocities that have taken place.
>
> I am sorry that the gentleman . . . does not recognize the difference between organized repression and atrocities, and those of isolated incidents which are, as he mentioned, a natural outcropping of warfare.[34]

Nevertheless, eyewitness testimony by Maryknoll Sister Nancy Donovan conveyed a different portrait of contra abuses. Sister Donovan, who was personally kidnapped by the rebels, detailed for Congress the way in which the contras "indiscriminately attacked civilian populations and . . . used terror tactics of kidnapping, torturing, raping, and killing."[35]

Despite the numerous forces opposed to the president's Nicaraguan policy and the concerns about human rights abuses, Reagan achieved a partial victory in 1985 by winning congressional approval for $27 million in non-lethal aid. When the debate was joined again in 1986, after further opposition had mounted, President Reagan beat the odds and secured $100 million in military and non-lethal aid. At that time, Congress also lifted the prohibition on CIA participation in the contra aid program. His vigorous propaganda and lobbying campaign paid great short-term dividends to the contras.

Nevertheless, as revelations of the secret Iran-contra deal were disclosed in late 1986, Reagan lost congressional support for continued military aid. The increasingly tarnished image of the contras as "freedom fighters," alongside continued concerns about illegal arms transfers, caused the administration and Congress to back away from the issue in 1988.[36] The confluence of influences on Capitol Hill had a strong but temporary effect, ultimately overtaken by the election of Violeta Chamorro as president on February 25, 1990.

Sanctions against South Africa

In the mid-1980s, apartheid in South Africa became the focus of an intense American foreign policy debate once more centered in the Congress. Despite official condemnation of the South African government's racial policies, the United States had remained a major trading partner and diplomatic friend of Pretoria's white minority government. The Reagan administration, through its policy of "constructive engagement," continued this rather conciliatory approach. President Reagan argued that through "quiet diplomacy" and sustained contact the white regime could most effectively be persuaded to embrace substantive reforms and power sharing measures. However, by the fall of 1984, there emerged a growing chorus of criticism of constructive engagement and a vigorous public outcry for punitive action against the country. The end result, almost two years later, was the passage over a presidential veto of the 1986 Comprehensive Anti-Apartheid Act. This legislation for the first time imposed substantive economic sanctions on the South African

Government. Moreover, it marked the first congressional override of a presidential veto on a foreign policy issue since the passage of the 1973 War Powers Resolution.[37]

The policy reversal affected by this congressional override illustrates the power of lobbies, advocacy groups, and influential private citizens to shape the course and outcome of the legislative process. The South African policy debate also demonstrates the capacity congressional leaders themselves possess to lobby and mobilize their fellow legislators.

A variety of factors and forces inspired the mounting public concern. Events in South Africa itself—escalating violence, intensified repression by the white minority government through widespread detentions, deaths, and deportations to "homelands," and a generally hostile posture to significant reform—were primarily responsible for raising the American public's consciousness about the brutal nature of the apartheid regime.[38] Media attention to the violence in South Africa increased dramatically in 1984. On an almost nightly basis, news broadcasts brought the repression and turmoil into America's living rooms. A 1985 *New York Times* editorial highlighted the extent to which the average American citizen was bombarded with disturbing images from South Africa:

> In the last nine months South Africa has penetrated the American consciousness with a breadth that it rarely has had during a quarter-century of racial strife in that troubled country. Significantly, this turnabout has coincided with sustained and vivid coverage of South Africa by American television.
>
> Funerals and riots, overturned cars aflame and armored vehicles rolling through black townships have all become familiar images. . . . Calls for disinvestment and sanctions have sounded with wider and more forceful emphasis in recent months from campuses to Congress.
>
> . . . With a few exceptions—a week of specials on ABC's Nightline, a series by Tom Brokaw on NBC and another by Charlayne Hunter-Gault on PBS—the coverage has centered on turbulence in South Africa's black townships. Of 39 ABC reports from South Africa between Aug. 2 and Sept. 30, for example, 14 dealt wholly or in part with funerals in the black townships.[39]

However, in addition to greater television coverage, there were other events that converged to heighten public awareness and concern about the deteriorating situation in South Africa. On November 21, 1984, three influential black leaders, Randall Robinson, executive director of TransAfrica, Walter Fauntroy, the District of Columbia's delegate to Congress, and Mary Frances Berry, a member of the U.S. Commission on Civil Rights, began daily picketing outside the South African embassy in Washington. All three were arrested for their refusal to abandon the sit-in. The leaders quickly established the Free South Africa Movement (FSAM) in an effort to bring greater American public attention and congressional response to the situation in South Africa. The goals of their largely grass-roots organization were threefold: to win the release of black leaders imprisoned in South Africa; to apply public pressure for direct negotiations between black leaders and the South African government; and to change American policy from constructive engagement to a more punitive posture designed to dismantle apartheid.[40]

Beyond question, the Free South Africa Movement and Robinson's TransAfrica lobbying group were the all-important agents of change ultimately responsible for altering Washington's South African policy. The daily pickets of the South African embassy continued without interruption for more than a year. In fact, the protests quickly spread to other cities and campuses across the country. Protesters picketed South African consulates and corporations and banks with investments in South Africa. By mid-July 1985, "2,900 people had been arrested in Washington and more than 4,000 at demonstrations at 26 other cities or college campuses." Twenty-two members of Congress, a number of mayors, and union and religious leaders were also arrested in public protests.[41]

The explosion of public concern about the violence in South Africa and growing criticism of the constructive engagement policy inspired renewed congressional resolve to impose economic sanctions against Pretoria. The widespread outcry against apartheid elicited not only liberal criticism of the president's policy, but conservative Republican opposition as well. On December 4, 1984, two Republican senators, Richard Lugar, newly appointed chairman of the Senate Foreign Relations Committee, and Nancy Kassebaum, sent a public letter to President Reagan urging him to take a stronger stand against apartheid.[42] The following day, 35 conservative Members of Congress handed a threatening letter to South Africa's ambassador to Washington. The letter stated that the signatories would support economic sanctions against Pretoria if the government did not undertake a greater effort to protect the civil rights of the black majority.[43] Domestic political concerns influenced these actions. Conservative Republicans, especially in the South, were sensitive to the degree to which their African American constituencies viewed the dismantling of apartheid as an extension of their own civil rights efforts.

From January 1985 until October 1986, Congress held seventeen hearings, many over the course of several days, to consider sanctions legislation. These hearings involved four full committees, one select committee, and six subcommittees of the House and Senate. Assistant Secretary for African Affairs Chester Crocker, who was both the architect and defender of the administration's constructive engagement policy, testified at a number of the hearings. Randall Robinson of TransAfrica was also a frequently heard witness.

Although many individuals testified, a large portion of the "witness docket" was reserved for those legislators eager to go on the record in opposition to constructive engagement and in support of economic sanctions. Many congressional leaders saw the hearings as an opportunity to appeal to their own black constituencies. Some observers claimed that Senator Edward Kennedy's widely publicized trip to South Africa in January 1985 was largely motivated by domestic political considerations.[44]

By the time the hearings began in early 1985, the criticism of constructive engagement and the demand for punitive measures had become so widespread, especially within the Congress, that the ensuing debate focused not so much on whether there would be legislation, but rather on what *form* it should take. Numerous voices repudiated the "quiet diplomacy" of the Reagan administration, arguing that subtle American pressure had failed to produce significant reforms. Senator Kennedy was an outspoken critic:

> I would like to address the arguments of some apologists for the South African government that there has in fact been change inside South Africa, and that the white leadership of that country is committed to fundamental reform. My experience in South Africa suggests otherwise. The conditions of life for most black people in South Africa are appalling and have become worse, not better, in recent years, and the system of apartheid has become more pervasive and pernicious than ever before.[45]

Randall Robinson went even further in denouncing the United States as "a major part of making apartheid possible."[46] In congressional testimony he offered a blunt indictment of Reagan's policies:

> The unending brutality of [the South African] government and
> the untold suffering of the black majority described here daily, bear
> incontrovertible witness that by placing our economic, diplomatic,
> and intelligence resources at the disposal of the Government of South
> Africa, and by couching that support in the guise of "quiet diplomacy"
> we encourage and accommodate what is essentially a minority-rule
> slave economy in South Africa. In response to current U.S. policy
> there have been dramatic increases in government forced removals to
> barren "homelands," police killings of black South Africans, bannings
> and detentions of peaceful protesters without judicial process, pass
> law arrests, and regional destabilization efforts.[47]

Administration officials continued to suggest that the reform process was
moving forward. Assistant Secretary Crocker repeatedly voiced this
conviction:

> It is indisputably true that changes that have occurred in South
> Africa fall far short of meeting the aspirations of the majority of the
> country's population, as well as our own standards in this country. But
> it is equally true that over the past 4 years, fundamental pillars of the
> apartheid system have eroded. The South African government has
> recognized the rights of at least some of those outside the white
> community to exercise political power at the center, by the inclusion
> of Asians and coloreds in the government. It has recognized and must
> soon act upon the principle that denying citizenship to South Africa's
> blacks is as unworkable as it is ludicrous. . . . It has moved increasingly
> to recognize that blacks are a central and permanent feature of the
> urban, industrial economy. As a consequence, we have seen important
> movement on urban residency and property rights, as well as trade
> union rights for blacks. Such moves implicitly recognize that it is
> utterly unworkable to govern South Africa on the basis of laws that
> ignore these realities.[48]

Crocker's testimony also refuted those critics who described the Reagan
administration's relationship with South Africa as a "cozy rapprochement." He called such characterizations a "severe distortion of reality."[49]

Congressional debate soon came to focus on whether or not sanctions and mandatory divestment legislation would adversely affect blacks
in South Africa. Supporters of sanctions claimed that their proposals had

widespread black support. Opponents, including administration officials and corporate leaders, suggested otherwise.

Representative Howard Wolpe, chairman of the House Foreign
Affairs Subcommittee on Africa, maintained that a majority of blacks
supported sanctions and divestment.

> Almost all of those whom blacks within South Africa regard as
> authentic political leaders from the ANC [African National Congress]
> to Bishop [Desmond] Tutu, the principal labor federations, the Na-
> tional Education Crisis Committee, patrons of the United Democratic
> Front, are all calling for tougher Western economic sanctions includ-
> ing general disinvestment. Recent polls within South Africa among
> urban blacks have indicated upwards of 70 percent of blacks support-
> ing disinvestment.[50]

The administration, through Chester Crocker, presented a different
perspective on black attitudes:

> There is no black view in South Africa about economic sanctions
> and disinvestment. We follow this very, very closely. . . . But we have
> very clear evidence of a wide diversity of views. A wide range of results
> from the polls that we have seen. We are aware that there are some in
> the trade union movement who have called for sanctions, but some
> have said disinvestment ought not to mean that the plant and the jobs
> go. . . . We have seen many results indicating that black workers don't
> want to see sanctions if it means they lose their jobs.[51]

Despite the contrasting depictions of the course of reform or the
black South African community's attitudes toward sanctions, by 1985 it
was clear that some type of punitive legislation would be endorsed by
Congress. A confluence of forces guaranteed it—the ongoing political
violence in South Africa, sustained American public concern, and the
determination of the aggressive lobbying campaign waged by FSAM in
the corridors of Congress.

In the summer of 1985 the House and Senate approved rather
extensive sanctions legislation. However, in an effort to thwart the bill's
passage and in response to Republican appeals, President Reagan issued
a surprising, last-minute executive order imposing more limited sanctions on South Africa. Nevertheless, the issue refused to die. The South
African government's June 1986 declaration of a state of emergency and
renewed violence once more intensified the demand for more stringent

measures against Pretoria. This time President Reagan was unsuccessful in blocking tougher sanctions. In early October 1986, the Senate voted with the House to override a presidential veto and adopt the 1986 Comprehensive Anti-Apartheid Act. This action signaled a final defeat for the policy of constructive engagement.

Although the Congress was responsible for crafting the actual sanctions legislation and for defying vigorous presidential opposition, it was never truly the "leader" in shaping public opinion on South Africa. Rather, this role was played by the FSAM and TransAfrica (with the help of other religious and trade union organizations). Their national campaign provided the necessary catalyst for galvanizing public support, harnessing sustained media attention, and ultimately shaping the course of congressional debate. Perhaps Congressman Don Edwards was not far off the mark when he suggested in December 1984 that Randall Robinson was "well on the way to becoming known as 'the most effective foreign policy catalyst in recent history.'"[52] The transformation of American policy toward South Africa in 1985-86 demonstrates the potential for activists to set the political agenda and to use the legislative process as a forum to advance their ideas.

Angola

The previous chapter's discussion of lobbies described how UNITA leader Jonas Savimbi used public and political pressure to create the image of a "freedom fighter" worthy of American support. The creation and selling of Savimbi's image through the high-priced public relations blitz undertaken in the mid-1980s by the Black, Manafort, and Stone lobbying firm was only part of the story. The creation of an image alone was not enough to achieve the political objectives of Savimbi and his supporters. The ultimate effectiveness of this effort depended on congressional action. This case study shows how that pressure was translated into legislative action.

The question of U.S. support for Savimbi in Angola's civil war was on the congressional agenda for more than a decade. Congress first addressed the Angolan situation in the aftermath of the 1974 Portuguese withdrawal. At that time, congressional hearings were initiated to explore the Ford administration's request for aid to groups opposing the Marxist MPLA government in Luanda. However, the adoption of the Clark amendment in 1975, which required prior congressional approval for any military assistance to rebel factions, was designed to block assistance to the Angolan resistance. This legislation effectively derailed any further attempt by President Ford or his successor to aid the Angolan rebels. The issue of offering U.S. aid to UNITA was not seriously reconsidered until the Reagan administration.

The significance of the Angolan issue in the U.S. is illustrated by the fact that from 1975 until 1992 Congress held at least twenty hearings to debate American policy. These hearings involved two full committees, two select committees, and four subcommittees.[53] These extensive proceedings demonstrate not only the importance attached to the Angolan conflict as a part of the Cold War, but also the ability of several groups and external events to create a persuasive image of Savimbi as an effective American ally.

To varying degrees, UNITA rebels had impressed three American administrations, both Republican and Democratic. Over time, diverse pockets of Washington's policy-making elite had come to perceive Savimbi as the most effective candidate for blocking Soviet-Cuban designs in southern Africa. Moreover, UNITA's surprising ability to block major MPLA offensives further established it as a viable option in Angolan politics.

Ronald Reagan's wholehearted embrace of Jonas Savimbi strengthened his appeal, especially among conservatives. Reagan's ideological commitment to aiding anti-communist rebels worldwide emboldened the image of Savimbi as another "freedom fighter" worthy of U.S. aid. In his 1986 State of the Union address, Reagan highlighted his administration's commitment to assisting freedom fighters everywhere, specifically mentioning Angola.

Reagan's rhetoric undoubtedly influenced congressional sentiment that eventually came to perceive Savimbi as a necessary and effective bulwark to communist encroachments in Africa. In July 1985, Congress voted to repeal the Clark amendment, which had stood since 1976 as an obstacle to American assistance to UNITA. The Clark repeal was perceived by many, including the Angolans and Congress, as a signal of heartfelt congressional interest in extending aid to Savimbi.

The public dimension of the debate over Angola became more focused after the Clark amendment's repeal, centering on legislative proposals to aid UNITA. The first of these, sponsored by UNITA supporters from both parties, proposed $27 million in nonlethal, open assistance.[54] At the same time, the administration revealed its intention to undertake a covert assistance program for Savimbi's forces.[55] The debate then turned not on whether to aid UNITA, but on what *type* of aid should be given—lethal or humanitarian—and most importantly, *how* it should be given—covertly or openly.

The administration's strategy was two-pronged. It quickly initiated a covert assistance program to Savimbi in late 1985 and stepped up its efforts to harness bipartisan congressional support for it. This was accompanied by official steps to reinforce Savimbi's image as a reliable ally and courageous "freedom fighter," including an invitation to the Angolan leader to visit the White House in January 1986. The administration relied upon extensive media coverage and high-profile meetings between Savimbi, Reagan, and other high-ranking administration officials to communicate publicly its support for UNITA's efforts. The purpose was to transform the image of Savimbi "the guerrilla fighter" into one of Savimbi "the statesman and Angolan democrat," and to reinforce efforts to win support in Congress.

Other influential public addresses and interviews were sponsored by leading conservative groups including the Heritage Foundation, the American Enterprise Institute, and the American Conservative Union. During his Washington visit, other more moderate and nonpartisan groups also hosted events in Savimbi's honor. These included an address at the National Press Club, an interview published in the journal *Foreign Policy*, a dinner hosted by the AFL-CIO, and a meeting convened by the Center for Strategic and International Studies.[56]

The Reagan administration's efforts met with some resistance on Capitol Hill. This opposition came from different corners and for widely divergent reasons. Conservatives were interested in offering both humanitarian and military aid to UNITA openly. Congressman Jack Kemp led the conservative charge in favor of open assistance. According to Secretary of State George Shultz, conservatives were eager to go on record in support of freedom fighters and saw the issue of aid to Savimbi as a means by which to embarrass and expose those who appeared "soft" on communism.[57]

Congressman Lee Hamilton was among those who questioned the wisdom of covert military assistance to UNITA that was not publicly acknowledged and debated. As chairman of the House Select Committee on Intelligence, he tried unsuccessfully to hold up assistance until an open disclosure and debate could take place.[58] Congressional opponents also attacked UNITA for its close ties and seeming reliance on South

Africa. Senator Claiborne Pell summarized this sentiment succinctly in congressional debate: "Given UNITA's ties with South Africa, championing UNITA's cause would certainly undermine our antiapartheid efforts and deal a serious blow to our relations with black African nations."[59] Randall Robinson was more blunt in his testimony before the House Foreign Affairs subcommittee on Africa:

> TransAfrica believes strongly that any United States aid to UNITA would not only alienate the peoples of Angola, southern Africa, and the rest of the African continent, but more importantly will adversely affect America's image, interest, and stated objectives in the area. The many reasons for these—for this include the following:
>
> First, and most important, aid to UNITA is aid to South Africa. We must understand clearly that these current attempts to shore up UNITA are merely the latest effort to weaken our opposition to apartheid. UNITA and the current war in Angola are very much the creations of the apartheid government in South Africa. But for Pretoria's advice, military supplies and intelligence, South African officers, troops, and equipment, UNITA would cease to be a credible threat. . . . For the United States to aid UNITA, therefore, would be to support apartheid militarily and to join in Pretoria's policy of external aggression and destabilization as a strategy of protecting apartheid.[60]

Critics also charged that aid to Savimbi would undermine the administration's own diplomacy aimed at securing a Cuban withdrawal from Angola and achieving Namibian independence from South Africa. In time, much of the debate came to focus on when and why the Cubans were involved in Angola. While conservatives argued it was part of a global, Soviet-inspired Marxist strategy, opponents of UNITA aid maintained that South Africa's presence dictated continued Cuban involvement. Gerald Bender, an Angolan specialist from the University of Southern California, was a frequent witness at many of the hearings from 1975 until 1992 addressing the Angolan situation. His academic analysis led him to conclude that South Africa's incursions into Angolan territory were responsible for the Soviet-Cuban involvement in the country. Bender made this argument repeatedly in congressional testimony:

> It is the South African regime's aggressive military strikes against its neighbors that are primarily responsible [f]or the Soviet and Cuban presence in the region.

The CIA accurately predicted in 1975—when less [than] 1,000 Cubans were in Angola—that the entry of South African troops would result in a 10 to 15 fold increase in the number of Cuban combat troops.

Moreover, the Washington-Pretoria axis, far more than any other factor, resulted in legitimizing the presence of thousands of Cuban troops in southern Africa.[61]

Assistant Secretary of State Chester Crocker defended the administration's strategy in southern Africa. His efforts to win congressional support for aid to Savimbi were undertaken at precisely the time he was called upon to defend the administration's policy of constructive engagement. The aid campaign also was concurrent with the domestic push for economic sanctions against South Africa. Crocker attempted to convince congressional opponents that aid to UNITA would strengthen the administration's diplomatic leverage at the negotiating table:

Some may perceive that the recent reception Savimbi received here signals a change in U.S. policy. It does not. Our strategy recognizes that the scene on the ground in Angola has changed, largely owing to Soviet actions, and that our ability to respond diplomatically and in other ways has been measurably increased by the repeal of the Clark amendment, effective October 1, 1985. I want, however, to categorically state here that the basis and the goals of our policy remain unchanged: We seek a negotiated solution that will bring independence to Namibia and the withdrawal of Cuban forces from Angola.[62]

Crocker also presented a far different view of the Cuban and Soviet involvement in Angola:

We have seen so much evidence of it ourselves, that the Cubans are there because of a certain temporary requirement, but that they are not loved, that they live high off the land, that they do not, in fact, engage in some of the fighting that one might have expected them to. They are not seeking to increase their own body count. As I said, they do pretty well and they live pretty well in a very, very poor country.

The same applies, to an extent, to the Soviet Union, which has helped to badly damage Angola's ocean fisheries and seems to be living off the relationship.[63]

Conservative groups and activists emphasized the menacing nature of Soviet designs in Angola and trumpeted the image of Savimbi as a committed democrat, a reliable ally and an effective counterweight to Marxist ambitions in Angola. Thomas Henriksen, senior research fellow at the Hoover Institution, conveyed this sentiment in congressional testimony:

> In my opinion, the United States, wherever possible, must provide moral and material support to peoples struggling against Communist-aided governments. Otherwise, in the case of Angola, we as a nation accept a Soviet dominated and a Communist state eventually analogous to that which is present in Eastern Europe.
>
> For another reason, UNITA has long formed and will continue to form an important factor in Angolan politics. UNITA deserves to be strengthened on account of its hostility to the USSR and Cuba, both open and avowed opponents of the United States.
>
> For another reason, the continued viability of UNITA is the best guarantee that the MPLA will not have the resources to make mischief in the states bordering Angola.
>
> . . . For another reason, for support for UNITA, the downfall of the MPLA will provide the greatest single factor toward the promotion of independence in Namibia from South African control. . . . The removal of a powerfully backed Soviet client in Angola will remove South African justification for continued occupation of Namibia.[64]

The Cuban American National Foundation, represented by Jose Sorzano, also spoke out in favor of aid to UNITA. It sought to highlight Savimbi's credentials as an effective "freedom fighter" and legitimate Angolan leader:

> In opposition to the MPLA, Dr. Jonas Savimbi over the last decade has forged UNITA, a grass roots nationalistic organization which has established effective government in the area it already controls and has waged an increasingly successful arms struggle against the Cuban and Soviet backed MPLA.
>
> UNITA's estimated 4,000 armed men fully control about half of Angola's territory and operate extensively over an additional 20 percent of the territory. And, just a few weeks ago, before the start of the rainy season, defeated a powerful MPLA offensive reportedly spearheaded by Cuban and Soviet officers.
>
> . . . while it is true that Dr. Savimbi has received assistance from Pretoria, it is equally true that UNITA has also received material

support from several other countries, including black African nations. As a matter of fact, I believe the proposed American assistance to Savimbi will lessen his relationship with neighboring South Africa.

. . . nobody can reasonably accuse Savimbi of racism or of supporting apartheid. On the contrary, Savimbi has fashioned an indigenous fighting force that is struggling against the presence of foreign troops in Angolan soil. It is precisely Savimbi's adversaries who, in a style reminiscent of past colonial times, are utilizing white troops, foreign troops to kill black Angolans.[65]

The debate ended and the intense effort to win the battle in Congress paid off when the House of Representatives voted in September 1986 to extend congressional support for the $15 million aid operation.[66] In time, this amount was increased to $40 million.[67] A significant foreign policy issue once more had been decided in the arena of Congress where private and official efforts converged.

The Twenty-First Century

Will the public dimension of U.S. foreign policy that has existed through the last half of the twentieth century continue into the twenty-first?

There can be little doubt that the interplay of public expression and its pressure on policy making in the last fifty years has had an impact. It is more difficult to argue that the activities of the various citizen institutions fundamentally altered the directions of U.S. diplomacy. The Soviet Union would have been seen as threatening after the Korean War and the takeovers in Eastern Europe without the Captive Nation lobbies. The U.S. would have been unlikely to stand by and see Israel destroyed whether AIPAC existed or not.

In areas where the national interest was less clear, however, public pressures challenged official credibility and restrained government action. Vietnam remains the prime example. Well-organized groups were able to circumvent commitments to international organizations as did the Rhodesian lobby on chrome. Other lobbies could affect significant allied relationships as the Greek lobby did with Turkey. Washington's international credibility suffered from the success of such pressures.

Narrow interest groups were only part of the picture. A wider and less easily defined political and ideological interaction in Washington was creating images and perceptions—often wrong and oversimplified—

that affected national opinion and distorted debate: Carter was a weak president and his administration a disaster; Reagan won the Cold War and reduced spending. Walter Wriston, former chairman of Citicorp, writing in the *Wall Street Journal,* addresses this phenomenon and the failure of the press to challenge it:

> According to the surveys, most Americans get the bulk of their news from television, and day after day the newscasters relay the latest Washington Beltway wisdom, which often is the "newspeak" that George Orwell wrote about.
>
> Examples abound: We hear over and over that President Reagan made deep cuts in social spending. But any cub reporter could easily determine that the spending on almost all social programs was higher when President Reagan left office than when he was first inaugurated. According to the official "Historical Tables, Budget of the United States, 1990," non-defense spending in 1980 was $456,925,000 and grew to an estimated $838,775,000 in 1989. This huge growth in non-defense spending is described on the evening news as a "deep cut."[1]

The national debate during the past five decades has also been clouded by an imprecise definition of the national interest. Once discussion moved away from a broad consensus on the Soviet threat, the divisions began. Helping the resistance in Afghanistan was broadly supported; the Soviets were directly involved. Reagan could not make an equally forceful argument on the national interest involved in Nicaragua. Not only was the Soviet role there less clear, but the president's efforts also encountered strong inhibitions against involvement in Central America.

Experience with public pressure during this period suggests that it can be successful where a dedicated, well-organized group takes the lead, a definable constituency exists, a favorable predisposition is present in the body politic, and no substantial opposition is encountered. Successes on behalf of Israel are one illustration; so are actions in support of the embargo on Cuba.

In the last decade of the century, the situation has begun to change. With the collapse of the Soviet Union, and despite the continued suspicion of Russia among conservatives, many of the international issues that sparked past ideological efforts have faded. National security is less bound up with the support of peripheral nations and questionable rulers. The nation has become indifferent to the fate of movements in

Afghanistan, Angola, and Cambodia that once were "allies." Steps toward the resolution of the Israeli-Palestinian issue and apartheid in South Africa have reduced the intensity of interest in two problems that bred particularly strong and expensive lobbying activities.

The nation has moved back to a pre-1939 mood of non-involvement. The world will be chaotic, but except for nearby areas such as Haiti and humanitarian disasters that occasionally capture the TV audience, Americans are turning to domestic concerns. Gun control at home is taking over from arms control abroad. Interests such as oil will remain significant, but future access may be challenged as much by political change in producing countries as by external threats. Although future challenges from the Eurasian land mass cannot be excluded, the Gulf War may represent the last great American military adventure.

The international political and strategic concerns that preoccupy Washington in 1996 still include putting the final touches on Middle East peace and establishing a satisfactory relationship with Russia. But, beyond these, the priorities are becoming commercial and economic.

In the area of public expression, official statements are still central to the policy process. In the Clinton administration, the focus of such statements has shifted to the White House and to the president himself. This can change with future administrations, although the secretary of state will probably not again occupy the central position of an Acheson or a Kissinger. One problem remains. Although the mood of the country is one of non-involvement, presidents and their advisers are likely to continue to use the rhetoric of the superpower era. An often troubling gap will exist between the promises of Washington and the reality of the national response.

National security, combat, terrorism, intelligence, and diplomacy— issues that were at the heart of many of the deep differences between the information media and government—have become less contentious with the end of the Cold War. Internal disputes over foreign issues that resulted in the breakdown of official discipline and a multitude of leaks should diminish. Continuing challenges to official secrecy should further lessen the need for unauthorized disclosures.

Overall, coverage of foreign affairs will decline as economies become more stringent in the news media and public interest fades. Coverage of national security and diplomatic issues may be reduced as the United States becomes less central to many of the world's problems. Combat and terrorist acts involving Americans will be exceptions. Although formal peace may come in areas of conflict such as the Middle East and, perhaps, ultimately in Bosnia, fringe groups, resisting concessions, may continue isolated violent acts.

The traditional print press and TV networks are experiencing new problems. Public respect for the news organizations is low. The impact on newspapers and broadcasting of the "communications revolution" may be exaggerated, but competing and influential public dialogues that bypass the mainstream media and government have developed in radio and TV talk shows and computer networks. Political correctness and ethnic sensitivities have, further, placed new restraints on total freedom. Even talk of the need for controls on the free press can be heard.

The think tanks that survive will be those that adapt to a new agenda. The institutes dominated by personalities that built their institutional reputations on the Cold War will still find the support and audiences to caution about Russia and too rapid a decline in defense budgets. In general, domestic issues will take priority in research, conferences, and funding. A few dedicated institutes will concentrate on emerging transnational causes: environment, health, communications, trade. David Abshire at CSIS has been particularly adept at transforming the center's agenda. One of its major releases of 1994 was the *Consensus Report of the CSIS Working Group on Global HIV/AIDS*.[2] Issues of peace and democratization have captured the interest of other institutes, including the U.S. Institute of Peace. How long these subjects will remain central public issues, however, is questionable. Efforts to promote such subjects will face a general U.S. reluctance to be involved abroad, complexities of the problems, limitations of citizen involvement in diplomacy, and disillusionment with attempts at democracy, especially in Eastern Europe. Funding for all but the most conservative causes may be more difficult to obtain.

The concerns promoted by advocacy organizations have broad support. Each, however, will face ongoing challenges. Their influence on policy will depend on rallying effective allies in Congress and the public to overcome serious resistance to rapid progress. As the case of China has demonstrated, human rights intervention may be subordinate to trade interests. Arguments about the validity of scientific data, cost estimates, and nationalistic resistance in other lands will plague the promotion of a cleaner environment. The Cairo conference on population in 1994 demonstrated the deep ideological and religious differences that surround this issue and efforts to expand family planning programs.

Lobbies will not fade from the Washington scene, but the clients and objectives will change. With the drop in interest in foreign aid and resources in the United States, the desire of foreign countries to lobby for a portion of that pie will decline. The end of the Cold War means, also, the end of major battles for U.S. opinion by anti-communist surrogates. Costly major campaigns on behalf of personalities such as Jonas Savimbi or white South Africa are unlikely to be repeated. Peace has overtaken much of the need for pressure groups in the Middle East; the U.S. Jewish community is less united on how best to support Israel. African American concerns will focus less on Pretoria and more on the inner cities of America. Ethnic groups from Eastern Europe may find that the reality of the post-communist era is harsher than their dreams, and their active campaigning for U.S. support could diminish. In 1995 even the ardent Cuban lobby is finding itself torn over approaches to the problems of Fidel Castro's regime.

In the final analysis, the vitality of the public dimension, whether expressed in think tanks, advocacy groups, or lobbies, will depend on available resources, both human and financial. The active involvement of academic institutions in the study and teaching of international affairs will continue, but the interests of the graduates will change to reflect the problems and opportunities of an era different from the last half-century. Because scholarship is retrospective, interest in the Cold War era will remain strong, but students looking to their future will seek opportunities in domestic affairs, trade, and the transnational problems that dominate the new agenda. There will be fewer specialists in national security and more in commerce, communications, health, science, and the environment.

As money has determined much of the structure of the public dimension in the past, so it will in the future. Most experts expect a decline in individual giving for foreign affairs institutions and projects. Major donors, especially for conservative causes, are likely to give more to domestic issues and less to those related to national security and foreign policy. With the emphasis on reducing government expenditures, Congress will be less forthcoming in areas of overseas aid and foreign policy. Congress could also change the tax laws that encourage giving. The institutions that depended on government favors will suffer. Some major foundations will confront generational changes; the grandchildren and great-grandchildren of founders may have different ideas. In a period of intense commercial competition, corporations may see less justification for giving.

Washington will remain the hub of patterns of expression and pressure that are part of the American system. The interests and resources to mold policy, however, will reflect a very different world than that existing in 1950.

NOTES

1. The Legal Basis

1. See Spencer Sherman, "Pack Journalism, Japanese Style," *Columbia Journalism Review* (September–October 1990): 37-42.

2. *The Federalist No. LXXXIV,* Modern Library edition (New York: Random House, 1937), 560.

3. Frank Luther Mott, *Jefferson and the Press* (Baton Rouge, LA: Louisiana State University Press, 1943), 14.

4. See William L. Chenery, *Freedom of the Press* (New York: Harcourt, Brace, 1955), 50.

5. See details of case of Peter Zenger in Frank Luther Mott, *American Journalism* (New York: Macmillan, 1941), 31-38.

6. Ibid., 528.

7. Ibid., 529.

8. Ibid., 623-24. See also Anthony Lewis, *Make No Law* (New York: Random House, 1991), 69-70.

9. For further details, see Lewis, *Make No Law,* 70-72.

10. *Schenck vs. U.S.,* 249 U.S. 47 (1919).

11. *Abrams et al. vs. United States,* 250 U.S. 616 (1919).

12. *Abrams et al. vs. United States,* 250 U.S. 628 (1919).

13. For a further discussion, see Laurence H. Tribe, *American Constitutional Law,* 2nd ed. (Mineola, NY: Foundation Press, 1988), 840ff.

14. For the full story of this case, see Fred W. Friendly, *Minnesota Rag* (New York: Random House, 1981).

15. Lewis, *Make No Law,* 97.

16. Quoted in Lewis, ibid., 93-94.

17. Tribe, *American Constitutional Law,* 1041.

18. Quoted in Lewis, *Make No Law,* 141.

19. James Reston, *Deadline* (New York: Random House, 1991), 210.

20. Ibid., 325-326.

21. Ibid., 294.

22. See Peter Braestrup, *The Big Story: How the American Press and Television Reported and Interpreted Views of Tet 1968 in Vietnam and Washington,* abridged ed. (New Haven: Yale University Press, 1983).

23. James Boylan, "Declarations of Independence," *Columbia Journalism Review* (November–December 1986): 29-45.

24. 50 U.S.Code 431.

25. 5 U.S. Code 552, Section (a)(6)(A).

26. "A General Loses His Case," *Time,* February 4, 1985, 64-66.

27. "Absence of Malice," *Newsweek,* February 4, 1985, 56-58.

28. Ibid.

29. Quoted in Lewis, *Make No Law,* 216.

30. Don Kowet, *A Matter of Honor: General William Westmoreland vs. CBS* (New York: Macmillan, 1984).

31. Robert G. Kaiser, "If Westy Wins, You Lose," *Washington Post,* December 23, 1984, pp. B1, B2.

32. Based on Lewis, *Make No Law,* 216-217.

33. Ibid., 241.

34. *Media Law Reporter* (BNA), 15 (1988): 1369, 1390; (844 F2d 1057 [4th Cir. 1988]).

35. Potter Stewart, "Or of the Press," *Hastings Law Journal* 26 (1975): 631.

36. Lee H. Hamilton, "The Costs of Too Much Secrecy," *Washington Post,* April 13, 1992, p. A21.

2. Government Speaks

1. For a contrary view of the noon briefing, see Nicholas F. Benton, "More Nuisance Than News: State's Daily News Briefing," *Foreign Service Journal* (November 1989): 41-44.

2. Howard Kurtz, "At Briefing, No News Is Old News," *Washington Post,* February 17, 1993, p. A17.

3. Sidney Blumenthal, "On Wings of Bull," *New Republic,* July 13/20, 1992, 12+.

4. George P. Shultz, *Turmoil and Triumph: My Years as Secretary of State* (New York: Charles Scribner's Sons, 1993), 361.

5. Ibid., 362.

6. Elaine Sciolino, "In Diplomacy, Plain Talk Is Often Just Plain Wrong," *New York Times,* April 10, 1994, sec. IV, p. 6.

7. Conversation with author, May 1994.

8. Anthony Marro, "When the Government Tells Lies," *Columbia Journalism Review* (March–April 1985): 29-41. See also Remarks of Benjamin C. Bradlee at the Frank E. Gannett Lecture, Capital Hilton Hotel, Washington, DC, November 25, 1986; William Safire, "More Lying in State," *New York Times,* December 25, 1989, p. A31; Benjamin C. Bradlee, "America's Truth-Ache: Access, Manipulation and the Large and Small Lies of America's Presidents," *Washington Post,* November 17, 1991, p. C1.

9. Stephen Hess, *The Government/Press Connection,* appendix (Washington, DC: Brookings Institution, 1984), 121.

10. Jody Powell, *The Other Side of the Story* (New York: William Morrow, 1984), 233.

11. Jeremiah O'Leary, "Concern Grows Over a Marxist Power Seizure," *Washington Star,* June 9, 1979, p. A1.

12. David D. Newsom, "Scoops and Secrets," *Gannett Center Journal* (Fall 1989): 175-187.

13. George P. Shultz, *Turmoil and Triumph: My Years as Secretary of State* (New York: Charles Scribner's Sons, 1993), 598.

14. *Public Papers of the Presidents of the United States: Ronald Reagan, 1981* (Washington, DC: U.S. Government Printing Office, 1982), 956.

15. *Public Papers of the Presidents of the United States: Ronald Reagan, 1983,* vol. I (Washington, DC: U.S. Government Printing Office, 1984), 359-364.

16. David Korn, *Assassination in Khartoum* (Bloomington: Indiana University Press, 1993), 150.

17. Transcript, MacNeil-Lehrer News Hour, Wednesday, March 24, 1993 (New York: WNET, Show #4591), p. 13.

18. Bernard Roshco,"When Policy Fails: How the Buck Was Passed When Kuwait Was Invaded," Discussion Paper D-15, Joan Shorenstein Barone Center, John F. Kennedy School of Government, Harvard University, December 1992.

19. Raymond Garthoff, *Reflections on the Cuban Missile Crisis,* rev. ed. (Washington, DC: Brookings Institution, 1989), 7.

20. "Joint Resolution Expressing the Determination of the United States with Respect to Cuba," *Department of State Bulletin,* October 22, 1962, p. 597.

21. Garthoff, *Reflections on the Cuban Missile Crisis,* 9.

22. *Public Papers of the Presidents of the United States: John F. Kennedy, 1961* (Washington, DC: U.S. Government Printing Office, 1962), 304.

23. *Official Records of the United Nations General Assembly,* 17th Session, Plenary Meetings, vol. I (New York: United Nations, 1962), 48-49.

24. *Public Papers of the Presidents of the United States: George Bush—1991,* vol. I (Washington, DC: U.S. Government Printing Office, 1992).

25. Clyde Haberman, "A Mideast Lexicon: Words That Wound and Pacify," *New York Times,* August 29, 1992, p. A2.

26. David Hoffman, "Coalition Diplomacy," in *The Diplomatic Record, 1990-91,* ed. David D. Newsom (Boulder, CO: Westview Press, l992), 66.

27. *Public Papers of the Presidents of the United States: George Bush, 1990,* vol. II (Washington, DC: U.S. Government Printing Office, 1991), 1107.

28. Ibid., 1138-39.

29. *US Department of State Dispatch,* vol. 1, no. 2 (September 10, 1990): 72.

30. Ibid., 69.

31. *Public Papers of the Presidents of the United States: George Bush, 1990,* vol. II, 1449.

32. *US Department of State Dispatch,* vol. 1, no. 15 (December 10, 1990): 310-312.

33. Ibid.

34. *Dispatch,* vol. 1, no. 14 (December 3, 1990): 295-296.

35. *Dispatch,* vol. 1, no. 17 (December 24, 1990): 349.

3. The Reporting Dimension

1. David Shaw, "Opinion Leaders Dictate the Conventional Wisdom," *Los Angeles Times,* August 26, 1989.

2. Ibid.

3. *Gale Directory of Publications and Broadcast Media,* vol. III (Detroit: Gale Research Inc., 1994), xxii. As of 1994, there were 1,714 daily newspapers.

4. Thomas R. Rosenstiel, "TV's Tour Guides to the World," *Los Angeles Times,* March 9, 1990, p. A1.

5. *National Opinion Ballot Report* (New York: Foreign Policy Association, October 1, 1991).

6. "The Media in the Dock," *Newsweek,* October 22, 1984, 66-72.

7. Walter Goodman, "Network News and the Push to Do Less and Do It Worse," *New York Times,* February 8, 1990, p. C22.

8. Katharine Q. Seelye, "Gingrich, New King of the Hill, Used Skill with Media to Climb to the Top," *New York Times,* December 14, 1994, p. A18.

9. Michael Mosettig, Address before the East-West Center and the Public Relations Society of America, Ilikai Hotel, Honolulu, Hawaii, December 1, 1989. Published by the East-West Center, Honolulu, Hawaii, 1990.

10. Peter J. Boyer, "Famine in Ethiopia, the TV Accident That Exploded," *Washington Journalism Review* (January 1985): 19-21.

11. Johanna Neuman, "The Media: Partners in the Revolution of 1989," Occasional Paper (Washington, DC: Atlantic Council of the United States, June 1991), 10-11.

12. Shanto Iyengar and Donald R. Kinder, *News That Matters: Television and American Opinion* (Chicago: University of Chicago Press, 1988). Summary of author's conclusions drawn from review by Ralph Braccio in the *Christian Science Monitor,* March 16, 1988, p. 20.

13. Marvin Kalb, "Late Night with the Gulf Crisis," *New York Times,* August 29, 1990, p. A21.

14. Letter from Mr. German to author, June 6, 1994.

15. *Newsweek,* Special Issue 8, November–December 1984, 104.

16. Paul Farhi, "Covering the Iraq Invasion," *Washington Post,* August 4, 1990, p. G1.

17. Walter Goodman, "The Iraq Conflict on American TV," *New York Times*, September 17, 1990, p. C18.

18. See Frank Smyth, "'Official Sources,' 'Western Diplomats,' and Other Voices from the Mission," *Columbia Journalism Review* (January–February 1993): 35.

19. Ibid.

20. Letter of June 12, 1992 from Murray Gart to author.

21. Kalb, "Late Night with the Gulf Crisis."

22. Stephen Hess, "Confessions of a Sound Bite: Want to Get Quoted on TV? Tell 'Em What They Want to Hear," *Washington Post*, October 22, 1989, p. C5.

23. Ibid.

24. Av Westin, "Inside the Evening News: How TV Really Works," *New York*, October 18, 1982, p. 48.

25. Richard Harwood, "Where Are the Wars of Yesteryear?" *Washington Post*, May 4, 1993, p. A21.

26. Edward Jay Epstein, "The Selection of Reality," in *What's News?*, ed. Elie Abel (San Francisco: Institute for Contemporary Studies, 1981), 123.

27. From a speech by Jack Smith to McDonough School, McDonough, MD, Spring 1981.

28. See Tom Shales, "The Blockbuster No One Watched: Upheaval in Europe Leaving Viewers Cold," *Washington Post*, November 29, 1989, p. B1.

29. Richard W. Jencks, "A Picture Isn't Always Worth a Thousand Words on TV," *Wall Street Journal*, August 20, 1987, p. 22.

30. Ibid.

31. Edwin Diamond, *The Media Show: The Changing Face of the News, 1985-1990* (Cambridge: MIT Press, 1992). Quoted from review in *Christian Science Monitor*, May 8, 1992, p. 13.

32. David D. Newsom, *The Soviet Brigade in Cuba* (Bloomington: Indiana University Press, 1987).

33. David Whitman, "The Press and the Neutron Bomb," Case History no. C-14-84-607, by the President and Fellows of Harvard College, 1983.

34. Shaw, "Opinion Leaders."

35. See David D. Newsom, "The Rear View Mirror," *Christian Science Monitor*, November 26, 1989, p. 18.

36. Shaw, "Opinion Leaders."

37. "Iranian Confirmation of Secret Contacts," *New York Times*, November 5, 1986, p. I-1.

38. Robert Pear, "Missing the Iran Arms Story: Did the Press Fail?" *New York Times*, March 3, 1987, p. I-15.

39. Scott Armstrong, "Iran-Contra: Was the Press Any Match for All the President's Men?" *Columbia Journalism Review* (May–June 1990): 27-35.

40. Russ W. Baker, "Iraqgate: The Big One That (Almost) Got Away," *Columbia Journalism Review* (March–April 1993): 54.

41. David Shaw, "How Media Gives Stories Same 'Spin,'" *Los Angeles Times,* August 25, 1989, p. I-1.

42. Ibid.

43. Tom Wicker, *On Press* (New York: Viking Press, 1978), 19.

44. Shaw, "How Media Gives Stories Same 'Spin.'"

45. Ibid.

46. These articles include Robin Wright, "Fighting the Fires of Islam," *Los Angeles Times,* July 4, 1993, pp. M1, M6; and "The Religious Legacy: A Special Report," *Christian Science Monitor,* April 1, 1992, pp. 9-12. Following the World Trade Center bombing, the *Christian Science Monitor* ran a six-part series on the Islamic resurgence. On this, see the April 21-23 and April 26-28, 1993, issues.

4. Conflicting Objectives

1. Thomas J. Schoenbaum, *Waging Peace and War* (New York: Simon and Schuster, 1988), 245.

2. John Finney, letter to author, October 28, 1993.

3. "The Constitution: A Delicate Balance—National Security and Freedom of the Press," Video produced by Media and National Security Seminars, an Annenberg/Corporation for Public Broadcasting Project (New York: Trustees of Columbia University, 1984).

4. Howard Simons, "Government and National Security," *Editor and Publisher,* April 26, 1986, 80.

5. Richard Halloran, "Soldiers and Scribblers: A Common Mission," *Parameters,* vol. XVII, no. 1 (Spring 1987): 16.

6. Alexander M. Haig, Jr., *Caveat* (New York: Macmillan, 1984), 93.

7. Hess, *The Government/Press Connection,* 77-78.

8. Seymour Hersh, "Kissinger Panel, in a Draft, Says Soviet Is a Threat in Latin Affairs," *New York Times,* January 8, 1984, pp. A1, A16.

9. Seymour M. Hersh, *The Price of Power: Kissinger in the Nixon White House* (New York: Summit Books, 1983), 254.

10. David Whitman, *The Press and the Neutron Bomb,* Case history no. 14-84-607 (Cambridge, MA: Harvard University, Kennedy School of Government, Center for Press, Politics, and Public Policy, 1983).

11. David D. Newsom, *The Soviet Brigade in Cuba* (Bloomington: Indiana University Press, 1987), 22.

12. Leslie Gelb, "U.S. Officials Refuse to Confirm That Ford Sent Israel Warning," *New York Times,* March 24, 1975, p. A14.

13. Rowland Evans and Robert Novak, "The Senate's Foreign Policy Punch," *Washington Post,* May 26, 1975, p. A25.

14. John Wallach, "Alleged CIA Plan to Sabotage Nicaraguan Harbors to Halt

Arms," *San Francisco Examiner,* July 17, 1983, p. 1. Information on source from author's interview with Wallach.

15. Monica Langley and Lee Levine, "Broken Promises," *Columbia Journalism Review* (July–August 1988): 21.

16. From text of Frank E. Gannett lecture, November 25, 1986.

17. Transcript, MacNeil-Lehrer News Hour, Thursday, May 20, 1993 (New York: WNET, Show #4632), p. 7.

18. Transcript, MacNeil-Lehrer News Hour, Friday, December 4, 1992 (New York: WNET, Show #4513), p. 8.

19. Transcript, NBC Nightly News, December 5, 1992, 6:30-7:00 p.m.

20. Kenneth I. Juster, "The Myth of Iraqgate," *Foreign Policy* no. 95 (Spring 1994): 112-113.

21. William Branigan, "The U.N. Empire," four-part series, *Washington Post,* September 20, 1992, pp. A1, A26; September 21, 1992, pp. A1, A16; September 23, 1992, pp. A1, A14; September 23, 1992, pp. A1, A32.

22. Thomas L. Friedman, "Bush, in Address to U.N., Urges More Vigor in Keeping the Peace," *New York Times,* September 22, 1992, p. A1.

23. John Wallach, "'I'll Give It to You on Background': State Breakfasts," *Washington Quarterly* (Spring 1982): 54.

24. Daniel Williams and John M. Goshko "Reduced U.S. World Role Outlined but Soon Altered," *Washington Post,* May 26, 1993, pp. A1, A24; Daniel Williams and John M. Goshko, "Administration Rushes to 'Clarify' U.S. Policy Statements by 'Brand X,'" *Washington Post,* May 27, 1993, p. A45; Lloyd Grove, "Who Was That Masked Official?" *Washington Post,* May 27, 1993, pp. D1, D2.

25. "U.S. Weighing View That Soviet Force Is Training Cubans," *New York Times,* September 13, 1979, pp. A1, A7.

26. Quoted in Monica Langley and Lee Levine, "Broken Promises," *Columbia Journalism Review* (July–August 1988): 23.

27. Ibid., 22.

5. Key Issues

1. Strobe Talbott, *Deadly Gambits* (New York: Alfred A. Knopf, 1984).

2. Robert Pear, "For the Patient Reader, Military Secrets Are Self-Revealing," *New York Times,* August 30, 1987, sec. IV, p. 5.

3. Benjamin C. Bradlee, "The Post and Pelton: How the Press Looks at National Security," *Washington Post,* June 8, 1986, p. F1.

4. "The Shuttle Story," *Washington Post,* December 20, 1984, p. A18.

5. Peter Braestrup, *The Big Story: How the American Press and Television Reported and Interpreted the Crisis of Tet 1968 in Vietnam and Washington* (Boulder, CO: Westview Press, 1977).

6. Richard Halloran, "Soldiers and Scribblers: A Common Mission," *Parameters* (1987): 22.

7. Brent Scowcroft, "Reflections on the Role of the Media," Occasional Paper (Washington, DC: Institute for the Study of Diplomacy, Georgetown University, 1987).

8. Malcolm W. Browne, "Conflicting Censorship Upsets Many Journalists," *New York Times,* January 21, 1991, p. A10.

9. Marvin Kalb, "Late Night with the Gulf Crisis," *New York Times,* August 24, 1990, p. A21.

10. "Liz Trotta on the Gulf War," *Christian Science Monitor,* June 13, 1991, p. 13.

11. Walter Goodman, "The Iraq Conflict on American TV," *New York Times,* September 17, 1990, p. C18.

12. Stefano Silvestri, "The Media and National Security," in *The Media and National Security: Foreign Policy, Defense, and Terrorism in the Information Society*, Marco Carnovale, ed. (Council for the United States and Italy, Milano: Edizioni del sole 24ore, 1988), 81.

13. Robert Oakley, "Media Coverage of Terrorism: Recent Cases and Lessons for the Future," pp. 94-95 in *The Media and National Security.*

14. Katharine Graham, "The Media and Terrorism: Coverage Should Be Complete and Reasonable," the Churchill Lecture, Guildhall, London, December 6, 1985. Text provided by the *Washington Post.*

15. Alex S. Jones, "TV in the Hostage Crisis: Reporter or Participant?" *New York Times,* July 2, 1985, p. I 7.

16. Morton Dean, "TV's Duty to Cover Terror," *New York Times,* July 12, 1985, p. I 27.

17. The NBC interview with Abbas was aired on May 5, 1986. *Television News Index and Abstracts* (Nashville, TN: Vanderbilt Television News Archive, May 1986), 801.

18. *Neiman Reports,* XL, no. 4, Winter 1986.

19. Ibid.

20. Katherine Graham, "The Media and Terrorism."

21. Bob Woodward, "CIA Paid Millions to Jordan's King Hussein," *Washington Post,* February 18, 1977, p. A1.

22. "The Shuttle Story," *Washington Post,* December 20, 1984, p. A18.

23. Bradlee, "The Post and Pelton: How the Press Looks at National Security."

24. David D. Newsom, *The Soviet Brigade in Cuba* (Bloomington: Indiana University Press, 1987), 14.

25. For a full discussion of Casey's relationship with the press, see Dom Bonafede, "Muzzling the Media," *National Journal,* July 12, 1986, pp. 1716-1720.

26. For a challenge to this "right to know," see chapter 4, p. 3.

27. Letter from the Secretary of State to the Prime Minister of Iran, August 20, 1980, Document no. 370 in *American Foreign Policy Basic Documents, 1977-1980* (Washington, DC: Department of State, 1983), 772-773.

28. Tom Shales, "The Gulf Crisis and the TV News Wars," *Washington Post,* August 20, 1990, p. B1.

29. "Moscow's Vigorous Leader," Special Section, *Time,* September 9, 1985, pp. 16-28+.

30. James Reston, *Deadline* (New York: Random House, 1991), 330-331.

31. Ted Koppel, "TV Diplomacy in South Africa," *Newsweek,* April 8, 1985, p. 14.

32. Walter Goodman, "Why the Tube Can Be Hussein's Worst Enemy," *New York Times,* August 30, 1990. p. A16.

33. Tom Shales, "Islands in the Swirl of the Storm: American TV's Extraordinary Role in the Philippine Crisis," *Washington Post,* February 24, 1986, pp. D1, D2.

34. William Borders, "Pakistani Dismisses $400 Million in Aid Offered by U.S. as 'Peanuts,'" *New York Times,* January 18, 1981, p. A1.

6. Money

1. Landrum R. Bolling, with Craig Smith, *Private Foreign Aid, A Council on Foundations Report* (Boulder, CO: Westview Press, 1982), 177.

2. Sources: annual reports of each organization for 1993.

3. Michael Weisskopf, "Backtracking to Back Winners," *Washington Post,* December 26, 1994, pp. A1, A23. See also Michael Weisskopf, "New Political Landscape Bountiful for Think Tank with Gingrich Ties," *Washington Post,* February 5, 1995, p. A10.

4. David M. Ricci, *The Transformation of American Politics: The New Washington and the Rise of Think Tanks* (New Haven: Yale University Press, 1993), 167.

5. Ibid., 171. See also James Allen Smith, *The Idea Brokers* (New York: Free Press, 1991), 200.

6. *Annual Report* (Washington, DC: Center for Strategic and International Studies, 1993), 60-63.

7. *Annual Report* (Washington, DC: Brookings Institution, 1993), 26-27.

8. *Annual Report* (Washington, DC: Heritage Foundation, 1993), 30.

9. Ibid., 32.

10. Ricci, *Transformation of American Politics,* 154.

11. Ibid., 166.

12. For a more detailed look at the history of major foundations, see Bolling, *Private Foreign Aid,* 45-98. At the time of writing, Bolling was chairman of the Council on Foundations.

13. The following foundations were the ten largest in terms of assets in 1994:

Ford Foundation	$6,253,006,737
Kellogg Foundation	5,396,889,094
J. Paul Getty Trust*	5,251,845,004
Robert Wood Johnson Foundation	4,085,941,388
Lilly Endowment	3,592,519,250
MacArthur Foundation	3,393,492,922
Pew Charitable Trusts	3,338,048,594
Rockefeller Foundation	2,171,548,237
Mellon Foundation	1,701,863,355
Woodruff Foundation	1,495,171,323

* Primarily an operating foundation with few grants
[Source: Stan Olson, ed., *Foundation Directory* (New York: Foundation Center, 1993), p. x.]

14. *The Foundation Grants Index: 1993,* 21st ed. (New York: Foundation Center, 1992).

15. Smith, *The Idea Brokers,* 196.

16. Ford Foundation International Affairs Grants, Sponsored Programs Information Network (SPIN), no. 3387.

17. Ibid.

18. Bolling, *Private Foreign Aid,* 46.

19. SPIN, no. 4990.

20. *Annual Report* (Chicago: John D. and Catherine T. MacArthur Foundation, 1990), 1.

21. SPIN, no. 06987.

22. Ibid., no. 5945.

23. Bolling, *Private Foreign Aid,* 76.

24. Smith, *The Idea Brokers,* 196.

25. Ricci, *Transformation of American Politics,* 161; also Smith, *The Idea Brokers,* 19, 279.

26. Sarah Scaife Foundation Grants Program, SPIN, no. 05252.

27. SPIN, no. 4177.

28. Ricci, *Transformation of American Politics,* 41-42.

29. Sec. 1701, Title XVII of the Defense Authorization Act of 1985, Public Law 98-525 (Oct. 19, 1984), 98 Stat. 2492, 22 U.S.C. 4601-4611, as amended.

30. *Building Peace: The First Decade and Beyond* (Washington, DC: United States Institute of Peace, 1994), 73.

31. Ibid., 72.

32. For details see Patrick Choate, *Agents of Influence* (New York: Alfred A. Knopf, 1990).

33. *New York Times*, February 24, 1981, p. A13.

34. For a fuller account of the separation of CSIS from Georgetown University from the CSIS point of view, see James Allen Smith, *Strategic Calling: The Center for Strategic and International Studies, 1962-1992* (Washington, DC: Center for Strategic and International Studies, 1993), 136-140.

35. Gail Russell Chaddock, "Universities, Seeing a Shrinking Fund-Raising Pool, Jump In," *Christian Science Monitor,* May 23, 1994, p. 13.

36. Thomas B. Edsall, "Thanks to the Clintons' Approach, Cash Flows into Conservative Coffers," *Washington Post,* February 10, 1994, p. A6.

7. Academia

1. William H. Honan, "At the Top of the Ivory Tower, the Watchword Is Silence," *New York Times,* July 24, 1994, p. E5.

2. Samuel Huntington, "The Clash of Civilizations," *Foreign Affairs,* vol. 72 (Summer 1993): 22-49.

3. Paul Kennedy, *Preparing for the Twenty-First Century* (New York: Random House, 1993).

4. "INR" (Washington, DC: Bureau of Intelligence and Research, Office of Research, United States Department of State), September 1994.

5. Robert Shaplen, "The Eye of the Storm," *New Yorker,* June 2, 9, and 16, 1980.

6. David D. Newsom, *The Soviet Brigade in Cuba* (Bloomington: Indiana University Press, 1987).

7. Robert Kaufman, "The Line in the Sand: What George Bush Learned from Winston Churchill," *Policy Review* no. 56 (Spring 1991): 36-43.

8. Michael Brenner, "The Alliance: A Gulf Post-mortem," *International Affairs* 67, no. 4 (October 1991): 665-678.

9. Graham Allison, *Essence of Decision: Explaining the Cuban Missile Crisis* (Boston: Little, Brown, 1971).

10. I. M. Destler, *Presidents, Bureaucrats, and Foreign Policy: The Politics of Organizational Reform* (Princeton, NJ: Princeton University Press, 1972).

11. *Annual Report* (New York: Social Science Research Council, 1988-89), 61.

12. Hans Morgenthau, *Politics Among Nations: The Struggle for Power and Peace,* 5th ed. (New York: Alfred A. Knopf, 1973), 21.

13. Charles W. Kegley, Jr. and Eugene R. Wittkopf, *American Foreign Policy, Pattern and Process,* 4th ed. (New York: St. Martin's Press, 1991).

14. Priscilla Stone and Paul Richards, "Social and Natural Science Conjoined: The View from the Program on African Studies," *Items* 47, nos. 2-3 (June-September 1993): 31.

15. David L. Featherman, "What Does Society Need from Higher Education?" *Items* 47, nos. 2-3 (June–September 1993): 39.

16. *Annual Report: 1988-89,* Social Science Research Council, 63.

17. These observations are based on the author's experience in initiating the program of case studies at Georgetown University.

18. Author was a member of the committee; analysis based on recollection.

19. For full details, see 1993 Case Catalog, *Enhancing Education in International Affairs* (Washington, DC: Institute for the Study of Diplomacy, Edmund A. Walsh School of Foreign Service, Georgetown University, Pew Case Study Center, 1993).

20. Roger Fisher with William Urey, *Getting to Yes: Negotiating Agreement without Giving In* (Boston: Houghton Mifflin, 1981).

21. David Mutch, "No Benefit to Aggression: Talk with Saddam, Experts Say," *Christian Science Monitor,* September 10, 1990, p. 8.

22. Laura Blumenfeld, "The Absent-Minded Miracle Worker: Yair Hirschfeld Quietly Taught History in Israel, and Very Quietly Made It in Oslo," *Washington Post,* September 22, 1993, p. C1; also, Stephen Franklin, "How A Scholarly Secret Agent Led the Way to Peace," *Chicago Tribune,* December 17, 1993, sec. 5, p. 1.

23. David E. Sanger, "Two Koreas Agree to Summit Meeting on Nuclear Issue," *New York Times,* June 19, 1994, p. A12.

24. Maureen Dowd, "Despite Role as Negotiator, Carter Feels Unappreciated," *New York Times,* September 21, 1994, pp. A1, A17.

25. Thomas W. Lippman, "The Mediator's Strength: I'm Not Taking Sides," *Washington Post,* December 15, 1994, p. A-39.

26. I. William Zartman and Maureen R. Berman, *The Practical Negotiator* (New Haven: Yale University Press, 1982).

27. James C. Garand, "An Alternative Interpretation of Recent Political Science Journal Evaluations," *PS: Political Science and Politics,* vol. 23 (September 1990): 448-451.

28. *Political Science and Social Policy* (Armonck, NY: M. E. Sharpe, Fall 1993).

29. David M. Ricci, *The Transformation of American Politics: The New Washington and the Rise of Think Tanks* (New Haven: Yale University Press, 1993), 136.

30. For a full description of this theory, see Karl-Dieter Opp, *The Rationality of Political Protest: A Comparative Analysis of Rational Choice Theory* (Boulder, CO: Westview Press, 1989).

31. Michael D. McGinnis and John T. Williams, "Policy Uncertainty in Two-Level Games: Examples of Correlated Equilibria," *International Studies Quarterly* 37, no. 1 (March 1993): 29.

32. Reprinted in Stanley Hoffmann, *Janus and Minerva* (Boulder, CO: Westview Press, 1987), 15. For a penetrating and amusing discussion of the efforts to make a science out of political studies, see Stanislav Andreski, *Social Sciences as Sorcery* (London: Penguin Books, 1974).

33. John Lewis Gaddis, "International Relations Theory and the End of the Cold War," *International Security* 17, no. 3 (Winter 1992/93): 56.

8. Think Tanks

1. Quoted in James Allen Smith, *Strategic Calling* (Washington, DC: Center for Strategic and International Studies, 1993), 68.

2. James Allen Smith, *The Idea Brokers* (New York: Free Press, 1991), 270-294.

3. David M. Ricci, *Transformation of American Politics: The New Washington and the Rise of Think Tanks* (New Haven: Yale University Press, 1993), 163.

4. *Annual Report* (Washington, DC: Brookings Institution, 1993), 2.

5. Smith, *The Idea Brokers,* 270.

6. For a full history of CSIS and its development, see Smith, *Strategic Calling.*

7. Smith, *The Idea Brokers,* 283; Ricci, *Transformation of American Politics,* 153.

8. *Annual Report* (Washington, DC: Joint Center for Political Studies, 1993), 3.

9. *Annual Report* (Washington, DC: Heritage Foundation, 1993), 3.

10. Ricci, *Transformation of American Politics,* 20.

11. Kim R. Holmes, ed., *A Safe and Prosperous America: A U.S. Foreign and Defense Policy Blueprint* (Washington, DC: Heritage Foundation, 1993), 1.

12. *Annual Report* (Washington, DC: American Enterprise Institute, 1993), 17.

13. *Annual Report* (Washington, DC: Cato Institute, 1993), 20.

14. *Annual Report* (Washington, DC: Center for Strategic and International Studies, 1993), 4.

15. Edmund S. Muskie, *Exploring Cambodia: Issues and Reality in a Time of Transition* (Washington, DC: Center for National Policy, February 1990).

16. *30th Anniversary Report* (Washington, DC: Institute of Policy Studies, 1993), 7-8.

17. *Leadership into the 21st Century: Annual Report, 1993-94* (Washington, DC: Center for Strategic and International Studies, 1994), 48.

18. *30th Anniversary Report,* IPS, 1.

19. Ricci, *Transformation of American Politics,* 160.

20. From the author's own long acquaintance with Abshire and the Center.

21. Ricci, *Transformation of American Politics,* 161.

22. Solicitation circular issued by the National Peace Academy Campaign, 110 Maryland Avenue, NE, Washington, DC, 20002, undated.

23. The United States Institute of Peace Act (Title XVII of the Defense Authorization Act of 1985, Public Law no. 98-525 (Oct. 19, 1984), 98 Stat. 2492, 22 U.S.C. 4601-4611, as amended), Sec. 1702 (a) (1). Printed as Appen-

dix H, *Biennial Report of the United States Institute of Peace, 1989* (Washington, DC: United States Institute of Peace, 1990), 129.

24. The United States Institute of Peace Act, Sec. 1702. (a) (2). *USIP Biennial Report*, 1991, 160-167.

25. For the full debate, see *Congressional Record*, vol. 130, no. 85, June 20, 1984, pp. S7785-S7816.

26. Francis Fukuyama, *The End of History and the Last Man* (New York: Free Press, 1992).

27. Patrick Glynn, "The Sarajevo Fallacy: The Historical and Intellectual Origins of Arms Control Theology," *The National Interest* 9 (Fall 1987): 3-32.

28. USIP *Special Report:* "Sudan: Ending the War, Moving Talks Forward—Report of a United States Institute of Peace Seminar." Undated.

29. For more detailed information on CSIS congressional study groups, see Smith, *Strategic Calling,* 52 and 67.

30. Katharine Q. Seelye, "Republicans Get a Pep Talk from Rush Limbaugh," *New York Times,* December 12, 1994, p. A16.

31. *Annual Report,* AEI, 29.

32. Smith, *Strategic Calling,* 56.

33. *Annual Report,* Heritage Foundation, 5.

34. For a further discussion of the motives of those who enter and leave think tanks, see Smith, *Strategic Calling,* 94.

35. Ricci, *Transformation of American Politics,* 142.

36. Ibid., 220.

37. Quoted in Smith, *Strategic Calling,* 168.

9. Advocacy

1. Landrum Bolling, *Private Foreign Aid* (Boulder, CO: Westview Press, 1982), 154.

2. Ibid., 9.

3. Ibid., 10.

4. Ibid., 12.

5. Except where otherwise indicated, information on individual organizations comes from the *Encyclopedia of Associations,* 3 vols. 28th ed. (Detroit: Gale Research, Inc., 1994).

6. "Questions and Answers," pamphlet published by Human Rights Watch, New York. Undated.

7. For further information on the Fraser hearings and human rights legislation, see David D. Newsom, ed. *The Diplomacy of Human Rights* (Lanham, NY: University Press of America, 1986), 13-20 and Appendix D.

8. International Human Rights Law Group, *U.S. Legislation Relating Human Rights to U.S. Foreign Policy,* 4th ed. (Buffalo, NY: William S. Hein, 1991).

9. "Angry Brazil Cancels Pact with U.S.," *Washington Post,* March 12, 1977, p. A1. The legislation was amended on August 14, 1979 as a part of Public Law 96-53, Sec. 504 (1) (B).

10. From an address by the Secretary of State at the University of Georgia School of Law, Athens, GA, April 30, 1977, published in *Department of State Bulletin,* May 23, 1977, pp. 505-508.

11. John M. Goshko and Helen Dewar, "Rejected 13 to 4, Lefever Withdraws," *Washington Post,* June 6, 1981, p. A1.

12. Jeane J. Kirkpatrick, "How Has the United States Met Its Major Challenges since 1945?" *Commentary* 80 (November 1985): 50-52.

13. Aryeh Neier, "An Unacceptable Accord," *The Recorder* (December 15, 1993): 9.

14. John P. Salzberg, "A View from the Hill: U.S. Legislation and Human Rights, in *The Diplomacy of Human Rights,* edited by David D. Newsom (Landham, MD: University Press of America, 1989), 15.

15. *Encyclopedia of Associations,* 2958-2960.

16. The entry for Human Rights Watch in the *Encyclopedia of Associations* for 1994 describes the extensive activities of this private advocacy organization and at the same time gives a full example of the scope of such associations:

"Evaluates the human rights practices of governments in accordance with standards recognized by international laws and agreements including the United Nations Declaration of Human Rights and the Helsinki Accords. Identifies government abuses of human rights such as kidnapping, torture, and imprisonment for nonviolent association, exile, psychiatric abuse and censorship; publicizes and protests against these violations. Also observes the human rights practices of nongovernmental groups, such as guerilla groups, that are in sustained armed conflict with governments and measures these practices against internal war standards set forth in the Geneva Conventions and Protocols. Reports on discrepancies between the claims made by governments with respect to human rights and their actual practices; urges governments to bring actual practices in line with stated claims; . . . Sponsors missions to countries accused of human rights abuses; meets with government officials, local human rights and relief groups, church officials, labor leaders, journalists, and others with information on human rights practices; conducts interviews with victims of human rights abuses, their families and witnesses. Attends court proceedings and examines court records. Observes elections and reports on conditions as a means to promote fair and free elections. Evaluates the U.S. government's performance in promoting human rights worldwide; observes U.S. domestic practices of human rights, particularly the treatment of visitors to the U.S. or refugees who are denied asylum or discriminated against on ideological, political or racial grounds; also generates pressure to enforce U.S. laws that require governments receiving U.S. economic, military, or diplomatic assistance to adhere to appropriate human rights practices. Testifies before congressional hearings."

17. "Summary Report of the United Nations Commission on the Truth about Atrocities in El Salvador," UN document 6/T77, March 15, 1993.

18. *Commonly Asked Questions,* pamphlet issued by Amnesty International, USA. Undated.

19. From an Amnesty International, U.S.A.'s general information brochure provided by Mid-Atlantic Regional Office, Washington, DC, 1984.

20. Virginia Leary, A. A. Ellis, and Kurt Madlener, *The Philippines: Human Rights after Martial Law: Report of a Mission* (Geneva, Switzerland: International Commission of Jurists, 1984).

21. Citation listed in *Encyclopedia of Associations,* 1813.

22. Ibid., 1808.

23. "Earth Count: 5.6 Billion and Growing," *Popline* World Population News Service, 16 (May-June 1994): 1.

24. David M. Kennedy, *Birth Control in America: The Career of Margaret Sanger* (New Haven: Yale University Press, 1970); and Lawrence Lader, *The Margaret Sanger Story* (Garden City, NY: Doubleday and Company, 1955).

25. *Encyclopedia of Associations,* 1282.

26. Landrum Bolling, *Private Foreign Aid,* 60.

27. *Population Policies and Programs: Proceedings of the United Nations Expert Group Meeting on Population Policies and Programs, Cairo, Egypt, 12-16 1992* (New York: United Nations, Department of Economic and Social Information and Policy Analysis, 1993), ST/ESA/SER.R/128.

28. *Encyclopedia of Associations,* 11497.

29. Ibid., 1338.

30. Ibid.

31. Ibid.

32. *Washington Post,* June 29, 1994, p. A9.

33. Werner Fornos, "A Return to Reason: U.S. International Population Policy," *Toward the 21st Century* (November 4, 1993): 2.

34. Mary Gray Davidson, "NGOs: Voice of the People?" *Courier* no. 16 (Summer 1994): 7.

35. *Encyclopedia of Associations,* 1338.

36. Attachment to "Population, Environment and Development: Proceedings of the United Nations Expert Group Meeting on Population, Environment, and Development, United Nations Headquarters, 20-24 January 1992. (New York: United Nations, 1994), Annex XXIX, ST/ESA/SER.R/129.

37. *Encyclopedia of Associations,* 4244.

38. *The Year in Review, 1993: Annual Report* (New York: Environmental Defense Fund, 1993), 5 and 7.

39. Peter Dykstra, "Twenty Years: No Time Off for Good Behavior," *Greenpeace* (January–February–March 1991): 2.

40. *Annual Report* (Washington, DC: Greenpeace, U.S.A., 1992): 11.

41. Ibid., 18.

42. *Encyclopedia of Associations*, 471.

43. Martha Hamilton and Warren Brown, "GM, Environmental Defense Fund Team Up," *Washington Post,* July 9, 1992, p. D9.

44. Michael Wines, "Bush Likely to Go to Ecology Talks," *New York Times,* May 7, 1992, p. A1.

10. Lobbies

1. 22 U.S. Code, pp. 611-621, as amended 1966. For a fuller explanation of the Act and its provisions, see John L. Zorack, *The Lobbying Handbook* (Washington, DC: Professional Lobbying and Consulting Center, 1990), 37-44.

2. This information is available to the public through the Foreign Agents Registration Unit of the Department of Justice.

3. 2 U.S.Code, pp. 261-270. For more detailed information, see Zorack, *The Lobbying Handbook,* 23-36.

4. This information is available through the Office of Records and Registration of the Clerk of the House of Representatives.

5. Zorack, *The Lobbying Handbook,* 584-618.

6. Charles Mathias, "Ethnic Groups and Foreign Policy," *Foreign Affairs* 59 (Summer 1981): 975-998.

7. Originally organized in 1954 as the American Zionist Council of Public Affairs.

8. The most complete account of AIPAC is Edward Tivnan, *The Lobby: Jewish Political Power and American Foreign Policy* (New York: Simon and Schuster, 1987). Tivnan's story ends in 1985; many significant events relating to the power of the lobby occurred after that date. Many of the observations about AIPAC come also from the author's personal experience in policy positions in the Department of State. A more recent analytical study is David Howard Goldberg, *Foreign Policy and Ethnic Interest Groups: American and Canadian Jews Lobby for Israel* (New York: Greenwood Press, 1990).

9. Comment to author.

10. Tivnan, *The Lobby,* 188.

11. Ibid., 188-191. For the case of George McGovern, see 127.

12. David McCullough, *Truman* (New York: Simon and Schuster, 1992), 606-7.

13. Tivnan, *The Lobby,* 52-53.

14. Ibid., 59.

15. Ibid., 69-72.

16. Lloyd Grove, "The Men with Muscle: The AIPAC Leaders, Battling for Israel and among Themselves," *Washington Post,* June 14, 1991, pp. B1, B4.

17. Jacob Weisberg, "The Lobby with a Lock on Congress," *Newsweek,* October 19, 1987, pp. 46ff.

18. Tivnan, *The Lobby,* 88.

19. Ibid., 183.

20. Peter Beinart and Hanna Rosin, "AIPAC Unpacked," *New Republic,* September 20-27, 1993, pp. 20ff.

21. David Hoffman, "Rabin Criticizes Congressional Lobby for Israel," *Washington Post,* August 17, 1992, p. A8.

22. Robert S. Greenberger, "Pro-Israel Lobby Sees Role Shrink as Enemies Turn into Friends and Leaders Forge Own Ties," *Wall Street Journal,* April 26, 1994, p. A24.

23. Gary Lee, "S. Africa's Low-Profile Lobbyists," *Washington Post,* July 15, 1991, p. A9.

24. *New York Times,* December 20, 1975, p. 8.

25. For a full account of this effort, see Elaine Windrich, *The Cold War Guerrilla: Jonas Savimbi, the U.S. Media, and the Angolan War* (New York: Greenwood Press, 1992).

26. Chester A. Crocker, *High Noon in Southern Africa: Making Peace in a Rough Neighborhood* (New York: W. W. Norton, 1992), 283.

27. Elaine Windrich, *The Cold War Guerrilla,* 45.

28. Ibid., 35.

29. Ibid., 50.

30. Crocker, *High Noon in Southern Africa,* 283.

31. "How Lobbyists Briefed a Rebel Leader," *Washington Post,* October 8, 1990, p. A21.

32. Steven Mufson, "The Privatization of Craig Fuller" *Washington Post Magazine,* August 2, 1992, p. 14-19+; Arthur E. Rowse, "How to Build Support for War," *Columbia Journalism Review* (September–October 1992): 28-29.

33. Susumu Awanohara, "Asian Lobbies: Cash and Connections," *Far Eastern Economic Review,* June 2, 1994, pp. 24-32.

11. The Congress

1. Heritage Foundation, Center for National Policy, Population Institute, and Amnesty International.

2. For a full description of Senate action on the Panama Canal treaties, see Cecil Crabb, Jr. and Pat Holt, *Invitation to Struggle: Congress, the President and Foreign Policy,* 2nd ed. (Washington, DC: Congressional Quarterly Inc., 1984), chapter 3.

3. "Relief Problems in Nigeria-Biafra," Hearings before the Subcommittee to Investigate Problems Connected with Refugees and Escapees of the Committee

on the Judiciary, United States Senate, Ninety-First Congress, First Session, July 15, 1969 (Washington, DC: U.S. Government Printing Office, 1969), 65-145.

4. Based on *Congress and Foreign Policy-1979* (Washington, DC: U.S. Government Printing Office, 1980), 19.

5. Ibid., 2.

6. Charles Mohr, "Kissinger Suggests Senate Link Treaty to More Arms Funds," *New York Times*, August 1, 1979, p. A1.

7. "Military Implications of the SALT II Treaty," Hearing before the Senate Armed Services Committee, October 16, 1979, p. 1255.

8. Ibid., 1307.

9. "SALT II Treaty," Hearing before the Senate Foreign Relations Committee, July 9, 1979, p. 97.

10. Ibid., 122.

11. Ibid., 437.

12. "Military Implications of the SALT II Treaty," Hearing before the Senate Armed Services Committee, October 10, 1979, p. 1080.

13. "Military Implications of the SALT II Treaty," Hearing before the Senate Armed Services Committee, October 16, 1979, p. 1328.

14. *Congress and Foreign Policy, 1985-86* (Washington, DC: U.S. Government Printing Office, 1988), 37.

15. These committees included: the House Committee on Foreign Affairs and its subcommittees on Human Rights and International Organizations, International Economic Policy and Trade, and Western Hemisphere Affairs; the House Committee on Appropriations and its subcommittee on the Department of Defense; the Senate Committee on Appropriations and its subcommittee on Defense; the Senate Committee on Foreign Relations; the House Committee on Armed Services; and the House Permanent Select Committee on Intelligence.

16. Mark Whitaker et al., "Playing Propaganda Games," *Newsweek*, March 18, 1985, p. 32.

17. Joanne Omang, "Contra Aid Fight Nears, Hill Besieged from All Sides," *Washington Post*, April 15, 1985, pp. A1, A14.

18. *Congress and Foreign Policy, 1985-86*, 39; and Elizabeth Kastor, "Reagan's Night for the Refugees," *Washington Post*, April 16, 1985, p. C1. Not surprisingly, the dinner event coincided with the start of congressional consideration of Reagan's request for renewed aid to the contras.

19. Omang, "Contra Aid Fight Nears," p. A14.

20. Ibid., A1.

21. Gerry Fitzgerald, "Religious Groups Orchestrate Opposition to 'Contra' Aid," *Washington Post*, April 23, 1985, p. A18.

22. "Playing Propaganda Games," *Newsweek*, p. 32.

23. Joel Brinkley, "Rights Report on Nicaragua Cites Recent Rebel Atrocities," *New York Times,* March 6, 1985, p. A10.

24. "Playing Propaganda Games," *Newsweek,* p. 32.

25. "U.S. Support for the Contras," Hearing before the House Subcommittee on Western Hemisphere Affairs, Committee on Foreign Affairs, 99th Congress, 1st session, April 16, 1985, p. 88.

26. Ibid., April 17, 1985, 114.

27. Ibid., April 16, 1985, 105.

28. Ibid., April 17, 1985, 226.

29. Ibid., April 16, 1985, 56.

30. Ibid., pp. 72, 79. For McGeorge Bundy's comments, see p. 88.

31. "Playing Propaganda Games," *Newsweek,* p. 32.

32. "U.S. Support for the Contras," April 18, 1985, 256.

33. Ibid., 248-249.

34. Ibid., April 17, 1985, 237.

35. Ibid. April 18, 1985, 267-268.

36. Although Congress was no longer willing to provide military assistance, legislators remained rather evenly split on the issue of non-lethal aid. The ongoing controversy surrounding the issue discouraged the administration from launching an aggressive campaign for support in 1988. That year Congress voted only $27 million in humanitarian assistance. On this, see *Congress and Foreign Policy, 1988* (Washington, DC: U.S. Government Printing Office, 1989).

37. *Congress and Foreign Policy: 1985-86* (Washington, DC: U.S. Government Printing Office, 1988), 3.

38. In the fall of 1984, the level of violence escalated dramatically in South Africa. The South African Government undertook a brutal crackdown against blacks participating in the widespread demonstrations, strikes, boycotts and political violence that erupted. The protests were a response to the adoption of a new constitution that created a tricameral legislature with chambers for whites, Asians, and mixed race ("colored") representatives, but offered no representation for the country's black majority. On this, see *Congress and Foreign Policy: 1985-86,* 14.

39. "News Reports Bring South Africa's Turmoil into America's Living Rooms," *New York Times,* November 3, 1985, p. A12.

40. "U.S. Drive Opposes South African Racial Policies," *New York Times,* November 24, 1984, p. 9; also, Barbara Gamarekian, "Lobbying with a Target: South Africa," *New York Times,* December 8, 1984, p. 9.

41. Barry Sussman, "Activists Stimulate S. African Sanctions," *Washington Post,* July 24, 1985, p. A25.

42. *Congress and Foreign Policy: 1985-86,* 15.

43. Ibid.

44. Alan Cowell, "Kennedy's Trip: 'Stirring Things Up' in South Africa," *New York Times,* January 15, 1985, p. A2.

45. "U.S. Policy toward South Africa," Hearing of the Senate Foreign Relations Committee, April 24, 1985, p. 12.

46. Gamarekian, "Lobbyist with a Target: South Africa," p. 9.

47. "U.S. Policy toward South Africa," Hearing before the Senate Foreign Relations Committee, May 22, 1985, p. 190.

48. "U.S. Policy toward South Africa," Hearing of the Senate Foreign Relations Committee, April 24, 1985, p. 37.

49. Ibid.

50. "Legislative Options on U.S. Policy toward South Africa," Hearing of the House Committee on Foreign Affairs, Subcommittees on International Economic Policy and Trade and on Africa, April 9, 1986, p. 8.

51. "Legislative Options and United States Policy toward South Africa," Markup session before the House Foreign Affairs Committee, Subcommittees on International Economic Policy and Trade and on Africa, June 4, 1986, p. 66.

52. Gamarekian, "Lobbyist with a Target: South Africa," p. 9.

53. The committees included: the House Committee on Foreign Affairs (then called the Committee on International Relations) and its subcommittees on Africa and International Resources, Food, and Energy; the House Select Committee on Hunger; the House Select Committee on Intelligence; and the Senate Committee on Foreign Relations and its subcommittee on African Affairs.

54. On this, see George P. Shultz, *Turmoil and Triumph: My Years as Secretary of State* (New York: Charles Scribner's Sons, 1993), 1118.

55. The Reagan administration's intention to extend covert aid to UNITA was first acknowledged by the president in late 1985. It was publicly affirmed by Assistant Secretary of State for African Affairs, Chester Crocker, in congressional testimony in February 1986. On this, see Crocker, *High Noon in Southern Africa*, 293-303; also, Stephen Engelberg, "House Backs Covert Aid to Rebels in Angola," *New York Times*, September 18, 1986, p. A8.

56. Bernard Gwertzman, "Angolan Rebel Sees Top U.S. Officials," *New York Times*, January 30, 1986, p. A3; also, Patrick Tyler and David Ottaway, "The Selling of Jonas Savimbi: Success and a $600,000 Tab," *Washington Post*, February 9, 1986, pp. A1, A8.

57. On this, see Shultz, *Turmoil and Triumph*, 1118-1119.

58. Engelberg, "House Backs Covert Aid to Rebels in Angola," *New York Times*, p. A8.

59. "Angola: Options for American Foreign Policy," Hearing before the Senate Foreign Relations Committee, February 18, 1986, p. 2.

60. "Angola: Intervention or Negotiation," Hearing before the House Foreign Affairs subcommittee on Africa, October 31, 1985, p. 31.

61. Ibid., 40.

62. "Angola: Options for American Foreign Policy," February 18, 1986, p. 5.

63. Ibid., 10-11.

64. Ibid., 30-31.

65. "Angola: Intervention or Negotiation," October 31, 1985, pp. 33-34.

66. The House of Representatives defeated a motion to bar further covert aid to UNITA on September 17, 1986. It then moved to approve the intelligence authorization bill which included an undisclosed amount of money (estimated to be about $15 million) for covert assistance to UNITA. On this, see Engelberg, "House Backs Covert Aid to Rebels in Angola," p. A8.

67. On this, see Shultz, *Turmoil and Triumph,* 1124.

The Twenty-First Century

1. Walter Wriston, "The Beltway-Media Complex," *Wall Street Journal,* October 29, 1990, p. A14.

2. *Panel Report: Global HIV/AIDS: A Strategy for U.S. Leadership: A Consensus Report of the CSIS Working Group on Global HIV/AIDS* (Washington, DC: Center for Strategic and International Studies, 1994).

SELECT BIBLIOGRAPHY

"A General Loses His Case." *Time,* February 4, 1985, 64-66.

A New Look at U.S.-Vietnam Relations. Report of a Center for National Policy Study Group, Washington, DC, June 1993.

Abrams et al. vs. *United States.* Title 250 U.S. Code, 616 and 628 (1919).

Abrams, Floyd. "Why We Should Change the Libel Law." *New York Times Magazine,* September 29, 1985, 34-35+.

Adatto, Kiku. "The Incredible Shrinking Sound Bite." *New Republic,* May 28, 1990, 20-23.

"Agenda for Earth's Future: The Sierra Club 1994 Congressional Platform." *Sierra* 79, no. 4 (July–August 1994): 84a-84h.

Albritton, Robert B., and Jarol B. Manheim. "News of Rhodesia: The Impact of a Public Relations Campaign." *Journalism Quarterly* (Winter 1983): 622-628.

Allison, Graham T. *Essence of Decision: Explaining the Cuban Missile Crisis.* Boston: Little, Brown, 1971.

Alter, Jonathan. "Prime-Time Revolution: How Technology Fueled a Year of Change." *Newsweek,* January 8, 1990, 25.

———. "The Network Circus: TV Turns Up the Emotional Volume." *Newsweek,* July 8, 1985, 21.

———. "Why the Old Media's Losing Control." *Newsweek,* June 8, 1992, 28.

Alter, Jonathan, Lucy Howard, and Nancy Stadtman. "The Media in the Dock." *Newsweek,* October 22, 1984, 66-68+.

Alter, Jonathan, Tony Clifton, and Ray Wilkinson. "Will We See the Real War?" *Newsweek,* January 14, 1991, 19.

American Foreign Policy Basic Documents, 1977-1980. Washington, DC: Department of State, 1983.

Anderson, Jim. "Delivering the Message: The Press as an Instrument of Diplomacy." *Foreign Service Journal* 71, no. 4 (April 1994): 32-36.

Andreski, Stanislav. *Social Science as Sorcery.* London: Penguin Books, 1974.

"Angola: Intervention or Negotiation." Hearing before the Subcommittee on Africa of the Committee on Foreign Affairs. U.S. House of Representatives. 99th Congress. 1st Session. October 31; November 12, 1985. Washington, DC: U.S. Government Printing Office, 1986.

"Angola: Options for American Foreign Policy." Hearing before the Committee on Foreign Relations. U.S. Senate. 99th Congress. 2nd Session. February 18, 1986. Washington, DC: U.S. Government Printing Office, 1986.

Armstrong, Scott. "Iran-Contra: Was the Press Any Match for All the President's Men?" *Columbia Journalism Review* (May–June 1990): 27-35.

Aronson, James. "The Press in the Seventies and the Eighties." *Hunter Magazine* VII (Summer 1988): 10-25.

Awanohara, Susumu. "Asian Lobbies: Cash and Connections." *Far Eastern Economic Review* 157, no. 22 (June 2, 1994): 24-26+.

Backer, Dana M., ed. "International Population Non-Governmental Organizations." *Toward the 21st Century.* A monograph published by the Population Institute, no. 2 (1993): 1-39.

Baker, James A., III. "Principles and Pragmatism: American Policy toward the Arab-Israeli Conflict." *Department of State Bulletin* 89 (July 1989): 24-27.

Baker, Russ W. "Iraqgate: The Big One That (Almost) Got Away." *Columbia Journalism Review* (March–April 1993): 48-54.

"Battling the Gods of War." *Time,* June 25, 1984, 30-32+.

Beal, John Robinson. *John Foster Dulles: A Biography.* New York: Harper, 1957.

Becker, Carol, and David Herschler. "Cuban Missile Crisis Was a Communications 'Watershed.'" *State* (June 1987): 24-26.

———. "How Cordell Hull Handled the Press: He Was 'At Home.'" *State* (May 1987): 28-29.

Beinart, Peter, and Hanna Rosin. "AIPAC Unpacked." *New Republic,* September 20-27, 1993, 20+.

Bell, Steve. "Reporting on the Bias." *Washington Journalism Review* (October 1985): 16, 54.

Benedick, Richard Elliot. *Ozone Diplomacy.* Cambridge, MA: Harvard University Press, 1991.

Benton, Nicholas F. "More Nuisance Than News: State's Daily Press Briefing." *Foreign Service Journal* (November 1989): 41-44.

Bernard, Joe. "Tomorrow's Edition." *TWA Ambassador* (July 1990): 38-40+.

Berry, Nicholas O. *Foreign Policy and the Press: An Analysis of the New York Times' Coverage of U.S. Foreign Policy.* New York: Greenwood Press, 1990.

Bibliography on Peace, Security, and International Conflict Management. Washington, DC: United States Institute of Peace, 1993.

Blight, James G. *The Shattered Crystal Ball: Fear and Learning in the Cuban Missile Crisis.* Savage, MD: Rowman and Littlefield, 1990.

Blumenthal, Sidney. "On Wings of Bull." *New Republic,* July 13–20, 1992, 12+.

Blyskal, Jeff, and Marie Blyskal. "Making the Best of Bad News." *Washington Journalism Review* (December 1985): 51-55.

Bolling, Landrum R., with Craig Smith. *Private Foreign Aid: A Council on Foundations Report.* Boulder, CO: Westview Press, 1982.

Bolling, Landrum R. "Questions on Media Coverage of Recent Wars." In *Reporters under Fire,* edited by Landrum Bolling. Boulder, CO: Westview Press, 1985.

Bonafede, Dom. "Muzzling the Media." *National Journal,* July 12, 1986, 1716-1720.

Boucher, Norman. "Learning Peace." *Atlantic* (September 1983): 12+.

Boyer, Peter J. "Famine in Ethiopia: The TV Accident That Exploded." *Washington Journalism Review* (January 1985): 19-21.

Boylan, James. "Declarations of Independence." *Columbia Journalism Review* (November–December 1986): 29-45.

———. "How Free Is the Press?" *Columbia Journalism Review* (September–October 1987): 27-31.

Bradlee, Benjamin C. "Reporters, Governments and National Security." Remarks at the Frank E. Gannett Lecture sponsored by the Washington Journalism Center, Capital Hilton Hotel, Washington, DC, November 25, 1986.

Braestrup, Peter. *The Big Story: How the American Press and Television Reported and Interpreted Views of Tet 1968 in Vietnam and Washington.* Abridged ed. New Haven: Yale University Press, 1983.

Bremer, L. Paul, III. "Terrorism and the Media." *Department of State Bulletin* 87 (September 1987): 72-75.

Brenner, Michael. "The Alliance: A Gulf Post-Mortem." *International Affairs* 67, no. 4 (October 1991): 665-678.

"Broadcasting Guidelines for Covering Crises." *Nieman Reports* XL, no. 4 (Winter 1986): 20-24.

Browne, Malcolm W. "The Military vs. the Press." *New York Times Magazine,* March 3, 1991, 27-30+.

Brzezinski, Zbigniew. "Recognizing the Crisis." *Foreign Policy* no. 17 (Winter 1974-75): 63-74.

———. "The Balance of Power Delusion." *Foreign Policy* no. 7 (Summer 1972): 54-59.

———. "The Cold War and Its Aftermath." *Foreign Affairs* 71 (Fall 1992): 31-49.

———. "The Deceptive Structure of Peace." *Foreign Policy* no. 14 (Spring 1974): 35-55.

Carlson, Peter. "The Image Makers." *Washington Post Magazine,* February 11, 1990, 12-17+.

Carnovale, Marco, ed. *The Media and National Security: Foreign Policy, Defense and Terrorism in the Information Society.* Milano: Council for the United States and Italy, Edizioni del sole 24 ore, 1988.

"The Carousels of Power." *Economist,* May 25, 1991, 23-24+.

Carter, Margaret G. "Boning Up for Overseas Duty." *presstime* (February 1988): 30-32.

"Censor Journalists Covering Wars?" *U.S. News and World Report,* November 14, 1983, 33-34.

Chauncey, Helen R. *On Watch in Cambodia: Notes of an Election Observer.* Report to the Center for National Policy, Washington, DC, June 1993.

Chaze, William L., et al. "What America Thinks on TV." *U.S. News and World Report,* May 13, 1985, 67-68.

Chenery, William L. *Freedom of the Press.* New York: Harcourt, Brace, 1955.

Choate, Patrick. *Agents of Influence.* New York: Alfred A. Knopf, 1990.

Christrup, Judy. "Our Twentieth Anniversary." *Greenpeace* (January–March 1991): 13-20.

"Civil and Political Rights: The Human Rights Committee." United Nations Fact Sheet no. 15. New York: Secretariat Centre for Human Rights, 1991.

Cloud, Stanley W. "How Reporters Missed the War." *Time,* January 8, 1990, 61.

Cohen, Bernard C. *The Press and Foreign Policy.* Princeton, NJ: Princeton University Press, 1963.

"Conflict and Conflict Resolution in Mozambique." A Conference report on *Discussions from Dialogues on Conflict Resolution: Bridging Theory and Practice,* United States Institute of Peace, Washington, DC, July 13-15, 1992.

Congress and Foreign Policy, 1979. Washington, DC: U.S. Government Printing Office, 1980.

Congress and Foreign Policy, 1985-86. Washington, DC: U.S. Government Printing Office, 1988.

Congress and Foreign Policy, 1988. Washington, DC: U.S. Government Printing Office, 1989.

Conly, Shanti R., and J. Joseph Speidel. *Global Population Assistance: A Report Card on the Major Donor Countries—Executive Summary.* Washington, DC: Population Action International, 1993.

Conly, Shanti R., J. Joseph Speidel, and Sharon L. Camp. *U.S. Population Assistance: Issues for the 1990s—Executive Summary.* Washington, DC: Population Crisis Committee, 1991.

"The Constitution: A Delicate Balance—National Security and Freedom of the Press." Video produced by Media and National Security Seminars, an Annenberg/Corporation for Public Broadcasting Project. New York: Trustees of Columbia University, 1984.

Cooper, Nancy. "Guerrilla Chic." *Newsweek,* March 17, 1986, 22.

Cose, Ellis. "Shopping in the News Bazaar." *Time,* March 26, 1990, 64.

"Covering the Gulf Crisis." *Deadline* VI, no. 1 (January–February 1991): 1-16.

Crabb, Cecil, Jr., and Patrick Holt. *Invitation to Struggle: Congress, the President and Foreign Policy.* 2nd ed. Washington, DC: Congressional Quarterly, 1984.

Crocker, Chester. *High Noon in Southern Africa: Making Peace in a Rough Neighborhood.* New York: W. W. Norton, 1992.

Crozier, Brian. "Staunch Allies? (Comparing Soviet Support of Allies to U.S. and British Policies)." *National Review,* April 24, 1987, 26.

Cutler, Lloyd N. "Foreign Policy on Deadline." *Foreign Policy* no. 56 (Fall 1984): 113-128.

David, Michael, and Pat Aufderheide. "All the President's Media." *Channels* (September–October 1985): 20-24.

Davidson, Mary Gray. "NGOs: Voice of the People?" *Courier* no. 16 (Summer 1994): 6-7.

Deakin, James. *The Straight Stuff.* New York: Morrow, 1984.

Denniston, Lyle. "Call to Judgment." *Washington Journalism Review* (January 1984): 60.

———. "War of Independence." *Washington Journalism Review* (October 1985): 17.

Department of State Bulletin.

Destler, I. M. *Presidents, Bureaucrats, and Foreign Policy: The Politics of Organizational Reform.* Princeton, NJ: Princeton University Press, 1972.

Diamond, Edwin. *The Media Show: The Changing Face of the News, 1985-1990.* Cambridge: MIT Press, 1992.

Diamond, Edwin, Adrian Marin, and Robert Silverman. "Bush's First Year: Mr. Nice Guy Meets the Press." *Washington Journalism Review* (January–February 1990): 42-44.

Dickey, Christopher. "Not Their Finest Hour." *Newsweek,* June 8, 1992, 66.

Divine, Robert, ed. *The Cuban Missile Crisis.* New York: Markus Wiener Publishing, 1988.

Dorman, William A., and Mansour Farhang. *The U.S. Press and Iran.* Berkeley: University of California Press, 1987.

Drinan, Robert F. "The Sanctuary Movement on Trial." *America,* August 17-24, 1985, 81-83.

Dykstra, Peter. "Twenty Years: No Time Off for Good Behavior." *Greenpeace* (January–February–March 1991): 2.

"Earth Count: 5.6 Billion and Growing." *Popline* World Population News Service, 16 (May–June 1994): 1.

Educating for Peace: A Summary of Completed Education and Training Grant Projects. Washington, DC: United States Institute of Peace, 1993.

Emerson, Steven. "No October Surprise." *American Journalism Review* (March 1993): 16-23.

———. "The Mistold Story of PanAm 103." *Washington Journalism Review* (September 1992): 15-20.

Encyclopedia of Associations. 3 vols. 28th ed. Detroit: Gale Research, 1994.

"Engulfed." *Commonweal* 114, no. 15 (September 11, 1987): 467-468.

Enhancing Education in International Affairs. Washington, DC: Institute for the Study of Diplomacy, Georgetown University, Pew Case Study Center, 1993.

The Environment Encyclopedia and Directory. London: Europa Publications Limited, 1994.

Epstein, Edward Jay. "The Selection of Reality." In *What's News?,* edited by Elie Abel, 119-130. San Francisco: Institute for Contemporary Studies, 1981.

Etheredge, Lynn, et al. *Health Care: How to Improve It and Pay for It*. Washington, DC: Center for National Policy, April 1985.

Fallaci, Oriana. "An Interview with Oriana Fallaci: Kissinger." *New Republic*, December 16, 1972, 17-22.

Farer, Tom J. *The Grand Strategy of the United States in Latin America*. New Brunswick, NJ: Transaction Books, 1988.

Fascell, Dante B. "Dynamo or Dinosaur." *Foreign Service Journal* (January 1984): 31-35.

Featherman, David L. "What Does Society Need from Higher Education?" *Items* 47, nos. 2–3 (June–September 1993): 38-43.

Feczko, Margaret Mary. *The Foundation Directory*. 1993 edition supplement. New York: Foundation Center, 1993.

The Federalist. New York: Modern Library, 1937.

Finder, Joseph. "Reporting from Russia: Three Correspondents in Moscow." *Washington Journalism Review* (June 1985): 54-58+.

Fisher, Roger. *Getting to Yes: Negotiating Agreement without Giving In*. Boston: Houghton Mifflin, 1981.

F.O.I. Computer Access: Maze or Miracle? 1989-1990 Report of the Society of Professional Journalists. Chicago: Society of Professional Journalists' National Freedom of Information Committee with USA Today and Gannett News Service, 1990.

"Foreign Aid Reform." Hearings before the Subcommittee on International Economic Policy, Trade, Oceans, and Environment Affairs of the Committee on Foreign Relations. U.S. Senate. 103rd Congress. 2nd Session. February 9, 22; March 3, 1994. Washington, DC: U.S. Government Printing Office, 1994.

Foreign Broadcast Information Service.

Fornos, Werner, and Hal Burdett. "A Return to Reason: U.S. International Population Policy." *Toward the 21st Century*. A monograph published by the Population Institute, no. 4 (1993): 1-15.

The Foundation Grants Index: 1993. 21st ed. New York: Foundation Center, 1992.

Francis, Fred. "Get Me to the Invasion on Time." *Communicator* (February 1990): 12-13.

Frank, Andre Gunder. "Third World War: A Political Economy of the Gulf War and the New World Order." *Third World Quarterly* 13, no. 2 (1992): 267-282.

Freedom of Information Act: Title 5 U.S. Code, 552.

Friedman, Thomas L. "Israelis and Palestinians Struggle in the Spotlight." *Washington Journalism Review* (October 1989): 30-33.

Friendly, Fred W. *Minnesota Rag*. New York: Random House, 1981.

Fukuyama, Francis. *The End of History and the Last Man*. New York: Free Press, 1992.

Gaddis, John Lewis. "International Relations Theory and the End of the Cold War." *International Security* 17, no. 3 (Winter 1992–93): 5-58.

Gale Directory of Publications and Broadcast Media. Vol III. Detroit: Gale Research, 1994.

The Gallup Poll: Public Opinion 1991. Wilmington, DE: Scholarly Resources, 1992.

Garand, James C. "An Alternative Interpretation of Recent Political Science Journal Evaluations." *PS: Political Science and Politics* 23 (September 1990): 448-451.

Garfield, Bob. "What if They Held a Press Conference and Nobody Came?" *Washington Post Magazine,* July 11, 1993, 17-20+.

Garthoff, Raymond L. *Reflections on the Cuban Missile Crisis.* rev. ed.Washington, DC: Brookings Institution, 1989.

Genovese, Margaret. "FOIA: More Trouble Ahead?" *presstime* (July 1986): 22-23.

Gergen, David. "Is the Press to Blame?" *U.S. News and World Report,* January 13, 1992, 54.

————. Remarks given at the Frank E. Gannett Lecture, Washington, DC, November 25, 1986.

————. "Why America Hates the Press." *U.S. News and World Report,* March 11, 1991, 57.

Gersh, Debra. "Survey: Print Readers More Aware About Campaign." *Editor and Publisher—The Fourth Estate* 125 (March 14, 1992): 8, 37.

Geyelin, Philip. "Managing the Media." *Fletcher Forum of World Affairs* 13, no. 1 (Winter 1989): 19-23.

Gilbert, Richard. "How Much Should the Public Know?" *Foreign Service Journal* (May 1990): 19-23.

Given, Deam W. "Do We Need an Official Secrets Act?" *Retired Officer* (May 1981): 18-21.

Global HIV/AIDS: A Strategy for U.S. Leadership. A Consensus Report of the CSIS Working Group on Global HIV/AIDS. Washington, DC: Center for Strategic and International Studies, 1994.

Glynn, Patrick. "The Sarajevo Fallacy: The Historical and Intellectual Origins of Arms Control Theology." *National Interest* 9 (Fall 1987): 3-32.

Goldberg, David Howard. *Foreign Policy and Ethnic Interest Groups: American and Canadian Jews Lobby for Israel.* New York: Greenwood Press, 1990.

Graham, Katharine. "Foreign Policy and the Media." Address presented at the Women's National Democratic Club, Washington, DC, July 24, 1986.

————. "Four Areas of Conflict in the American Press." Address presented at the "Conflict and the Press" conference sponsored by the Star, Johannesburg, South Africa, October 8, 1987.

————. "The Media and Terrorism: Coverage Should Be Complete and Reasonable." Churchill Lecture before the English-Speaking Union of the Commonwealth, Guildhall, London, December 6, 1985.

Gray, Madeline. *Margaret Sanger: A Biography of the Champion of Birth Control.* New York: Richard Marek Publishers, 1979.

Greenfield, Jeff. "Technology and News." Conference paper presented at the Gannett Center for Media Studies' Technology Studies Seminar, Columbia University, New York, February 1, 1987.

Grunwald, Henry A. "The Post–Cold War Press." *Foreign Affairs* 72, no. 3 (Summer 1993): 12-16.

Haig, Alexander M., Jr. *Caveat: Realism, Reagan, and Foreign Policy.* New York: Macmillan, 1984.

Halliday, Fred. "The Gulf War and Its Aftermath: First Reflections." *International Affairs* 67, no. 2 (April 1991): 223-234.

Halloran, Richard. "Soldiers and Scribblers: A Common Mission." *Parameters* 17, no. 1 (Spring 1987): 10-28.

Harter, John J., and Anne Stevenson-Yang. *Energy, the Environment and the World Economy: Critical Linkages for the 1990s.* Report from a Symposium at the Department of State, Washington, DC, April 8, 1993.

Healy, Melissa. "Triumph and Defeat in the International Arena." *U.S. News and World Report,* October 7, 1985, 43.

Henry, III, William A. "'McPaper' Stakes Its Claim." *Time,* July 9, 1984, 69.

———. "The Ten Best U.S. Dailies." *Time,* April 30, 1984, 58-63.

Herman, Edward S. "The Media's Role in U.S. Foreign Policy." *Journal of International Affairs* 47 (Summer 1993): 23-45.

Herring, George C., ed. *The Secret Diplomacy of the Vietnam War: The Negotiating Volumes of the Pentagon Papers.* Austin: University of Texas Press, 1983.

Hersh, Seymour M. *The Price of Power: Kissinger in the Nixon White House.* New York: Summit Books, 1983.

Hess, Stephen. "A Washington Perspective." Address presented at the Donald S. MacNaughton symposium on "Informing America: Who Is Responsible for What?" Syracuse University, New York City, April 23-24, 1985.

———. "How Foreign Correspondents Cover the United States." *Transatlantic Perspectives* no. 10 (December 1983): 3-5.

———. *The Government-Press Connection: Press Officers and Their Offices.* Washington, DC: Brookings Institution, 1984.

———. *The Washington Reporters: Newswork.* Washington, DC: Brookings Institution, 1981.

Hill, Kevin A. "The Domestic Sources of Foreign Policymaking: Congressional Voting and American Mass Attitudes toward South Africa." *International Studies Quarterly* 37, no. 2 (June 1993): 195-214.

Hoffman, David. "Coalition Diplomacy." In *The Diplomatic Record, 1990-91,* edited by David D. Newsom, 59-81. Boulder, CO: Westview Press, 1992.

Hoffman, Stanley. *Janus and Minerva.* Boulder, CO: Westview Press, 1987.

Holmes, Kim R., ed. *A Safe and Prosperous America: A U.S. Foreign and Defense Policy Blueprint.* Washington, DC: Heritage Foundation, 1993.

Holsti, Ole R. "Theories of Crisis Decision Making." In *International Relations*

Theory: Realism, Pluralism, Globalism, 2nd ed., edited by Paul Viotti and Mark Kauppi, 304-341. New York: Macmillan, 1993.

Human Rights Watch: Questions and Answers. New York: Human Rights Watch, undated.

Huntington, Samuel. "The Clash of Civilizations." *Foreign Affairs* 72 (Summer 1993): 22-49.

"Influence and Affluence." *Economist,* June 19, 1993, 93-94.

International Media Fund Report. Vol. 3, no. 2 (July 1993): 1-11.

"Is Reagan Getting a Fair Shake from Press?" *U.S. News and World Report,* December 7, 1981, 25-26.

Iyengar, Shanto, and Donald R. Kinder. *News That Matters: Television and American Opinion.* Chicago: University of Chicago Press, 1988.

Joffe, George. "Middle Eastern Views of the Gulf Conflict and Its Aftermath." *Review of International Studies* 19, no. 2 (April 1993): 177-199.

Johnson, Paul. "The Media and the Presidency: A Balance-Sheet of an 'Ongoing Confrontation Situation.'" *Encounter* (November 1984): 8-14.

Jordan, Donald L. and Benjamin I. Page. "Shaping Foreign Policy Opinions." *Journal of Conflict Resolution* 36, no. 2 (June 1992): 227-241.

Journalists on Journalism. Published by the Global Newsroom, Columbia University Graduate School of Journalism, New York, June 1993.

Kalb, Marvin, and Frederick Mayer. *Reviving the Presidential News Conference.* Report of the Harvard Commission on the Presidential News Conference, Joan Shorenstein Barone Center on the Press, Politics, and Public Policy, Harvard University, 1988.

Kalven, Harry, Jr. "The New York Times Case: A Note on 'The Central Meaning of the First Amendment.'" In *Supreme Court Review, 1964,* edited by Philip B. Kurland, 191-221. Chicago: University of Chicago Press, 1964.

Katz, Jon. "Beyond Broadcast Journalism." *Columbia Journalism Review* (March–April 1992): 19-23.

Kaufman, Robert. "The Line in the Sand: What George Bush Learned from Winston Churchill." *Policy Review* no. 56 (Spring 1991): 36-43.

Kedourie, Elie. "Iraq: The Mystery of American Policy." *Commentary* 91, no. 6 (June 1991): 15-19.

Kegley, Charles W., Jr., and Eugene R. Wittkopf. *American Foreign Policy: Pattern and Process.* 4th ed. New York: St. Martin's Press, 1991.

Kelly, Frank K. *The United States Academy of Peace: A Long Step toward Real Security.* Washington, DC: National Peace Academy Foundation, 1983.

Kelly, James. "Three Years Old and Counting." *Time,* August 5, 1985, 48-49.

Kelly, James, with Kenneth W. Banta. "A General Loses His Case." *Time,* February 4, 1985, 64-66.

Kelly, Michael. "David Gergen, Master of the Game." *New York Times Magazine,* October 31, 1993, 62-71+.

Kennedy, David M. *Birth Control in America: The Career of Margaret Sanger.* New Haven: Yale University Press, 1970.

Kennedy, Paul. *Preparing for the Twenty-First Century.* New York: Random House, 1993.

Kinsley, Michael. "The Envelope, Please." *New Republic,* September 20-27, 1993, 6, 57.

Kirkpatrick, Jeane J. "How Has the United States Met Its Major Challenges Since 1945?" *Commentary* 80 (November 1985): 50-52.

Kondracke, Morton. "Grecian Formula." *New Republic,* June 6, 1988, 22-24.

Konner, Joan. "Moral Traditions as a Guideline for Journalists. "Address presented as part of the Andrew R. Cecil Lectures on Moral Values in a Free Society, University of Texas at Dallas, November 10, 1992.

Koppel, Ted. "TV Diplomacy in South Africa." *Newsweek,* April 8, 1985, 14.

Korn, David. *Assassination in Khartoum.* Bloomington: Indiana University Press, 1993.

Kowet, Don. *A Matter of Honor: General William Westmoreland vs. CBS.* New York: Macmillan, 1984.

Kuralt, Charles. "If He Could See It Now." *Communicator* (December 1988): 106.

Kurian, George Thomas. *World Press Encyclopedia.* 2 vols. New York: Facts on File, 1982.

Kurtz, Howard. "Read All About It." *Washington Post Magazine,* April 18, 1993, 8-11+.

Lader, Lawrence. *The Margaret Sanger Story.* Garden City, NY: Doubleday, 1955.

Landler, Mark, and Mark Lewyn. "The Networks and Affiliates May Be Falling Out of Love." *Business Week,* June 15, 1992, 41.

Langley, Monica, and Lee Levine. "Broken Promises." *Columbia Journalism Review* (July–August 1988): 21-24.

Laqueur, Walter. "Foreign News Coverage: From Bad to Worse." *Washington Journalism Review* (June 1983): 32-35.

Laron, James F. *Television's Window on the World: International Affairs Coverage on the U.S. Networks.* Norwood, NJ: Ablex, 1984.

Larson, David L., ed. *Anthology of Syllabi of Basic Courses in International Relations.* 3rd ed. New Hampshire Council on World Affairs, New England Division of the International Studies Association, April 1978.

"Leaking Ship Fires Warning Shots." *U.S. News and World Report,* June 2, 1986, 18.

Leary, Virginia, A. A. Ellis, and Kurt Madlener. *The Philippines: Human Rights After Martial Law: Report of a Mission.* Geneva, Switzerland: International Commission of Jurists, 1984.

Legislation on Foreign Relations Through 1984. Vol. 1. Committee on Foreign Relations. Washington, DC: U.S. Government Printing Office, 1985.

"Legislative Options and U.S. Policy toward South Africa." Hearing and Markup before the Subcommittees on International Economic Policy and Trade and on Africa of the Committee on Foreign Affairs. U.S. House of Representatives. 99th Congress. 2nd Session. April 9, 16; June 4, 5, 1986. Washington, DC: U.S. Government Printing Office, 1987.

Leiser, Ernest. "The Decline of Network News." *Washington Journalism Review* (January–February 1988): 49-52.

Leslie, Jacques. "The Anonymous Source: Second Thoughts on 'Deep Throat.'" *Washington Journalism Review* (September 1986): 33-35.

"Letter from London." *New Yorker,* March 5, 1990, 91-92+.

Lewenstein, Marion. "Global Readership." *presstime* (September 1987): 10, 12.

Lewis, Anthony. "A Public Right to Know about Public Institutions: The First Amendment as Sword." *Supreme Court Review* (1980): 1-25.

———. *Make No Law.* New York: Random House, 1991.

Lewy, Guenter. "Can Democracy Keep Secrets?" *Policy Review* no. 26 (Fall 1983): 17-29.

Lieberthal, Kenneth. *The Future of United States-China Relations: A Proposal for a Sustainable, Bipartisan Policy.* Report presented to Policy Impact Panel of the Council on Foreign Relations, Washington, DC, May, 1994.

Lippmann, Walter. *Public Opinion.* New York: Free Press, 1965.

Little, Michael R. *A War of Information: The Conflict between Public and Private U.S. Foreign Policy on El Salvador, 1979-1992.* Lanham, MD: University Press of America, 1993.

Lovell, John P. "The Limits of 'Lessons Learned' from Vietnam to the Gulf War." *Peace and Change* 17, no. 4 (October 1992): 379-401.

Lucan, Alice Neff. "The Boundary Lines of Free Speech." Lecture presented at graduate seminar, University of Virginia, Charlottesville, Virginia, September 17, 1991.

MacArthur, Douglas, II. "Lessons the Media Can Learn from the Korean Experience and the Problems and Challenges of the Media Today." Keynote Address presented at the Sixth World Media Conference, Seoul, Korea, October, 1982.

Maoz, Zeev, and Allison Astorino. "The Cognitive Structure of Peacemaking: Egypt and Israel, 1970-1978." *Political Psychology* 13, no. 4 (December 1992): 647-662.

———. "Waging War, Waging Peace: Decision Making and Bargaining in the Arab-Israeli Conflict, 1970-1973." *International Studies Quarterly* 36, no. 4 (December 1992): 373-399.

Mapes, Milton C., Jr. "The National Peace Academy and Conflict Resolution at All Levels of Society." An Address to the Tenth Annual Scientific Meeting of the American Association of Social Psychiatry, Washington, DC, September 25, 1982.

Marro, Anthony. "When the Government Tells Lies." *Columbia Journalism Review* (March–April 1985): 29-41.

Martz, Larry, et al. "The Contra Crusade." *Newsweek,* March 17, 1986, 20+.

Massing, Michael. "The Libel Chill: How Cold Is It Out There?" *Columbia Journalism Review* (May–June 1985): 31-39+.

Mathias, Charles M., Jr. "Ethnic Groups and Foreign Policy." *Foreign Affairs* 59 (Summer 1981): 975-998.

McCullough, David. *Truman.* New York: Simon and Schuster, 1992.

McDaniel, Ann, and Evan Thomas. "Bush the Communicator." *Newsweek,* October 14, 1991, 28.

McGinnis, Michael D., and John T. Williams. "Policy Uncertainty in Two-Level Games: Examples of Correlated Equilibria." *International Studies Quarterly* 37, no. 1 (March 1993): 29-54.

McGrath, Peter, and Nancy Stadtman. "Absence of Malice." *Newsweek,* February 4, 1985, 52-56+.

McGuire, Stryker. "The 'Fun' Times Are Over." *Newsweek,* December 13, 1993, 70.

McLoughlin, Merrill, et al. "Television's Blinding Power." *U.S. News and World Report,* July 27, 1987, 18-21.

Media Law Reporter. (BNA), 15 (1988): 1369, 1390; (844 F2d 1057 (4th Cir. 1988).

"The Media in the Dock." *Newsweek,* October 22, 1984, 66-72.

"Media's Role in Foreign Policy." *The National Opinion Ballot Report.* Published in *Great Decisions* by the Foreign Policy Association, New York, 1991.

Mendelson, Sarah E. "Internal Battles and External Wars: Politics, Learning, and the Soviet Withdrawal from Afghanistan." *World Politics* 45 (April 1993): 327-360.

Merrill, John C., ed. *Global Journalism: A Survey of the World's Mass Media.* New York: Longman, 1983.

"Message to the Medium." *Economist,* July 20, 1985, 11-12.

Michel, Robert. Remarks presented at the National Press Club, Washington, DC, December 6, 1989.

"Military Implications of the SALT II Treaty." Hearings before the Committee on Armed Services. U.S. Senate. 96th Congress. 1st Session. Part 3, October 9-16, 1979. Washington, DC: U.S. Government Printing Office, 1979.

Moberly, John. "Iraq in the Aftermath of the Gulf War." *Asian Affairs* XX (October 1989): 306-314.

Morgenthau, Hans. *Politics among Nations: The Struggle for Power and Peace.* Revised by Kenneth W. Thompson. New York: McGraw-Hill, 1993.

"Moscow's Vigorous Leader." *Time,* Special Section, September 9, 1985, 16-28+.

Mosettig, Michael D. Address before the East-West Center and the Public Relations Society of America, Ilikai Hotel, Honolulu, Hawaii, December 1, 1989. Published by the East-West Center, Honolulu, Hawaii, 1990.

———. "Panama and the Press." *SAIS Review* 10, no. 2 (Summer–Fall 1990): 179-189.

Mott, Frank Luther. *American Journalism.* 3rd ed. New York: Macmillan, 1962.
————. *Jefferson and the Press.* Baton Rouge, LA: Louisiana State University Press, 1943.
Mudd, Roger. ". . . After the Television Machine Got Hooked Up to the Money Machine." *RTNDA Communicator* (June 1988): 6-8.
Mufson, Steven. "The Privatization of Craig Fuller." *Washington Post Magazine,* August 2, 1992, 14-19+.
Muskie, Edmund S. *Exploring Cambodia: Issues and Reality in a Time of Transition.* Findings and recommendations from the visit to Thailand, Vietnam and Cambodia by Edmund Muskie, Center for National Policy, Washington, DC, February 1990.
Myers, Norman. *Not Far Afield: U.S. Interests and the Global Environment.* Washington, DC: World Resources Institute, 1987.
Mylroie, Laurie. "After the Guns Fell Silent: Iraq in the Middle East." *Middle East Journal* 43, no. 1 (Winter 1989): 51-67.
————. "How We Helped Saddam Survive." *Commentary* 92, no. 1 (July 1991): 15-18.
————. "Still Standing." *New Republic,* April 13, 1992, 11-12.
————. "The Baghdad Alternative." *Orbis* 32, no. 3 (Summer 1988): 339-354.
————. "Trial and Error." *New Republic,* June 3, 1991, 17-18.
————. "Why Saddam Hussein Invaded Kuwait." *Orbis* 37 (Winter 1993): 123-134.
"National Security and the Press: An Interview with CIA Chief William Casey." *Washington Journalism Review* (July 1986): 14-17.
Neier, Aryeh. "An Unacceptable Accord." *Recorder* (December 15, 1993): 9.
Neiman Reports XL, no. 4 (Winter 1986).
Neuman, Johanna. *The Media: Partners in the Revolution of 1989.* Occasional Paper. Washington, DC: Atlantic Council of the United States, June 1991.
New York Times Company vs. *Sullivan* 376 U.S. Code 254 (1964).
Newhouse, John. "A Reporter at Large: Socialism or Death." *New Yorker,* April 27, 1992, 52-53+.
Newman, Edwin. Excerpts of remarks at Williamsburg Conference, sponsored by the Center for Strategic and International Studies, May 1984.
Newsom, David D. *Diplomacy and the American Democracy.* Bloomington: Indiana University Press, 1988.
————. Prepared Remarks at University Forum on Proposed U.S. Peace Academy, Georgetown University, Washington, DC, November 3, 1983.
————. "Scoops and Secrets: Diplomacy and the Press." *Gannett Center Journal* (Fall 1989): 175-187.
————, ed. *The Diplomacy of Human Rights.* Lanham, NY: University Press of America, 1986.
————. "The Media and Foreign Policy." Lecture presented at the University of Ulster, Belfast, Northern Ireland, October 15, 1986.

———. *The Soviet Brigade in Cuba: A Study in Political Diplomacy.* Bloomington: Indiana University Press, 1987.

"Newspaper Coverage of Health Care Reform: April 1-July 31, 1993—A Content Analysis." Kaiser Health Reform Media Monitoring Project. *Columbia Journalism Review* Supplement (November–December 1993): 1-8.

"Newspaper Money Can Still Be Sweet." *Economist,* October 31, 1992, 67-68+.

Nye, Joseph S., Jr. "Peering into the Future." *Foreign Affairs* 73, no. 4 (July–August 1994): 82-93.

Oberdorfer, Don. "Missed Signals in the Middle East." *Washington Post Magazine,* March 17, 1991, 19-23+.

Odom, William E. "American Intelligence: Current Problems in Historical Perspective." Address before the Association of Former Intelligence Officers, Washington, DC, October 10, 1987.

Official Records of the United Nations General Assembly. 17th Session. Plenary Meetings, vol. I. New York: United Nations, 1962.

Olin, Dirk. "When FOIA Means Business." *Washington Journalism Review* (September 1986): 40-41.

Olson, Stan, ed. *The Foundation Directory.* 1993 ed. New York: Foundation Center, 1993.

Olsson, Peter A. "Media Power: The Vietnam and Gulf Wars." *Mind and Human Interaction* 3 (May 1992): 85-87.

Opp, Karl-Dieter. *The Rationality of Political Protest: A Comparative Analysis of Rational Choice Theory.* Boulder, CO: Westview Press, 1989.

Ornstein, Norman, Andrew Kohut, and Larry McCarthy. *The People, the Press, and Politics: The Times Mirror Study of the American Electorate.* Reading, MA: Addison-Wesley, 1988.

Ornstein, Norman J., and Shirley Elder. *Interest Groups, Lobbying and Policy-making.* Washington, DC: Congressional Quarterly Press, 1978.

Pearce, David D. "Packaging the Message: Dealing with Reporters Means Watching Your P's and P's." *Foreign Service Journal* 71, no. 4 (April 1994): 38-42.

Pell, Claiborne. "The Future of Public Diplomacy: A Congressional View." Remarks presented before the conference on Public Diplomacy in the Information Age, Department of State, September 16, 1987.

Peterzell, Jay. "Can the CIA Spook the Press?" *Columbia Journalism Review* (September–October 1986): 29-34.

Pew Case Studies in International Affairs—1993 Case Catalog. Washington, DC: Pew Case Study Center, Institute for the Study of Diplomacy, Georgetown University, 1993.

Poland, James M. *Understanding Terrorism: Groups, Strategies, and Responses.* Englewood Cliffs, NJ: Prentice Hall, 1988.

"Policy Impact Panel on the Future of U.S.-China Relations." A public hearing chaired by Henry Kissinger and Cyrus Vance, Council on Foreign Relations, Washington, DC, March 15, 1994.

Political Science and Social Policy. Armonck, NY: M. E. Sharpe, Fall 1983.

Porter, Bruce. "The Newsweeklies: Is the Species Doomed?" *Columbia Journalism Review* (March–April 1989): 23-29.

Postman, Neil. *Amusing Ourselves to Death: Public Discourse in the Age of Show Business.* New York: Viking Press, 1985.

Powell, Jody. *The Other Side of the Story.* New York: William Morrow, 1984.

Powell, Stewart, et al. "The War of Words." *U.S. News and World Report,* October 7, 1985, 34-39+.

Prato, Lou. "Pentagon Wants to Make It Work, Williams Says." *Communicator* (February 1990): 15, 18.

Prichard, Peter. *The Making of McPaper: The Inside Story of USA Today.* Kansas City: Andrews, McMeel and Parker, 1987.

Privat, Pascal, Peter McKillop, and Carol Hall. "The BBC's New Baby." *Newsweek,* October 28, 1991, 40.

Prochnau, William. "If There's a War, He's There." *New York Times Magazine,* March 3, 1991, 30-31+.

"Proposals to Establish a U.S. Academy of Peace." Joint hearing before the Subcommittee on International Security and Scientific Affairs, and the Subcommittee on International Operations of the Committee on Foreign Affairs, and the Subcommittee on Postsecondary Education of the Committee on Education and Labor. U.S. House of Representatives. 97th Congress. 2nd Session. July 20, 1982. Washington, DC: U.S. Government Printing Office, 1982.

Public Engagement in U.S. Foreign Policy After the Cold War. Final report of the Eighty-third American Assembly, Columbia University, Harriman, New York, June 3-6, 1993.

Public Papers of the Presidents: George Bush, 1990. Vol II. Washington, DC: U.S. Government Printing Office, 1991.

Public Papers of the Presidents: Gerald Ford, 1975. Vol. I. Washington, DC: U.S. Government Printing Office, 1977.

Public Papers of the Presidents: Jimmy Carter, 1980-1981. Vol. I. Washington, DC: U.S. Government Printing Office, 1981.

Public Papers of the Presidents: John F. Kennedy, 1961. Washington, DC: U.S. Government Printing Office, 1962.

Public Papers of the Presidents: Ronald Reagan, 1981. Washington, DC: U.S. Government Printing Office, 1982.

Public Papers of the Presidents: Ronald Reagan, 1982. Vol. II. Washington, DC: U.S. Government Printing Office, 1983.

Public Papers of the Presidents: Ronald Reagan, 1983 Vol I. Washington, DC: U.S. Government Printing Office, 1984.

"Regulations Governing Department of State Press Building Passes," 49 *Federal Register* 26 (February 7, 1984), pp. 4465-4467.

"Relief Problems in Nigeria-Biafra." Hearings before the Subcommittee to Investigate Problems Connected with Refugees and Escapees of the Committee on the Judiciary. United States Senate. 91st Congress. First Session. July 15, 1969. Washington, DC: U.S. Government Printing Office, 1969.

Reston, James. *Deadline.* New York: Random House, 1991.

"Review of the President's Report on Assistance to the Nicaraguan Opposition." Hearing before the Subcommittee on Western Hemisphere Affairs of the Committee on Foreign Affairs. U.S. House of Representatives. 99th Congress. 1st Session. December 5, 1985. Washington, DC: U.S. Government Printing Office, 1986.

Ricci, David M. *The Transformation of American Politics: The New Washington and the Rise of Think Tanks.* New Haven: Yale University Press, 1993.

Roberts, Brad, Stanton H. Burnett, and Murray Weidenbaum. "Think Tanks in a New World." *Washington Quarterly* 16, no. 1 (Winter 1993): 169-182.

Roehm, John F., Jr. "Congressional Participation in U.S.-Middle East Policy, October 1973-1976: Congressional Activism vs. Policy Coherence." In *Congress, the Presidency and American Foreign Policy,* edited by John Spanier and Joseph Nogee, 22-43. New York: Pergamon Press, 1981.

Rosenblatt, Roger. "Journalism and the Larger Truth." *Time,* July 2, 1984, 88.

Roshco, Bernard. "When Policy Fails: How the Buck Was Passed When Kuwait Was Invaded." Discussion Paper D-15. Joan Shorenstein Barone Center, Harvard University, December 1992.

Rowse, Arthur E. "How to Build Support for War." *Columbia Journalism Review* (September–October 1992): 28-29.

Ruane, Michael E. "The Medium and the Messenger." *Inquirer,* November 14, 1993, 18, 20+.

Rubin, Barry. "Drowning in the Gulf." *Foreign Policy* no. 69 (Winter 1987-88): 120-134.

Rubinstein, Alvin Z. "New World Order or Hollow Victory?" *Foreign Affairs* 70 (Fall 1991): 53-65.

Saikal, Amin. "The United States and Persian Gulf Security." *World Policy Journal* IX, no. 3 (Summer 1992): 515-531.

"The SALT II Treaty." Hearings before the Committee on Foreign Relations. U.S. Senate. 96th Congress. 1st Session. 6 parts. July 9-12, 16-19; July 25-August 2; September 6-12, 18-24; October 15-November 9, 1979. Washington, DC: U.S. Government Printing Office, 1979.

"Sanctuary for Salvadorans?" *Economist,* May 2, 1987, 31-32.

Sanoff, Alvin P. "All the News—or Trends—That's Fit to Print." *U.S. News and World Report,* March 7, 1988, 64-65.

Scheer, Robert. *With Enough Shovels: Reagan, Bush and Nuclear War.* New York: Random House, 1982.

Scheinin, Richard. "Cathleen Black: USA Today's President with a Mandate." *Washington Journalism Review* (June 1984): 37-40.

Schenck vs. U.S.. Title 249 U.S. Code, 47.

Schickel, Richard. "How TV Failed to Get the Real Picture." *Time,* May 11, 1992, 29.

Schlesinger, Arthur M., Jr. *A Thousand Days: John F. Kennedy in the White House.* Boston: Houghton Mifflin, 1965.

———. "Four Days with Fidel: A Havana Diary." *New York Review of Books,* March 26, 1992, 22-29.

Schmertz, Herbert. "Turned Off: Why Executives Distrust T.V. Reporters." *Washington Journalism Review* (July–August 1984): 45-47.

Schneider, William. "Bang-Bang Television: The New Superpower." *Public Opinion* (April–May 1982): 13-15.

Schoenbaum, Thomas J. *Waging Peace and War: Dean Rusk in the Truman, Kennedy, and Johnson Years.* New York: Simon and Schuster, 1988.

Schooling for Democracy: Reinventing UNESCO for the Post–Cold War World. A Report of the American Panel on UNESCO of the United Nations Association of the USA. New York, 1993.

Schorr, Daniel. "Ten Days that Shook the White House." *Columbia Journalism Review* (July–August 1991): 21-23.

Schudson, Michael. "Watergate: A Study in Mythology." *Columbia Journalism Review* (May–June 1992): 28-33.

Scowcroft, Brent. "Reflections on the Role of the Media." Occasional Paper. Washington, DC: Institute for the Study of Diplomacy, Georgetown University, 1987.

Seeger, Murray. "Towards a Global Village — Bridging Cultural and Professional Values." *Nieman Reports* (Autumn 1989): 13-16+.

Serfaty, Simon., ed. *The Media and Foreign Policy.* New York: St. Martin's Press, 1990.

Shaplen, Robert. "The Eye of the Storm." 3-part series. *New Yorker,* June 6, 13, and 20, 1980, pp. 43-46+; 48-50+; 44-46+ respectively.

Sharkey, Jacqueline. "When Pictures Drive Foreign Policy." *American Journalism Review* (December 1993): 14-19.

"Sharon Case: *Time's* Bittersweet Victory." *U.S. News and World Report,* February 4, 1985, 10.

Sheehan, Edward R. F. *The Arabs, Israelis, and Kissinger.* New York: Reader's Digest Press, 1976.

Sherman, Spencer. "Pack Journalism, Japanese Style." *Columbia Journalism Review* (September–October 1990): 37-42.

Shultz, George P. *Turmoil and Triumph: My Years as Secretary of State.* New York: Charles Scribner's Sons, 1993.

Sidle, Winant. "The Military and the Press: Is the Breach Worth Mending?" *Army* (February 1985): 22-25+.

Sigal, Leon V. *Reporters and Officials.* Lexington, MA: D. C. Heath, 1973.

Simons, Howard. "Government and National Security." *Editor and Publisher,* April 26, 1986, 80+.

Singer, Amy. "How Prior Restraint Came to America." *American Lawyer* (January–February 1991): 88, 90-93.

Singer, David, and Ruth R. Seldin., eds. *American Jewish Yearbook, 1992.* New York: American Jewish Committee and Jewish Publication Society, 1992.

Smith, James Allen. *Strategic Calling: Center for Strategic and International Studies, 1962-1992.* Washington, DC: Center for Strategic and International Studies, 1993.

———. *The Idea Brokers: Think Tanks and the Rise of the New Policy Elite.* New York: Free Press, 1991.

Smyth, Frank. "'Official Sources,' 'Western Diplomats,' and other Voices from the Mission." *Columbia Journalism Review* (January–February 1993): 35.

Steele, Janet E. "Experts and the Operational Bias of Television News: The Case of the Persian Gulf War." Unpublished paper, University of Virginia, May 1994.

Stewart, Potter. "Or of the Press." *Hastings Law Journal* 26 (1975): 631.

Stone, Priscilla, and Paul Richards. "Social and Natural Science Conjoined: The View from the Program on African Studies." *Items* 47, nos. 2-3 (June–September 1993): 29-34.

Strong, Robert A. *Decisions and Dilemmas.* Englewood Cliffs, NJ: Prentice Hall, 1992.

Sussman, Leonard R. "Press Freedom, Secrecy and Censors." *Freedom at Issue* (January-February 1986): 7-12.

Taketoshi, Yamamoto. "The Press Clubs of Japan." *Journal of Japanese Studies* 15, no. 2 (1989): 371-388.

Talbott, Strobe. *Deadly Gambits.* New York: Alfred A. Knopf, 1984.

———. "Post-Victory Blues." *Foreign Affairs* 71 (Special Issue 1992): 53-69.

Television News Index and Abstracts. Nashville: Vanderbilt Television News Archive, May 1986.

Tillman, Seth. *The United States in the Middle East.* Bloomington: Indiana University Press, 1982.

Timberg, Robert. "The Hill Handlers: Who's Hot, Who's Not, among the Press Secretaries." *Washington Journalism Review* (June 1985): 39-43.

Times Mirror News Interest Index: Public Interest and Awareness of the News. Washington, DC: Times Mirror Center for the People and the Press, January 1991.

Tivnan, Edward. *The Lobby: Jewish Political Power and American Foreign Policy.* New York: Simon and Schuster, 1987.

de Tocqueville, Alexis. *Democracy in America.* New translation by George Lawrence, edited by J. P. Mayer. Garden City, NY: Anchor Books, Doubleday, 1969.

Tribe, Laurence H. *American Constitutional Law.* 2nd ed. Mineola, NY: Foundation Press, 1988.

Tripp, J. T. B., D. J. Dudek, and Michael Oppenheimer. "Equity and Ozone Protection." *Environment* 29, no. 6 (July–August 1987): 43-45.

Tucker, Robert W. "The Protectorate." *New Republic,* August 10, 1992, 19-20+.

"TV: Does It Box in President in a Crisis?" *U.S. News and World Report,* July 15, 1985, 23+.

U.N. Department for Economic and Social Information and Policy Analysis. Proceedings of the United Nations Expert Group Meeting on Population, Environment and Development. *Population, Environment and Development,* United Nations Headquarters, New York, 20-24 January 1992 (ST/ESA/SER.R/129). 1994 (mimeo).

U.N. Department of Economic and Social Information and Policy Analysis. Proceedings of the United Nations Expert Group Meeting on Population Policies and Programmes. *Population Policies and Programmes,* Cairo, Egypt, 12-16 April 1992 (ST/ESA/SER.R/128). 1993 (mimeo).

U.N. Economic and Social Council. List of Non-Governmental Organizations in Consultative Status with the Economic and Social Council as of 31 December 1993. (E/1994/INF/5). 13 May 1994 (mimeo).

Underwood, Doug. "The Newspapers' Identity Crisis." *Columbia Journalism Review* (March–April 1992): 24-27.

United Nations Handbook. Wellington, New Zealand: Ministry of Foreign Affairs and Trade, 1993.

United States Advisory Commission on Public Diplomacy—1989 Report. Washington, DC: United States Information Agency, 1989.

"U.S. Academy of Peace Act, 1983." Hearing before the Subcommittee on Education, Arts, and Humanities of the Committee on Labor and Human Resources. U.S. Senate. 98th Congress. 1st Session. March 16, 1983. Washington, DC: U.S. Government Printing Office, 1983.

"U.S. Army Field Manual 100-37," *Terrorism Counteraction.* July 1987.

"U.S. Army Training Circular 19-16," *Countering Terrorism on U.S. Army Installations.* April 1983.

U.S. Department of State Dispatch.

U.S. Legislation Relating Human Rights to U.S. Foreign Policy. 4th ed. Buffalo, NY: William S. Hein, 1991.

U.S. National Report on Population. A Report for the U.S. Department of State in Preparation for the 1994 International Conference on Population and Development. Prepared by the Population Reference Bureau, October 1993.

"U.S. Policy toward Nicaragua: Aid to Nicaraguan Resistance Proposal." Hearings before the Committee on Foreign Relations. U.S. Senate. 99th Congress. 2nd Session. February 27; March 4, 1986. Washington, DC: U.S. Government Printing Office, 1986.

"U.S. Policy toward South Africa." Hearings before the Committee on Foreign Relations. U.S. Senate. 99th Congress. 1st Session. April 24, May 2 and 22, 1985. Washington, DC: U.S. Government Printing Office, 1985.

"U.S. Support for the Contras." Hearing before the Subcommittee on Western Hemisphere Affairs of the Committee on Foreign Affairs. U.S. House of Representatives. 99th Congress. 1st Session. April 16, 17, and 18, 1985. Washington, DC: U.S. Government Printing Office, 1985.

"USA Today Tries to Take on the World." *Business Week,* August 13, 1984, 78.

"VOA: A Bridge to Iran." *Voice of America* no. 29 (October–November 1988): 2-5.

"The Voice of America: A Brief History and Current Operations." United States Information Agency, Office of Public Liaison, Washington, DC, June 1985.

Walcott, John. "Land of Hype and Glory: Spin Doctors on Parade." *U.S. News and World Report,* February 16, 1992, 6.

Waldman, Steven. "Consumer News Blues: Are Advertisers Stifling Local TV Reporting?" *Newsweek,* May 20, 1991, 48.

Wallace, Michael D., Peter Suedfeld, and Kimberley Thachuk. "Political Rhetoric of Leaders under Stress in the Gulf Crisis." *Journal of Conflict Resolution* 37, no. 1 (March 1993): 94-107.

Wallach, John P. "'I'll Give It to You on Background': State Breakfasts." *Washington Quarterly* (Spring 1982): 53-66.

Weinberg, Steve. "Hits and Misses: FOIA at 20." *Washington Journalism Review* (September 1986): 38-39.

———. "Trashing the FOIA." *Columbia Journalism Review* (January–February 1985): 21-28.

Weisberg, Jacob. "The Lobby with a Lock on Congress." *Newsweek,* October 19, 1987, 46+.

Weisman, Steven R. "The President and the Press: The Art of Controlled Access." *New York Times Magazine,* October 14, 1984, 35-37+.

Westin, Av. "Inside the Evening News: How TV Really Works." *New York,* October 18, 1982, 48-54+.

"Where the Money Is." National Survey conducted by the School of Journalism at the University of Missouri, Columbia. *Washington Journalism Review* (March 1986): 14-17.

Whitaker, Mark, et al. "Nicaragua: A War of Words." *Newsweek,* March 11, 1985, 20-22.

———, et al. "Playing Propaganda Games." *Newsweek,* March 18, 1985, 32.

Whitman, David. *The Press and the Neutron Bomb.* Case History no. 14-84-607. Cambridge, MA: Harvard University Press, Kennedy School of Government, Center for Press, Politics, and Public Policy, 1983.

Wick, Charles Z. "Public Diplomacy in the Global Marketplace of Ideas." Address presented at the 40th Anniversary U.S. Advisory Commission on Public Diplomacy, Department of State, September 16, 1987.

Wicker, Tom. *On Press.* New York: Viking Press, 1978.

Windrich, Elaine. *The Cold War Guerrilla: Jonas Savimbi, the U.S. Media, and the Angolan War.* New York: Greenwood Press, 1992.

World Conference on Human Rights: The Vienna Declaration and Programme of Action. United Nations pamphlet. June 1993.

Yoffe, Emily. "Peace of Mindlessness." *New Republic,* March 12, 1984, 16-18.

Zartman, William I., and Maureen R. Berman. *The Practical Negotiator.* New Haven: Yale University Press, 1982.

Zimmerman, Paul D. "But Will He, She or It Play in Peoria?" *U.S. News and World Report,* July 27, 1987, 22.

Zorack, John L. *The Lobbying Handbook.* Washington, DC: Professional Lobbying and Consulting Center, 1990.

INDEX

hearings and, 205; demonstrators and, 52; events covered, 47-48; future concerns, 234; hostages and, 90-92; impact on other media, 64; limitations of, 61; lobbies and, 196; public view of, 10; simplified reports, 231-32; technology and, 46-47

Terrorism, 87-92; confidentiality and, 88; hostages and, 88, 89, 90-92; media guidelines for, 91-92

Thatcher, Margaret, 89

Think tanks, 113-14, 141-62; activities of, 156-59; AIPAC and, 189; audience, 141, 161; conferences, 157; conflicts of interest and, 162; corporate funding, 108-9; diplomacy and, 149; exclusive clubs, 142; executive branch and, 160; funding for, 103-4, 112-13, 161; future concerns, 234; incomes, 114; influence of, 159-62; informal, 141-42; institutions, 145-47; listing of, 143; peace and, 153-56; personalities in, 150-52; policies of, 147-50; professionals in, 158-59; publications, 157-58; purposes of, 143-45

Thomas, Franklin, 115

Thompson, Llewellyn, 54

Time, 13-14, 96, 99

Times Mirror Center for the People and the Press, 46

Tivnan, Edward, 187

Trading-with-the-Enemy Act, 6

Trotta, Liz, 86-87

Truman, Harry, 188

Turmoil and Triumph (Shultz), 29

Turner, Ed, 52

U.S. Institute of Peace, 116-17

Uniao Nacional pro Indepencia Total de Angola (UNITA), 194-97, 223-29

UNITA, 194-97, 223-29

United Nations, 35, 77; environment and, 178; human rights and, 166, 169; population and, 174, 175, 176

United States: global responsibilities of, 82; human rights and, 166-67; self-image of, 6; view of as powerful, 36

United States Constitution, 3. *See also* First Amendment

United States Institute of Peace (USIP), 153-56, 158

Universal Declaration of Human Rights, 166, 169

Universities, 103, 105, 117-18. *See also* Academia

USIP. *See* United States Institute of Peace

Vance, Cyrus, 20, 31, 77, 168

Vietnam War, 11, 47, 82; academia and, 121; access to, 84-86; human rights and, 167; think tanks and, 149

Viguerie, Richard, 104

Wallach, John, 73, 77

Warnke, Paul, 208

Washington. *See also* Government; Think tanks; media and, 55, 62; networks, 203; think tanks in, 141-43

Washington, George, 4

Washington Post, 10; on Clinton administration, 21; on Gulf War, 39; intelligence reports and, 93-94; national security and, 83; Pentagon Papers and, 12; think tanks and, 142; use of stereotypes, 61

Washington Star, 26

Watergate affair, 12

Watson, Thomas, 106

Weinberger, Caspar, 29, 84

Weiss, Ted, 214

Westin, Av, 57

Westmoreland, William, 14

White, Robert, 163

Wicker, Tom, 64-65

Wilkerson, J. Harvey, 15-16

Will, George, 55, 98

Williams, Eddie N., 152

Williams, Hayden, 116

Wilson, Woodrow, 7

Witness for Peace, 213

Wolpe, Howard, 222

Woodward, Bob, 12, 79

Woolsey, James, 150

World Affairs Council, 142

Wriston, Walter, 232

Zero Population Growth, 175

David D. Newsom, since 1991, has been Hugh S. and Winifred B. Cumming Memorial Professor of International Relations at the University of Virginia. In 1995 he was appointed interim dean of the School of Foreign Service, Georgetown University. A graduate of the University of California at Berkeley with an M.S. from the Columbia University School of Journalism, he served 35 years in the U.S. Foreign Service. His career included three ambassadorships (Libya, Indonesia, Philippines) and appointments as Assistant Secretary and Under Secretary of State. Following retirement from the Foreign Service in 1981, he was for ten years associate dean and director of the Institute for the Study of Diplomacy at the Georgetown University School of Foreign Service. He has written two other books, *Diplomacy and the American Democracy*, and *The Soviet Brigade in Cuba*, and edited *The Diplomacy of Human Rights*, and *The Diplomatic Record* for 1989-90, 1990-91.